ARTH[illegible]EDIA

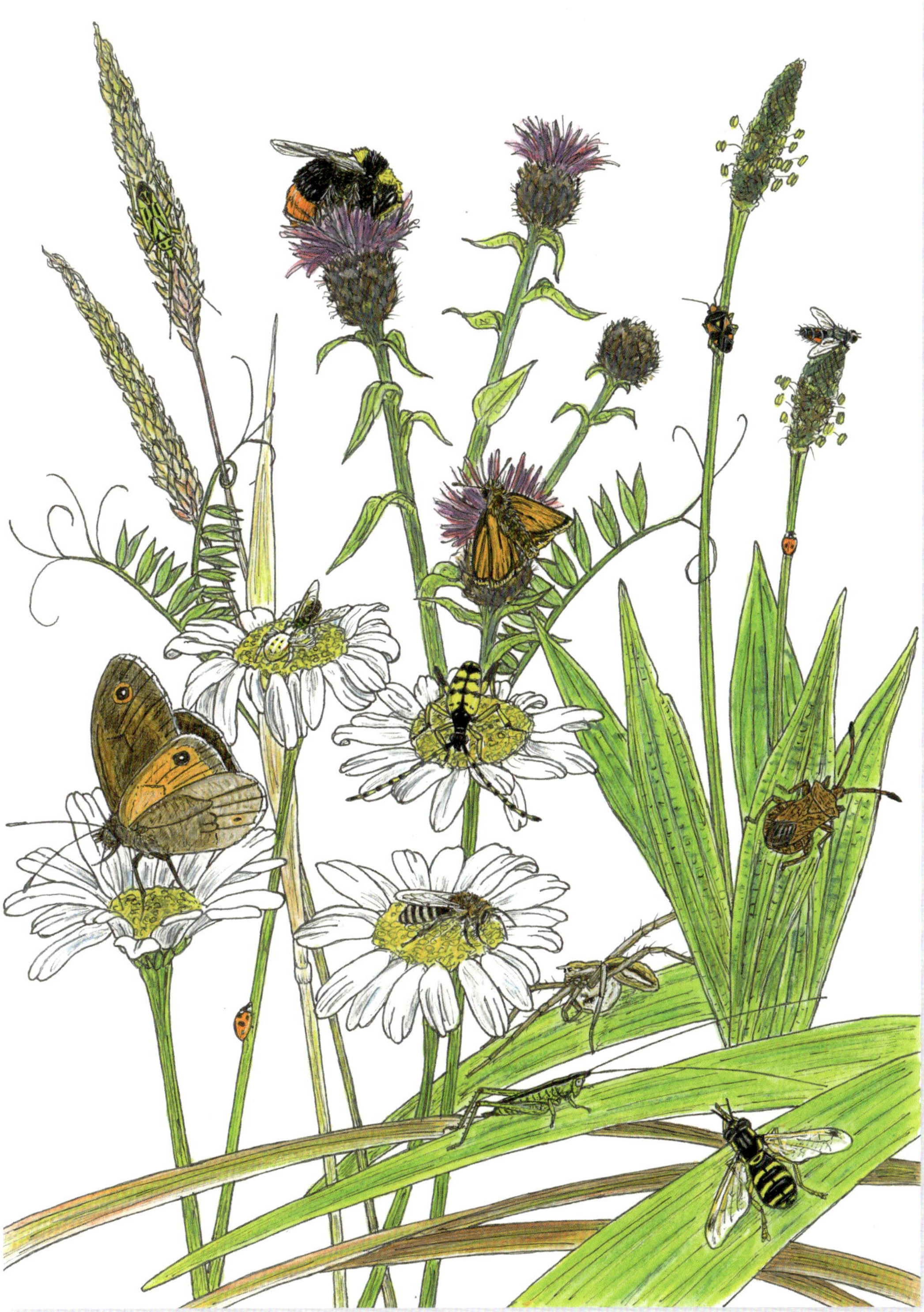

Made in Norfolk by Mascot Media

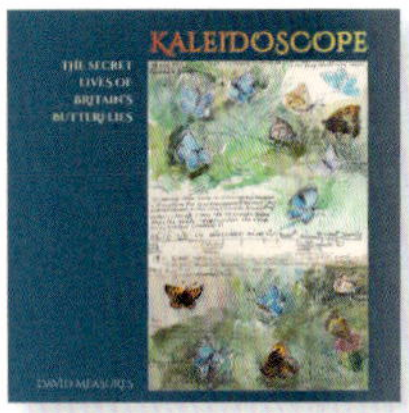

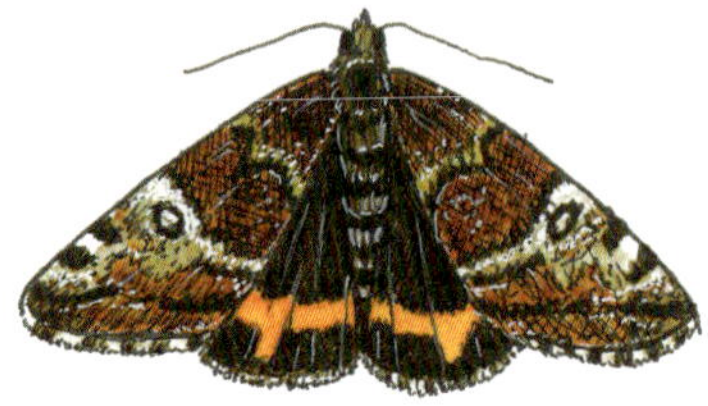

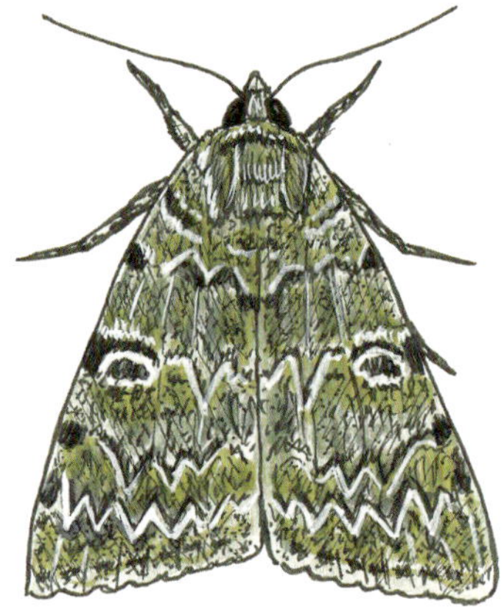

'ARTHROPEDIA'
Published in Great Britain in 2020 by Mascot Media, Norfolk.
A CIP catalogue record for this book is available from the British Library.

ISBN: 978-1-9164783-6-7

Scanning, image processing and book design by Alan Marshall.
Edited by Marion Scott Marshall and Jeremy Bartlett.

Printed by Swallowtail Print, Drayton Industrial Park, Taverham Road, Drayton, Norwich, Norfolk NR8 6RL.
Email: contact@swallowtailprint.co.uk
www.swallowtailprint.co.uk

FSC www.fsc.org MIX Paper from responsible sources FSC® C113523

Planting trees to catch carbon
19119900620
Printed on Carbon Captured paper

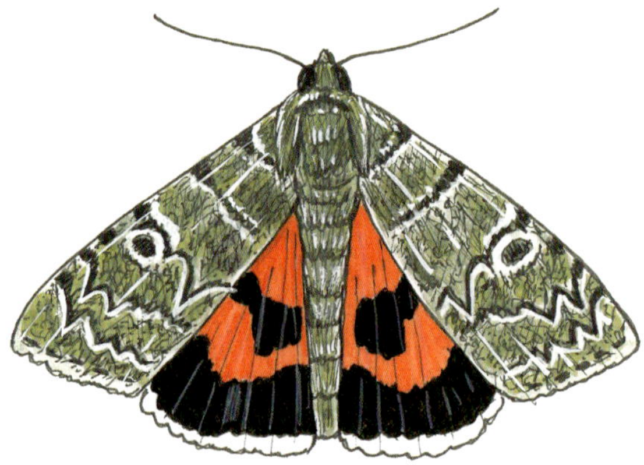

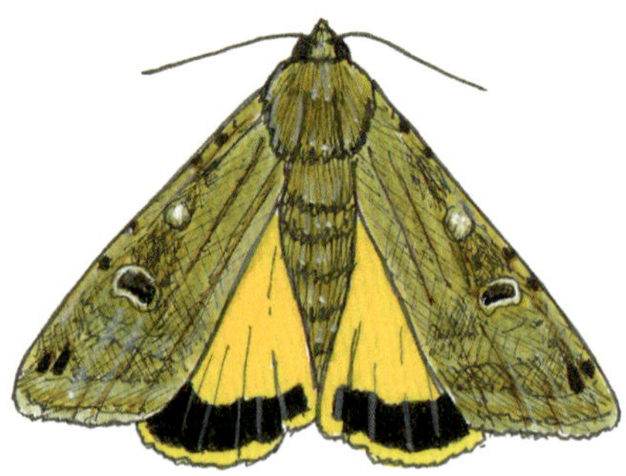

DEDICATION

This book is dedicated to my fellow invertebrate enthusiasts, past, present and future. Without their records and observations, our knowledge of invertebrates would be so much less. Happy (true) bug-hunting, one and all!

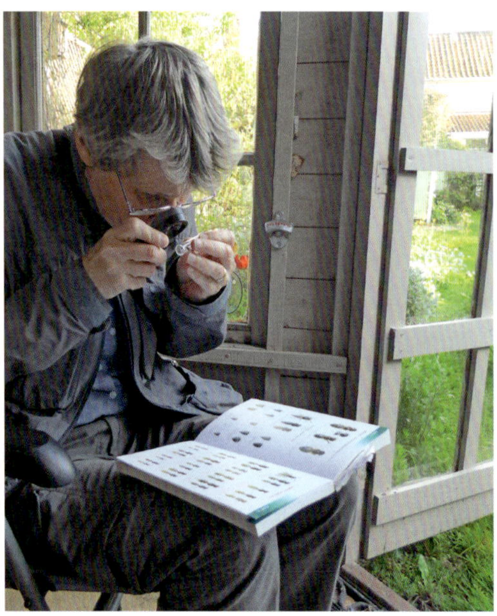

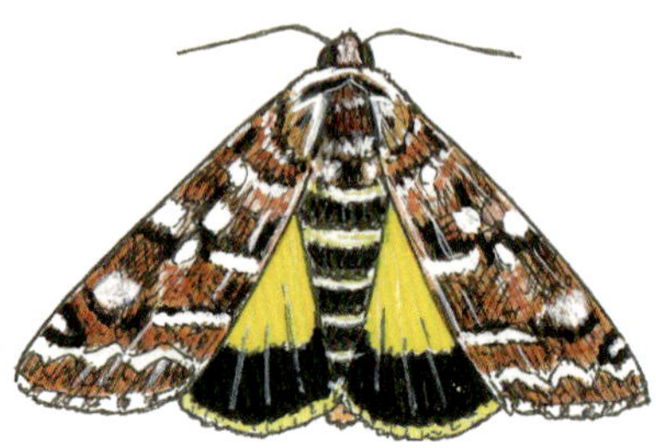

All creatures small and smaller...

Norfolk is at the heart of *Arthropedia*, not least because the author (and artist) resides here, and the book itself was produced and printed in the county. Of perhaps greater significance is the remarkably high proportion of insect and spider species observed on a small patch of garden in urban Norwich.

It is a lesson to us all that wildlife requires relatively little encouragement to make a garden its home. We simply have to become less selfish in our plant selection and garden management. Manicured lawns (worse still, plastic ones), orderly beds of showy cultivars and a heavy hand with the pesticide spray do not make for a healthy wildlife habitat.

Most of us would miss the gentle background music of bees seeking pollen and the seasonal procession of butterflies adorning our flowering shrubs. Surprisingly few people are, however, prepared to compromise their gardening habits to ensure that this sound and spectacle survives. Vanna Bartlett would like to see this change.

By retaining 'wild' sections complete with nettles, thistles, ivy, etc, the species count will rise rapidly. Letting the lawn sprout daisies, dead nettles, dandelions and clover, coupled with less frequent mowing, creates another world of possibilities.

You don't have to sacrifice colour and beauty in order to create a wildlife habitat. Planting for invertebrates allows for water, grass, rockeries, walls and paving, evergreen interest and a riot of flowering plants. Can you imagine the impact if every gardener turned over even 10 per cent of their garden to wildlife?

As a niche publisher, our specialisation is art books, but often with a bias towards natural history and the environment. This, however, is no ordinary art book. Drawing an analogy with the garden, the pictures here aren't simply decorative but have a higher function. Vanna hasn't drawn and painted only the most attractive arthropods, but has given equal billing to the plain or downright unappealing. She is championing the cause of all creatures small and smaller.

At every level of nature, there are threats to the creatures and the environment. Concern and awareness is on the rise, belatedly, and there has been an encouraging surge in interest as regards insects and spiders. This book aims to help with identification, understanding and appreciation of species that are all too often overlooked, but play a vital role in the wellbeing of our planet.

This book was inspired by a Norfolk garden and is inhabited by many creatures found in and around Norwich, but the images, information and messages contained in these pages are relevant to everyone, everywhere.

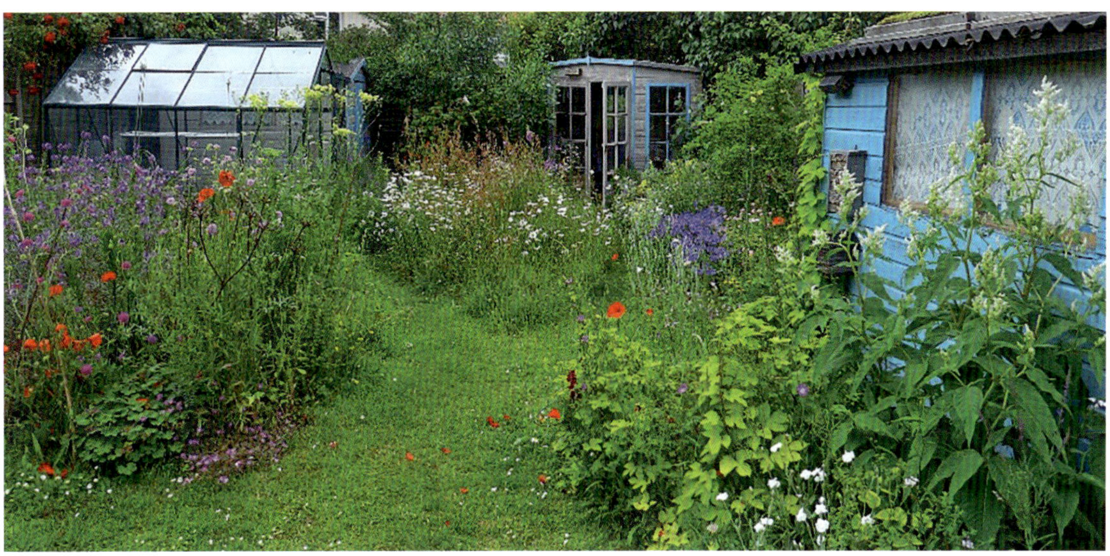

Introduction

Arthropedia is my personal alphabet of invertebrates. It is a pictorial celebration of the rich diversity of life that sits towards the bottom of the food chain, wisely described by the great American biologist E. O. Wilson as the little things that make everything work. While many go about their lives largely unnoticed, others are well known and even admired for their perceived usefulness: bees and ladybirds, for example. Some are pretty to look at while others have very un-pretty habits. Some are reviled and some are loved. They all have a place in the worldwide ecological web and, considering their small size, we should really be able to find a place for them to live out their often amazing little lives.

Like almost everything on the planet, arthropods are in decline. Most people wouldn't notice or mind if a few beetles, flies or moths disappeared – but we would, and do, mourn the loss of birds such as Cuckoos, Spotted Flycatchers and Red-backed Shrikes. While these birds are migratory and have declined through habitat loss both in Britain and in their overwintering quarters overseas, as well as through changes in climate, they are also disappearing because their food supply – the beetles, flies and moths – is shrinking.

Many of the animals depicted here will be familiar; others less so. There are well-known common or garden species alongside rare or localised specialities. Most can be found with a little bit of detective work – knowing where to look for them, what time of year they are around, what they feed on. All you really need is to be observant and have an inquiring mind. But often it's just luck, being in the right place at the right time. It's great when you go out looking for something specific and find it, through knowledge and a bit of fieldcraft, but there's a real wow factor when something unexpected turns up. A lot of my favourite finds have been in my own back garden, and it's a real pleasure to think that we've made our few square metres attractive enough to be chosen as a home.

This book started out as an insect alphabet but I wanted to include spiders so it grew to include other arthropods. The majority of species covered are still insects, largely because I love them but also because they are the largest group of the arthropods with the most species. There are a fair few spiders, limited by my ability to identify them to species (which requires microscopic examination of mature adults). Myriapods (centipedes and millipedes) are another tricky group, so there aren't many of those, but I have managed to include representative examples. Crustaceans are all but omitted, represented only by the largely terrestrial isopods (woodlice). I always intended to portray only land invertebrates (with the odd aquatic bug as an exception), mainly because of the inherent difficulties of finding, drawing and photographing (not to mention identifying) marine or freshwater life.

My aim has been to showcase the amazing diversity and beauty of life at the smaller end of the scale – what I like to call the charismatic microfauna. It is a celebration of the rich invertebrate life that can be found, with a little searching sometimes, in the British Isles. There are so many brilliant creatures literally on our doorsteps without the need to travel around the world – plant up a wildlife-friendly garden or visit a local wild patch and let this amazing world come to you.

Most of the species are not particularly rare; indeed, a lot have been found in my modest suburban back garden, but some have very limited distributions and there are a few extreme rarities that I am very lucky to have seen. There are no 'exotics' as they can all be found (for the time being at least) in Britain, although a couple of my encounters were in continental Europe.

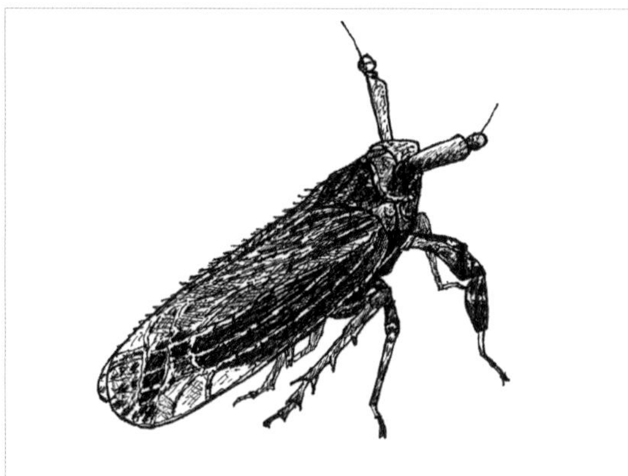

One of the strangest creatures I've come across is the 'true bug' Asiraca clavicornis. *It is only a couple of millimetres long, and if I'd been looking for it I would probably never have found one. As it was, I was sitting in the garden sketching when this one landed on a leaf in front of me.*

I hope this book will whet your appetite and inspire you to go and look at this miniature world and make your own observations and discoveries, to be as enthralled as I am. I hope you'll also want to contribute in any way you can to helping our invertebrates, from putting plants for pollinators in a window-box, gardening more benevolently for wildlife or even volunteering in conservation work or wildlife recording and monitoring.

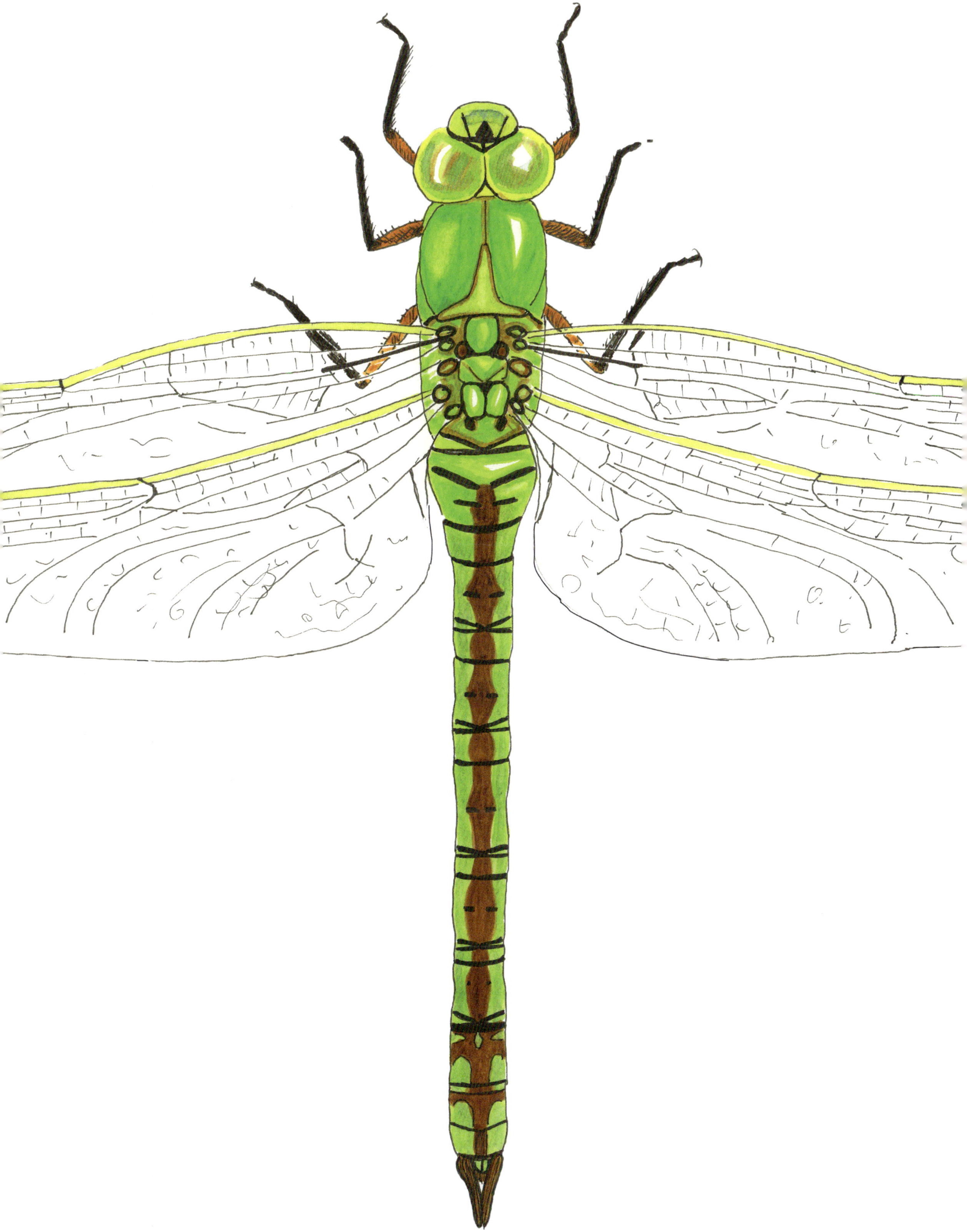

What is an arthropod?

The animal kingdom is divided into vertebrates and invertebrates (animals with and without a backbone) and then sub-divided into various phyla with further sub-divisions into classes, orders, families, genera and species. These divisions are based on shared characteristics. Arthropoda is the largest phylum within the animal kingdom, with more than 80 per cent of all invertebrates being arthropods.

All arthropods have a hard external skeleton (exoskeleton) made of chitin, similar to armour plating. In order to grow, arthropods have to shed their skin, known as moulting. This can be a difficult time, fraught with danger. Not only is the arthropod vulnerable until its new skin hardens, it is also possible to get stuck during the process. Sometimes limbs get damaged or lost. Spiders will actually chew off a leg if it can't be extricated from the old skin. These limbs can be re-grown if they are lost during a very early moult. Sometimes a spider will have all eight legs but one may be noticeably shorter where it hasn't had time to grow back completely.

The word arthropod literally means 'jointed foot', although it is also taken to mean jointed leg. Within a basically similar form, the arthropods (divided into groups depending on the number of limbs and the configuration of the body parts) have evolved and diversified to such an extent that they are known as the Swiss army knives of the invertebrate world – they have a tool for every purpose, and have colonised all but the most inhospitable places on Earth.

The arthropod phylum is divided into four main groups (and a few minor ones): insects, arachnids (which includes spiders), crustaceans (including the isopods that are the woodlice) and myriapods (centipedes and millipedes).

The insects are the largest group and they are characterised by having a body divided into three distinct parts (head, thorax and abdomen) and having six legs (in three pairs). The majority of adult insects are also winged and have the power of flight, although for some this amounts to no more than gliding; and some steadfastly refuse to take to

MEET THE ARTHROPODS

Some typical examples

Insects

1 Small Tortoiseshell Butterfly (Aglais urticae)
2 Common Wasp (Vespula vulgaris)
3 Gymnochaeta viridis
4 Southern Hawker Dragonfly (Aeshna cyanea)
5 Green Shieldbug (Palomena prasina)
6 7-Spot Ladybird (Coccinella septempunctata)

Arachnids

7 Cricket-bat Spider (Mangora acalypha)
8 Harvestman (Odiellus spinosus)
9 Pseudoscorpion (Chthonius ischnocheles)

Myriapods

10 Centipede (Lithobius forficatus)
11 Millipede (Ophiodesmus albonanus)

Crustaceans

12 Water Flea (Daphnia sp.)
13 Green Shore Crab (Carcinus maenas)
14 Woodlouse (Porcellio spinicornis)

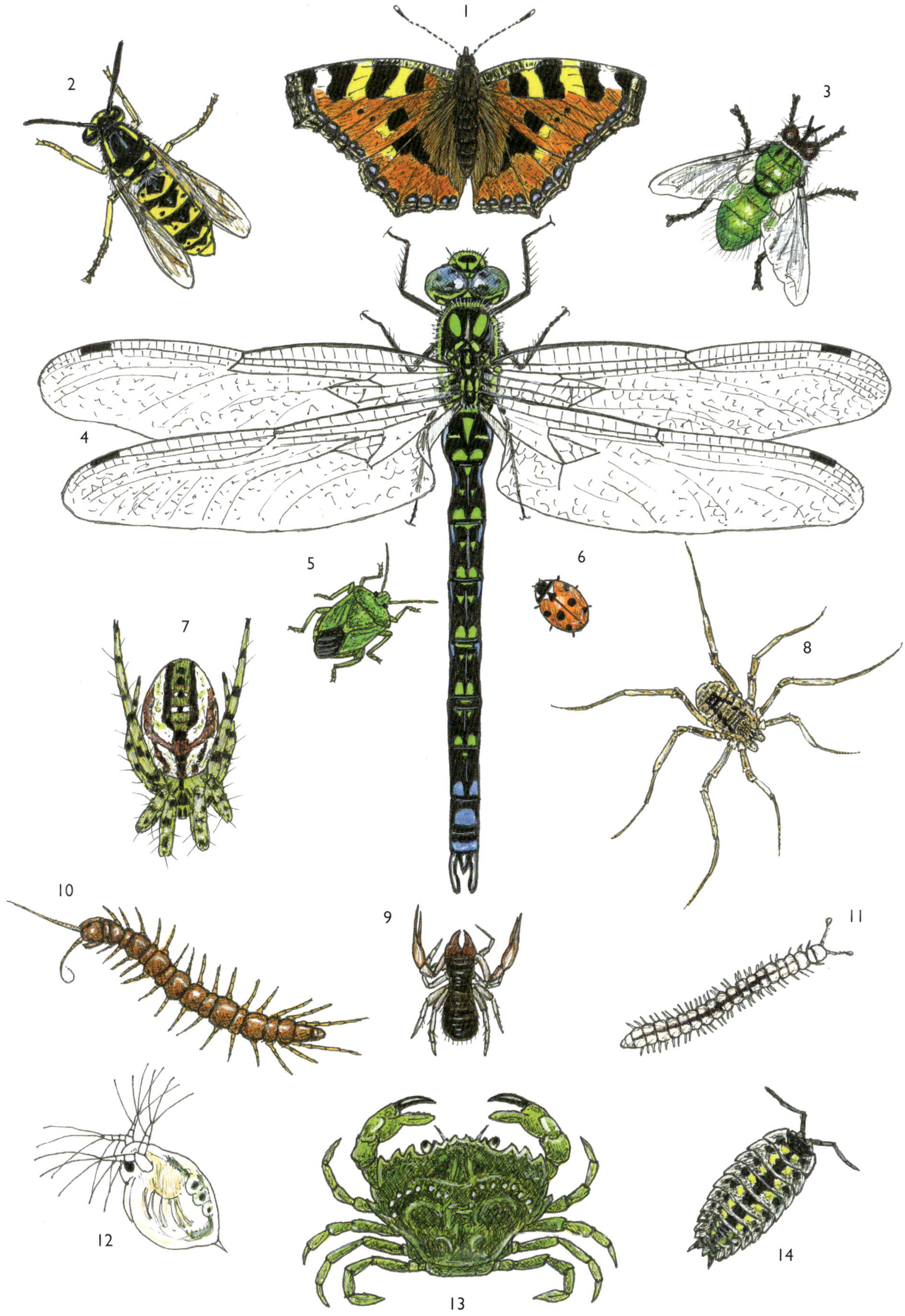
1
2
3
4
5
6
7
8
9
10
11
12
13
14

the air at all even though they do have wings. Some have vestigial wings and cannot fly, and a few never actually develop them. Although all the arthropod groups undergo a certain amount of change as they moult and grow, from juveniles to adults, it is only the insects that undergo the dramatic changes of metamorphosis (see chapter M).

Arachnids differ from insects in having eight legs and a body divided into two parts (the cephalothorax and the abdomen) although in some this is fused into what appears to be one part (eg, the harvestman). As well as spiders, the class contains the harvestmen (Opiliones), mites and ticks, and scorpions and pseudoscorpions. There are no native species of scorpion in Britain but we do have 27 species of pseudoscorpion which are very small, most only 2mm or 3mm long, some less. I saw my first one many years ago and only recently found a second. They can be found in a variety of habitats in leaf litter, compost heaps, under bark on decaying trees and under stones. Both the ones I found were indoors in bathrooms!

Spiders are unique in having spinnerets on the underside of their abdomens, linked to special glands from which they produce silk. Not all spiders make webs but they do all produce silk. They use silken strands for migrating – known as ballooning – spinning out a fine thread and then letting themselves be carried off with the breeze.

I have only recently started looking at spiders properly. There are around 670 species in Britain and they can be rather challenging to identify. Even with the new field guides that are available it is still hard (sometimes impossible) to identify many spiders to species, especially in the field. Quite often only mature adults can be identified for certain, and even then close examination under a microscope may be necessary. So I have been limited not only by the number I've seen but by those I could actually put a name to. On several plates you will see something 'sp.' for species, meaning that I couldn't identify a creature to a specific species.

Myriapods are the centipedes and millipedes. Myriapod means many legged, centipede means a hundred legs, and millipede a thousand, but none have that actual number of legs. Centipedes always have an odd number of pairs of legs: there is one with 49 pairs (ie, 98 legs), and another with 51 (ie, 102).

Millipedes are distinguished by having two pairs of legs on most of their body segments. These are generally short, and the millipede moves along rather slowly – they used to be known as galley worms because the action of all the little legs looked like rows of oars on a galley ship.

Centipedes have only one pair of legs per segment, which are generally much longer than those of millipedes; and they move faster, especially the so-called stone centipedes. The soil or earth centipedes resemble long, thin bootlaces and tend to writhe about and move a lot more slowly.

The Crustacea are the well-known crabs, lobsters, shrimps, etc. None of these marine or freshwater creatures have been included as I decided early on to cover virtually only terrestrial invertebrates. So the crustaceans are represented by the isopods (meaning equal legs), which include the woodlice with seven pairs of legs. See chapter 'I is for Isopods' for a diagram of a woodlouse.

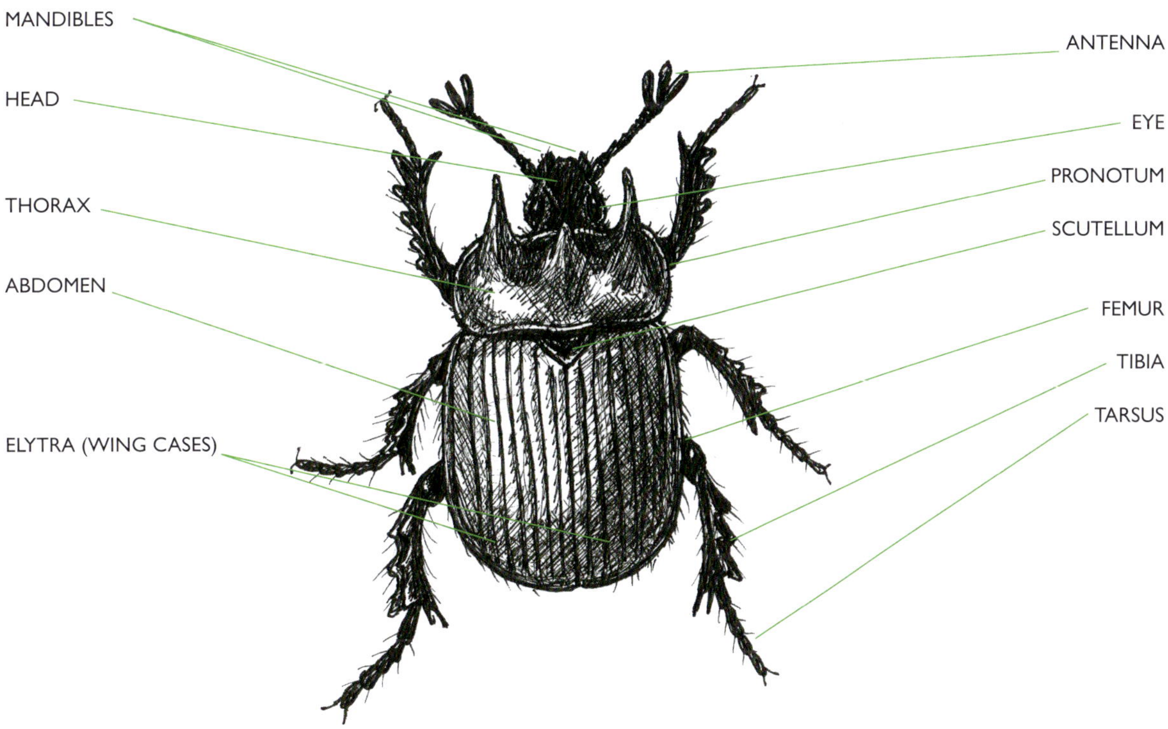

Minotaur Beetle (Typhaeus typhoeus), a typical insect with three pairs of legs and a body divided into head, thorax and abdomen.

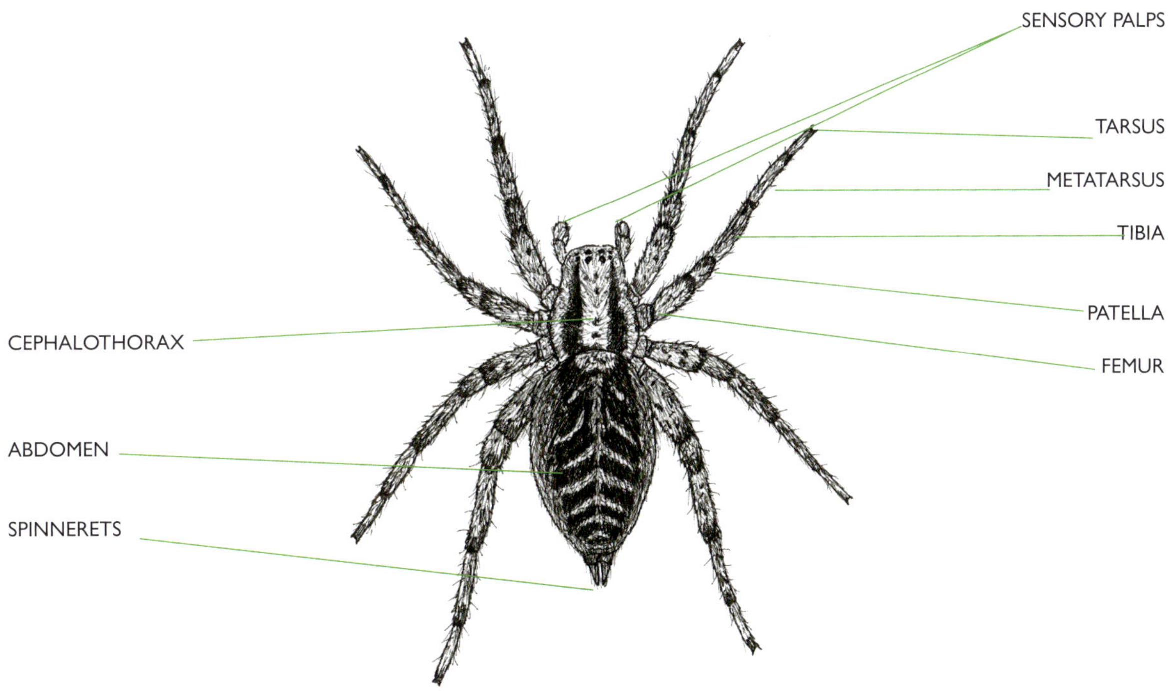

Female Labyrinth Spider (Agelena labyrinthica), a typical arachnid with four pairs of legs and a body divided into two distinct parts, cephalothorax and abdomen.

What's in a name?

Throughout this book I have used a mixture of English and scientific (ie, Latin or Greek) names reflecting current usage, in that English names are generally used for well-known groups such as butterflies and larger moths; whereas others, such as flies and spiders, very often don't have English names.

This made creating the alphabet a lot easier as I then had more options to choose from for each letter. I could also play around with names, having pages for Reds and Yellows, Emperors and Tigers as well as Flies and Shieldbugs and then Coleoptera, Isopods and Orthoptera. I also like a lot of the old English names, although I'm not so keen on some of the more modern ones – for *Helophilus pendulus* (a hoverfly), the English name 'The Footballer' really doesn't do it for me. And don't get me started on Wasp Spider... (see Arachnids page).

There is a danger in just using English names. When I was growing up, a 'Daddy-long-legs' was a harvestman, but my husband gave the name to the cranefly. It can also be applied to the spindly-legged spider *Pholcus phalangioides*. Ironically, we both knew what we were talking about when using the term harvestman or cranefly.

A lot of English names are not commonly adopted, and vernacular names can vary greatly around the country, so using a species' scientific name is really the only sure way of knowing that you are talking to someone about the same thing.

Long-legged beasties – who's the Daddy?

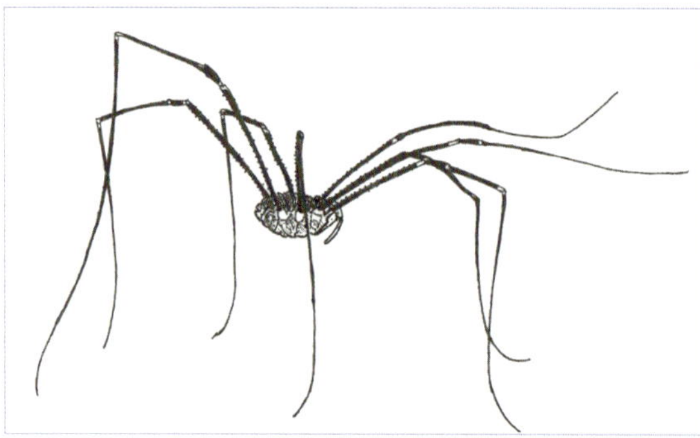

Harvestman such as Opilio canestrinii (left), cranefly Tipula sp. (below left) and spider Pholcus phalangioides (below right) are all commonly called 'Daddy-long-legs' by different people. Using their scientific names is the only sure way of knowing which species you mean.

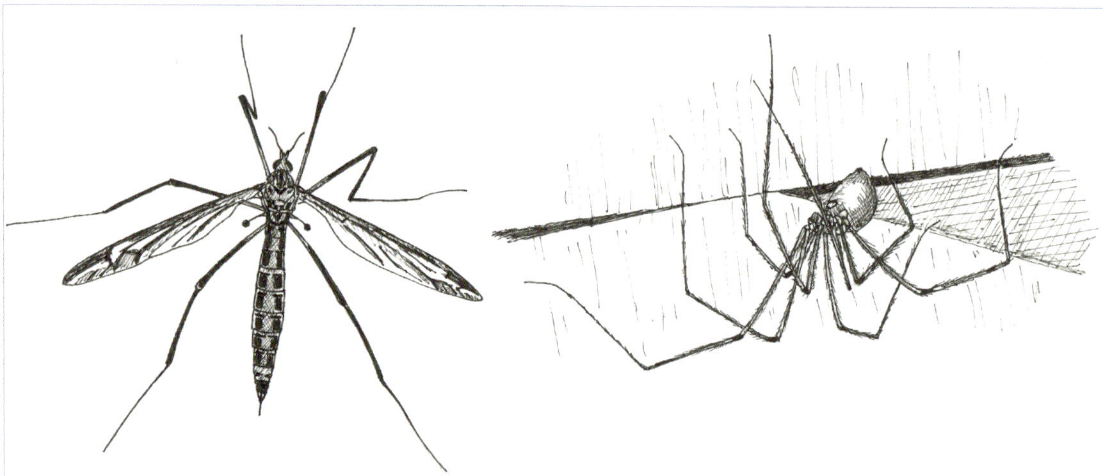

This is especially important if the person you are talking to is from another country altogether.

Scientific names consist of two parts. The first name refers to the genus and always starts with a capital letter; and the second is the specific name, which is all lower case. Scientific names are generally written in italics, too. So the solitary bee *Andrena cineraria* belongs to the genus *Andrena* (think of it as the equivalent to a surname), and its specific name is *cineraria* meaning ashy, which neatly gives it its English name Ashy Mining Bee (*Andrena* species being known as mining bees).

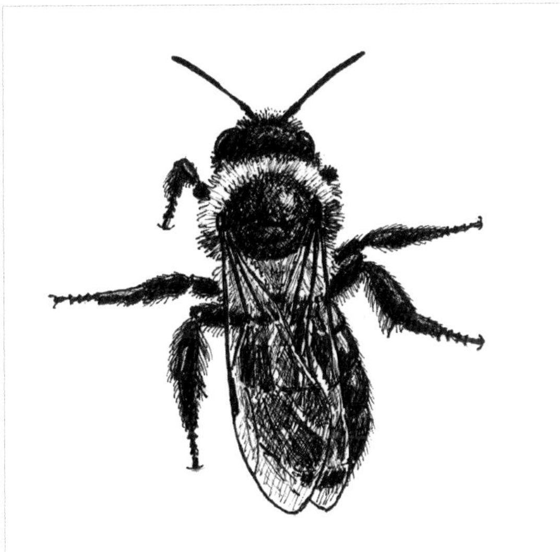

The rather lovely Ashy Mining Bee. The English name is a pretty straightforward translation of the scientific name Andrena cineraria.

As mentioned previously, sometimes on the plates I have used the letters sp. after a generic name. This stands for species and indicates that the invertebrate that has been illustrated could not be identified to species. For example, *Lucilia* sp. (plate F) shows that the greenbottle fly is known to be in the genus *Lucilia* but there is insufficient detail to determine the exact species. This is often the case when specific details need to be checked, such as the number of bristles on legs or some feature that can only be seen from a certain angle. To identify most spiders a mature adult needs to be examined under magnification.

Using a mixture of English and scientific names will probably annoy some readers. But anyone who says that scientific names are difficult should remember that most of us know what a *Rhododendron* is, and children are quite happy to talk about *Tyrannosaurus rex*.

Many people, including naturalists, use English names when talking about birds, mammals and butterflies. A lot of invertebrates don't have a generally accepted English name, anyway, although more are being coined to help encourage an interest in less well-known groups of species. Some find scientific names off-putting, but they become easier to remember the more you begin to know and it's interesting deciphering them – I almost wish I'd studied Latin at school now. I have given English names alongside the scientific ones where they are well established.

An example of possible confusion arising from English names is the Pine Ladybird. When English names were being assigned to ladybirds, *Exochomus quadripustulatus* (a small black species with four red spots) had been recorded pretty much exclusively on conifers and especially Scots Pine, so it was given the name Pine Ladybird. As further survey results came in, it was soon clear that it wasn't such a conifer specialist after all and was recorded from a whole host of other trees and shrubs – in fact, wherever scale insects were found upon which it preyed. However, I'm quite happy with it being called the Pine Ladybird (especially as I know to look for it elsewhere) as it is much more memorable and easy to pronounce than its scientific name.

Another example is to do with flowers rather than invertebrates, but deserves mention. The poet William Wordsworth loved the flowers of Lesser Celandine (*Ficaria verna*), dedicating three poems to them. After his death, therefore, it was deemed only proper to grace his memorial tablet with his favourite flower. The only problem is that the carving appears to represent the Greater Celandine (*Chelidonium majus*) which isn't at all related to the Lesser Celandine, being in the poppy

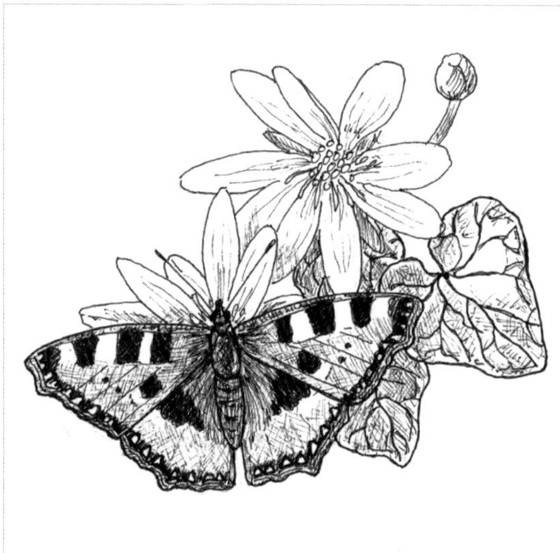

Which is the Celandine? Despite sharing a common name, Lesser and Greater Celandines are not remotely related and belong to different families. Wordsworth's beloved Lesser Celandine has small bright-yellow 'star-burst' flowers and is pictured above being visited by a Small Tortoiseshell butterfly (Aglais urticae) in early March sunshine. The larger flowers of Greater Celandine are also yellow, but it is a taller, more upright plant with distinctive seedpods and is related to the poppy. Flowering in late April and May, it is attractive to various insects including the solitary bee Andrena nigroaenea, as pictured below.

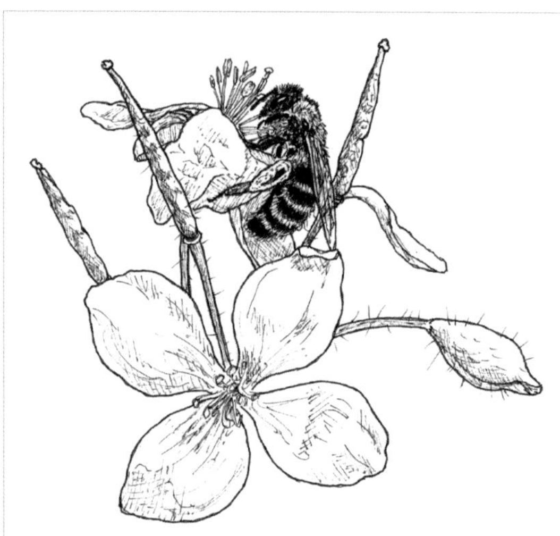

family (Papaveraceae) rather than the buttercup family (Ranunculaceae). This might be down to stylised artistic interpretation, but those who know about these things and have seen it agree it looks more like a Greater Celandine. It is an altogether different flower, blooming later in the year and makes little sense of the poems, which are all about the Lesser Celandine heralding the arrival of spring when it flowers as early as February, lifting its golden face to the first warm rays of sunshine, closing against the stinging pelts of hail and rain then opening again to greet the sun.

Having said all that, I had to make the decision not to include the scientific names of all the plants mentioned in the book for reasons of space. Most English names are pretty well used, and it is easy enough to find the scientific name in a good plant identification guide. After all, this is meant to be a celebration of invertebrates – not flowers. There are plenty of lovely, beautifully illustrated botanical books if you do want to find out more. Personally, I'm sticking with the 'creepy-crawlies'!

A note on the plates

The invertebrates featured on the plates are not drawn to scale, and each plate has creatures depicted at different sizes to the others. Most are larger than life size. Each plate has been carefully designed to showcase the variety of invertebrates, balancing colours and shapes into some kind of artistic design. The only criteria for inclusion were that they had to be found in Britain and that I had actually seen them, for in order to draw a species I was relying on my own field sketches, observations and photographs as reference material.

I have therefore personally encountered every species that appears on the plates, and usually have been able to sketch and/or photograph them. While the photographs have been the major material from which I have produced the illustrations, my field sketches of living creatures have provided me with invaluable insights into behaviour and movement and hopefully have allowed my artwork to look alive, rather than like a case of museum specimens. Dead specimens that I've found have been very useful for making detailed drawings to work out how complex invertebrates fit together.

Two books have been a great influence on my work. Moses Harris's *The Aurelian* (published in 1766) is a beautiful collection of hand-coloured engravings showing many of our butterflies and moths along with their larvae and food plants, most of which were reared by Harris himself. He was the foremost entomological artist of his time, and his work is still greatly admired. ('Aurelian' is the name the early butterfly and moth enthusiasts gave themselves; it is derived from the Latin word *aureoles*, meaning golden, which was sometimes used to describe a butterfly chrysalis. 'Entomologist' was coined by the Victorian collectors.)

The other book is Ernst Haeckel's *Art Forms in Nature*, where science and art are brought together to great effect. The wonders of the natural world are showcased with as much attention to artistic beauty in the symmetrical layout of each plate as to the accurate scientific portrayal of the subjects. The pages are a delight to behold from a purely artistic perspective, never mind the scientific interest of the subjects depicted, which include a host of microscopic organisms.

My plates were completed in pen and ink to get the finest details and then hand coloured with watercolour washes in the manner of old engravings. The black and white illustrations in the text also hark back to the traditions of our earliest illustrated books.

This is not an identification guide, although I do hope that I've drawn things well enough to be recognised. There are bound to be mistakes, though hopefully not too glaring, due to having a poor photograph, too rough a sketch, a slip of the pen or tired eyes, but I've tried to do my subjects justice and represent them to the best of my ability.

Some days this has been easier than others. There are species that I'm more familiar with; others that I just find simpler to draw. Spiders go together very oddly when you're used to insects, and who knew how complicated woodlice are? A lot of the species are extremely small and it's hard to see the detail, even with a macro photograph. Often interpreting my sketches or old blurry photos has led to errors that I've detected and changed before completing the plates. I'm sure others have slipped through...

There are just over 400 individual invertebrates depicted on the colour plates, covering more than 300 species. Most of them were found in Norfolk, with a high percentage in my garden, so there is a definite south-east bias to the species covered. But part of the point of the book was to highlight what amazing creatures can be found literally on our own doorsteps.

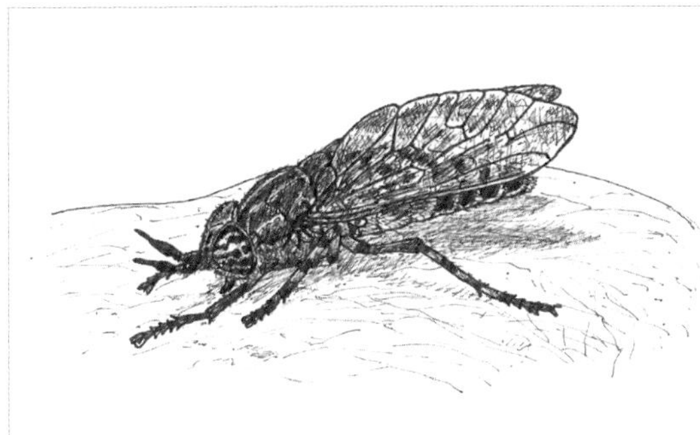

Suffering for my art: in order to get a close view of this beautiful fly Haematopota pluvialis (commonly called the Notch-horned Cleg) I had to let it draw blood, albeit briefly. The minor irritation of an itchy, swollen bump on the back of my hand for the rest of the day was more than worth it, although I don't feel it is necessary to repeat the encounter any time soon!

I discovered a lot of fascinating invertebrates as I was working on the book, usually just after I'd finished the plate they would have appeared on! In order to include some of these gems, I decided to make extra drawings to go with the text. These are very different to the colour plates: not only are they black and white, but generally they portray invertebrates in a natural setting – how you would encounter them.

In the accompanying text, species in blue refer to those depicted on the plate.

A is for... ARACHNIDS

1 *Araneus quadratus*
2 *Enoplognatha ovata*
3 *Garden Spider (Araneus diadematus)*
4 *Nuctenea umbratica*
5 *Argiope bruennichi*
6 *Misumena vatia*
7 *Araniella sp.*
8 *Alopecosa barbipes*
9 *Zelotes latreillei*
10 *Pardosa sp*

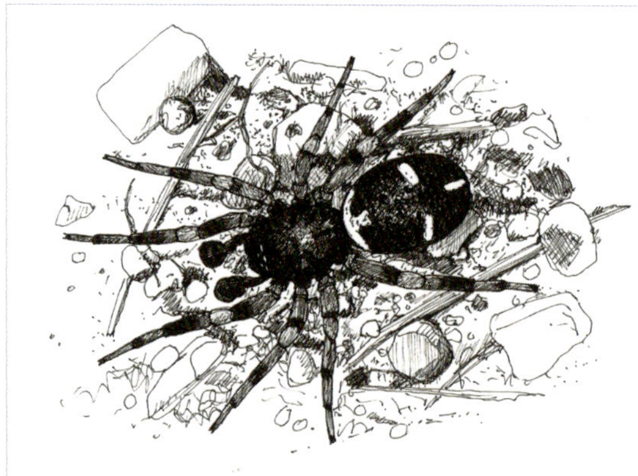

Asagena (formerly Steatoda) phalerata can easily be mistaken for an ant when first seen moving rapidly across the ground. The white markings on the abdomen and the dark annulations (rings) on the legs break up the outline of the spider when it is stationary, making it almost impossible to spot on a stony background. They are widespread but uncommon, generally being found on heathland or dry grassland where they do actually prey almost exclusively on ants.

Arachnids include mites, ticks, pseudoscorpions and harvestmen, but I decided to concentrate here on the most widely known arachnids, the spiders. (Examples of the other types of arachnid can be found on plate L.)

Spiders tend to be loved or loathed, especially when found indoors, scuttling fast across the floor at a rate of knots or crouching in the plughole when you want to have a bath. In the garden they are generally seen as a very welcome pest control, trapping flies and other 'unwanted' insects in their sticky silken webs.

I must admit that I used to be a bit scared of spiders, but have largely overcome this by trying to identify the ones in my garden and those that venture indoors. Spiders are amazing in so many respects. They can re-grow limbs that are lost in their early developmental stages, and several species show a surprising level of parental care, sitting guard over their eggs and newly hatched spiderlings. Taking a closer look at spiders and finding out more about their lives has led to an increasing fascination with them, and I now actively seek out new species – although I still tend to keep the larger ones at arm's length!

The orbweb spiders (family Araneidae) are perhaps the most frequently encountered, with their obvious webs strung across gardens in late summer, perfectly hung so that you walk into them. I've lost count of the times I've blundered into one and ended up with some web-wrapped insect adorning my clothes or an inadvertent spider earring dangling from an earlobe.

The plate depicts the well-known Garden Spider, *Araneus diadematus*, familiar to gardeners with its distinctive white cross on the abdomen. The large plump spiders that you come across late summer into autumn are the mature females, the males being smaller and less obvious as they are out

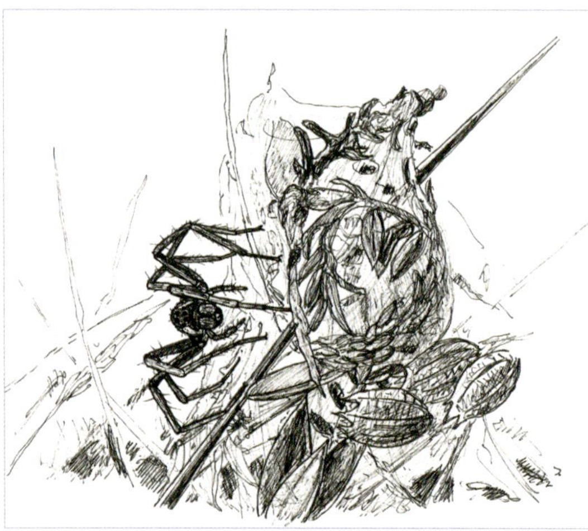

Pisaura mirabilis female sitting guard on her nursery web after most of the spiderlings have hatched and dispersed. Among our most distinctive and easily recognised spiders, they are commonly called Nurseryweb Spiders after the tent-like web they construct to house their young. They start off carrying their large, pale, spherical egg sac around underneath the body, held firmly in their chelicerae (jaws), before depositing it in a protective web where they sit guard.

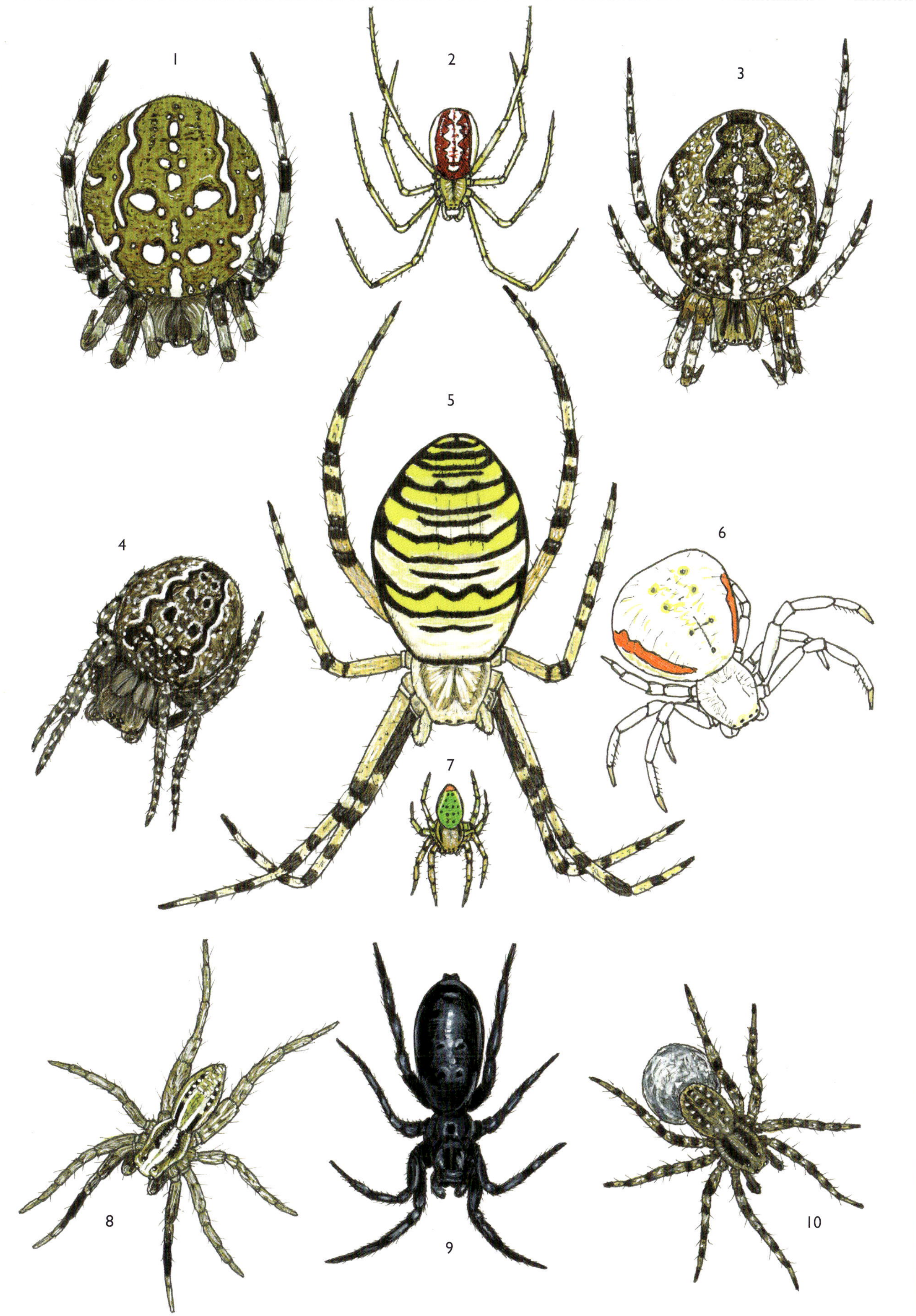
1
2
3
4
5
6
7
8
9
10

searching for a mate rather than sitting in a web. They vary in colour from very dark brown through pale fawn to terracotta and even deep orange.

A slightly less abundant spider is *Araneus quadratus*, another of the orbweb spiders like the Garden Spider. It is considerably bigger than the latter and has the distinction of being Britain's heaviest arachnid. It is beautifully marked, reminding me of an exotic octopus, with four large white spots on its abdomen amongst smaller wavy lines and spots. Again, the ground colour can vary.

On a much smaller scale are the *Araniella* species, the so-called cucumber spiders. There are five species in Britain, only one of which is readily identifiable; the others all share the same beautiful light apple-green abdomen. The red spot above the spinnerets is often more obvious in immature specimens. The two commonest species (*A. cucurbitina* and *A. opisthographa*) are easily overlooked, but I regularly find one or two in our garden – sometimes tucked up inside rose petals when dead-heading the flowers.

The star of the plate is *Argiope bruennichi*. It is an exotic beast for me, having first seen it on a Greek island, eventually catching up with it in Britain many years later. It inhabits areas with long grass where it spins its substantial webs and where there are plenty of grasshoppers, its favoured food. The web is constructed fairly low down and with a characteristic zigzag of thickened silk in the centre, known as a stabilimentum. The female is a truly handsome spider both in size and colour. The powers-that-be have sadly saddled it with the English name Wasp Spider. Memorable, yes (like the animal itself), but doubly damned as a lot of people dislike wasps as vehemently as spiders. In our house it is given the cuddlier epithet of The Stripy Jumper Spider. What's not to like?

The last orbweb on the plate is *Nuctenea umbratica*, the Walnut Orbweb Spider. This is a large, beautiful spider, shiny like polished wood with subtle light markings on the abdomen. It is mostly nocturnal and has to be searched for at night by torchlight. We had one living under the cap of a linen post, but they are often found under the eaves of sheds or on fences where they have somewhere secluded to hide away during the day.

Misumena vatia is one of the crab spiders (family Thomisidae). They do not build webs to snare their prey but instead sit on top of or in flowers. Here they wait for some unsuspecting insect to come and visit for pollen or nectar, before pouncing on them. A couple of the crab spiders are able to change colour to blend in with their surroundings – *Misumena* can be a pale ghostly white or bright yellow but usually has red lateral stripes on the abdomen.

Enoplognatha ovata is another variable spider, being pale greenish-yellow with varying amounts of red. It is known as the Common Candy-striped Spider (there are other similar species). In my garden they tend to live in webs under the flower heads of umbellifers, their presence given away by the corpses of flies in their webs. It is one of the comb-footed spiders from the family Theridiidae. Females are often found tucked up in a leaf with their pale blue-grey egg sac.

The wolf spiders (Lycosidae) are so called after their habit of running down their prey. There are eight different genera in Britain, with *Pardosa* being the largest with 15 species, all of which are rather similar and challenging to tell apart. The females are often to be seen running about on the ground or amongst low vegetation carrying their egg sac attached to their spinnerets at the back of the abdomen, as in the one illustrated. They also carry the newly hatched spiderlings for the first few days.

Alopecosa barbipes is another wolf spider which is found in fairly open habitats such as sandy heathland and dry grassland. Unlike the *Pardosa* spiders, the female *Alopecosa* digs a burrow to lay her egg sac in and remains inside with it until the baby spiders hatch out.

Zelotes are members of the Gnaphosidae or ground spiders. They are distinctive in appearance, being glossy black and somewhat elongated. *Zelotes latreillei* is the commonest and can be found on sandy heathlands, lurking under stones or, on sunny days, seen running rapidly across the ground.

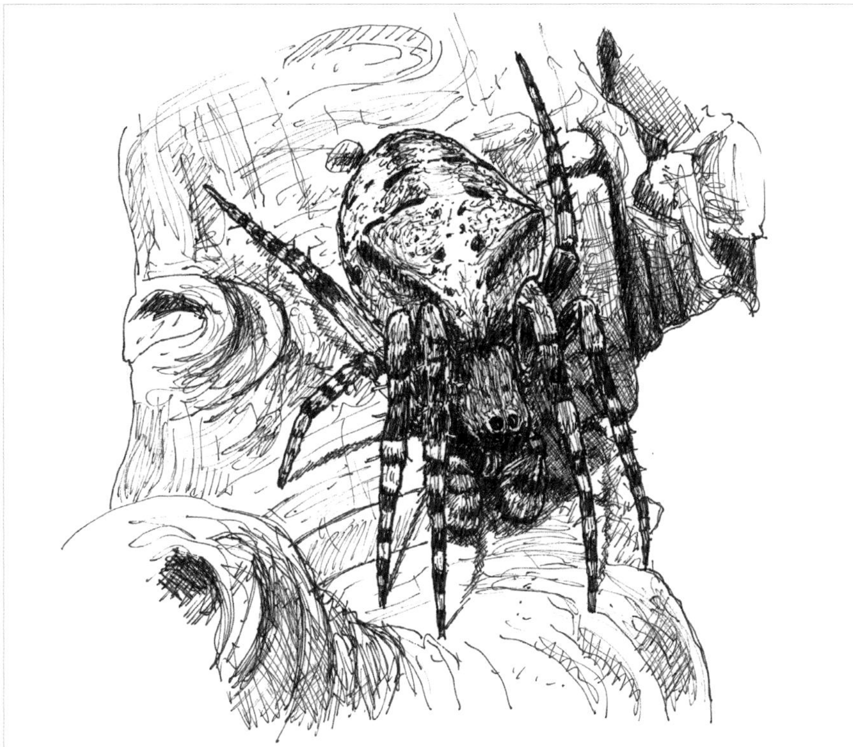

I didn't 'discover' Gibbaranea gibbosa until long after the plate for arachnids was finished, which is a shame as it is a lovely spider. It is another of the orb weavers, easily recognised by the 'shoulder pad' humps on the front of the abdomen and the delicate green tinge to its sides – which makes it difficult to spot hidden away amongst the foliage of trees.

B is for... BEES

1 Bombus pascuorum
2 Colletes hederae
3 Anthophora quadrimaculata
4 Andrena hattorfiana
5 Bombus terrestris
6 Dasypoda hirtipes
7 Nomada goodeniana
8 Melecta albifrons
9 Hylaeus signatus
10 Anthidium manicatum
11 Epeolus cruciger
12 Lasioglossum smeathmanellum
13 Megachile centuncularis
14 Osmia bicolor
15 Andrena fulva

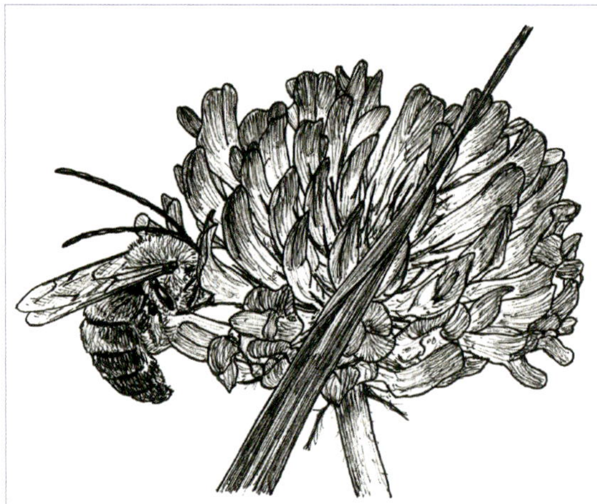

Eucera longicornis. The extremely long antennae of the male Long-horned Bee makes it unmistakable, even when its head is buried in a Red Clover flower.

There are more than 270 species of bee in Britain. Ignoring the Honeybee (only one species and, as nearly all are reared in artificial hives, it should really be considered livestock), there are 25 species of bumblebee and the rest are so-called solitary bees. The bumblebees are known as social bees as they live communally with one fertile female (the queen) in a nest and lots of worker bees (non-breeding females) that collect pollen and nectar, help rear the young and defend the nest. The solitary bees have individual nest holes that they provision with food, although often they are closely packed together into nesting aggregations. These aggregations range from a few nest holes to hundreds, usually of one species but sometimes several species together exploiting suitable habitat.

In Britain we have 25 genera of solitary bee. The largest is *Andrena*, the mining bees. There are also mason bees (*Osmia*), plasterer bees (*Colletes*), leafcutters (*Megachile*), wool carders (*Anthidium*), etc. The English names reflect their nesting behaviour – mining bees tunnel into soil, mason bees use holes in walls (and readily take to artificial bee hotels), plasterers line their nest cells with a waterproof substance, leafcutters cut sections out of leaves to make nest cells, and wool carders use plant fibres for theirs.

Then there are the bees that don't really behave like bees – the cleptoparasites, sometimes called cuckoo bees. They invade the nest of another species of bee, lay their eggs in it, and the larva that hatches out either eats the food store (thus starving the original larva) or simply kills the larva and then eats its food store. Either way, the outcome is the same – a dead host larva. Examples of these cleptoparasites are the wasp-like *Nomada* species, the black and yellow *Nomada goodeniana* being a typical example, although many of the smaller species are red and black. These prey mainly on *Andrena* species. Other cleptoparasites include two species of *Epeolus*, whose hosts are *Colletes* bees; *Melecta albifrons*, which can be found around the nests of *Anthophora plumipes*; and the sharp-tailed bees, *Coelioxys* sp. (see plate K), which go for *Megachile* species.

Most solitary bees nest in tunnels that they excavate in the ground. Bare, sandy soils are especially good, and sometimes lawns are used or sunny banks and cliffs. Some woodland species use tree root plates (the root and soil exposed when a tree falls down) if they are facing the sun. Others tunnel into mortar in old walls, excavate holes in dead wood, utilise hollow plant stems, and one even uses the vacated gall of a fly in reed stems (see chapter F for Flies). Artificial bee hotels provide useful nest sites for these so-called aerial nesters – mason bees, leafcutters and some *Hylaeus* species (yellow-face bees).

Osmia bicolor is rather special in that the females nest in the empty shells of banded snails, usually making three nest cells but sometimes as many as

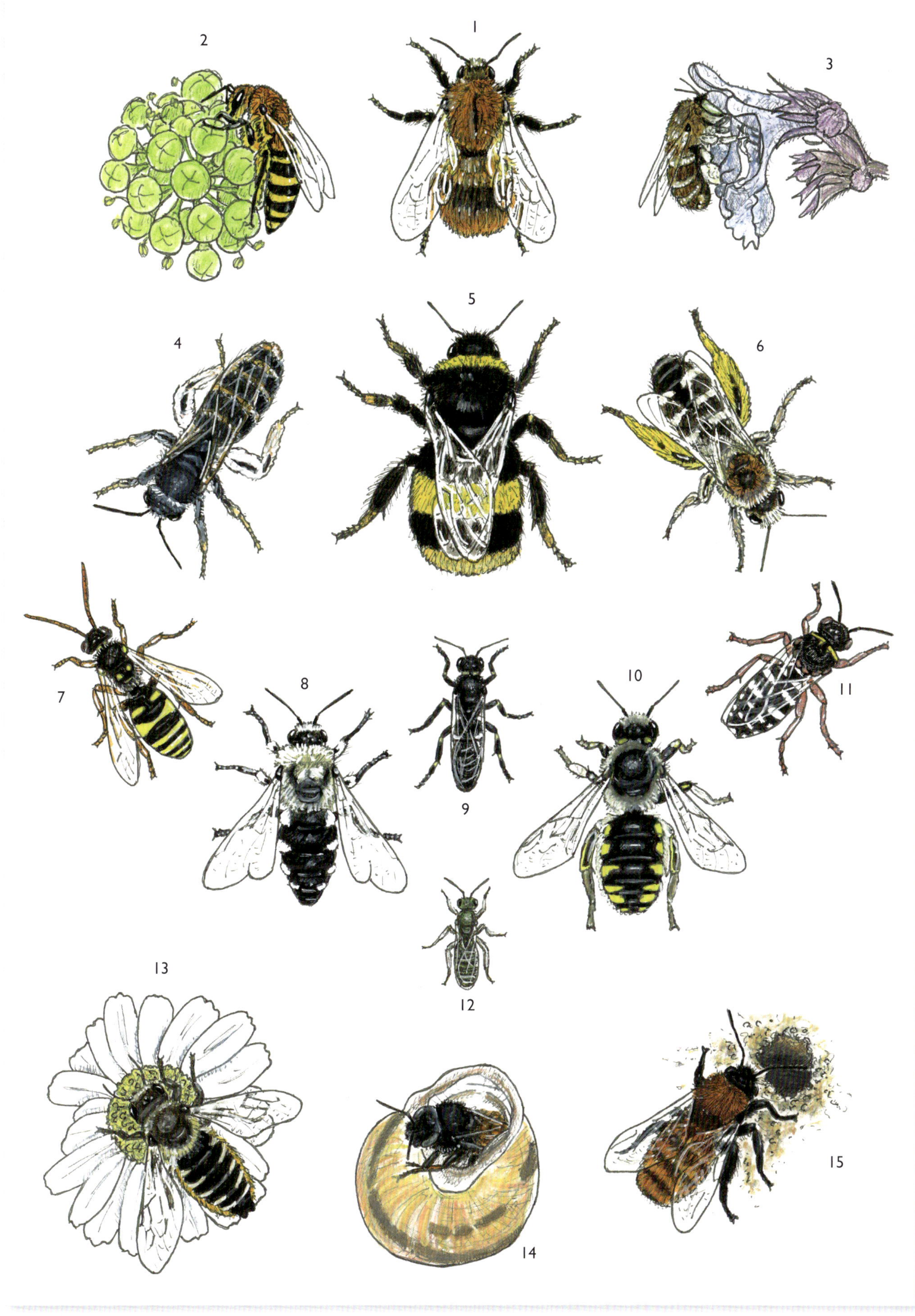
2
1
3
5
4
6
7
8
10
11
9
12
13
15
14

five depending on the size of the snail shell. When she has completed the last cell, she seals up the entrance and then covers the entire shell in dry grass stems or pine needles either to disguise it or to help regulate temperature, or possibly both.

Andrena hattorfiana, the Large Scabious Mining Bee, is our largest *Andrena*, slightly bigger than a Honeybee. The females gather pollen exclusively from scabious flowers although they will take nectar from other flowers. The females are very attractive when their hind legs are laden with pink pollen as depicted. *Andrena fulva* is a common spring species with lovely rich, foxy-red thorax and abdomen contrasting with a black head and legs. They like to nest in bare ground, leaving a little tell-tale cone of soil around the hole. We always get a few on our allotment in the asparagus bed.

There are several species of leafcutter, with *Megachile centuncularis* being one of the commoner ones. Rather than gathering pollen on their hind legs, the females have a pollen brush (scopa) on the underside of the abdomen. When they visit flowers they often look as though they are standing on their heads as they brush the anthers with their abdomen to pick up pollen (particularly on knapweed flowers).

Female *Dasypoda hirtipes* are endowed with the most enormous orangey hair fringes on their hind legs for gathering pollen, which they do exclusively from yellow flowers of the Asteraceae, such as hawkweeds. This magnificent accoutrement has led to them being given the name Pantaloon Bee. As the flowers from which they gather pollen often close up in the afternoon, this is a bee that should be searched for in the morning. I have found them in Norfolk nesting on the cliff tops on the north coast and in the car park at Weeting Heath in the Brecks. We have also had them collecting pollen in our back garden from Common Catsear, which flowers prolifically in our deliberately unkempt lawn.

Another regular visitor to our garden is *Anthidium manicatum*, the Wool Carder Bee. So far they haven't nested in the garden, but we have had males roosting overnight in a bee hotel and both males and females come in to take nectar from Purple Toadflax flowers. We have planted *Stachys lanata* (Lamb's Ears) in the hope that the females will collect the soft hairs off the leaves (so-called wool-carding) for their nest cells.

Of the smaller species of bee, *Hylaeus* are unusual in that they do not collect pollen externally. Instead, these small black bees ingest pollen and nectar, storing it internally (a bit like a bird's crop) to take back to

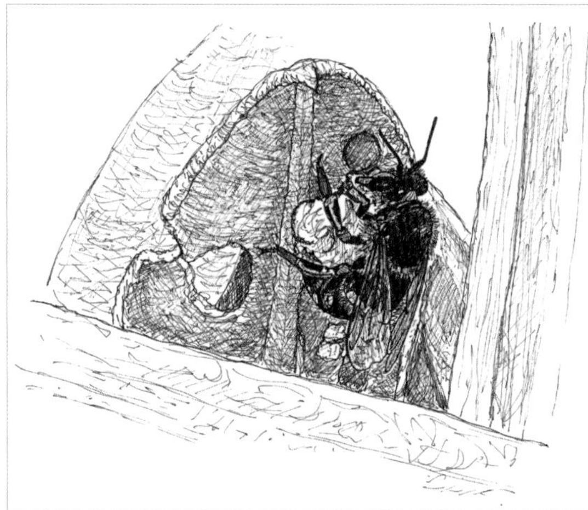

A female Wool Carder (Anthidium manicatum) collecting plant fibres from a Stachys leaf. The fibres are chewed off the leaf and gathered into a ball, rather like rolling up a duvet. The female then flies off to her nest site with the 'wool' tucked under her abdomen. Telltale bare patches on the underside of Stachys leaves are often a sign that one of these bees has been at work.

the nest where they regurgitate it. These bees have characteristic yellow patches on their faces that vary between species. *Hylaeus signatus* is the largest.

The *Lasioglossum* species are sometimes known as furrow bees from the small groove apparent at the tip of the abdomen in females. It isn't actually a groove but a bare patch surrounded by raised hairs, giving the appearance of a depression, and is called a rima. This is a very obvious characteristic, shared only with *Halictus* species, that helps differentiate them from other types of bee. There are more than 30 species in Britain, varying in size from very small to almost Honeybee size. Although a few are quite distinctive, most look much alike; as such, they are challenging to identify. They have been described, rather unkindly, as 'monotonously morphologically similar'. *Lasioglossum smeathmanellum* is one of four metallic greenish species. They generally nest in holes in masonry, and I discovered a small colony in the cracks in lime mortar in a mediaeval building in the centre of Norwich. I hope that nobody decides to re-point the wall and accidentally make them homeless.

Of all the bees in all the world, I love *Anthophora quadrimaculata* the best. These are truly charismatic little bees with beautiful grey-green eyes, a nicely banded furry abdomen and a characteristic loud buzz as they zip around flowers. They appeared in our garden the year we moved in, exploiting the newly planted Catmint, and have been with us every summer since. Their appearance each summer is as eagerly awaited as the return of the local Swifts, and I shall be bereft if one year neither turns up. We didn't know what they were to start with as there weren't any good bee guide books available; and as they age the brown hairs fade to grey, adding to the confusion. We named them 'Mouse Bees' from the small size, grey colour and how they actively dart about foraging. When we did get to put a name to them, we discovered that they are pretty rare in our neck of the woods with very few records other than ours. This has led to my intense interest in bees – some would say I'm obsessed – and we have clocked up more than 60 species in our garden.

If *Anthophora* bees are my all-time favourites, then *Colletes* come a very close second. There are eight species in Norfolk, and we managed to track them all down in one year, a feat accomplished by several train journeys, taxis and long walks in the Brecks on interminably hot days during one of the hottest summers on record, as well as a couple of visits to the coast. I'm not sure I'll be trying that again. *Colletes hederae*, the Ivy Bee, has only been in Britain since 2001, and was discovered to be a separate species as recently as 1993.

Over the last few years its range has increased dramatically, spreading around the coast and heading north, its progress tracked by eager bee enthusiasts logging their sightings. It is one of our latest flying solitary bees, timing its emergence to coincide with an abundance of ivy flowers in September and October. Ivy Bees can nest in huge aggregations of several hundred individuals. They are very docile and can easily be observed at close quarters. The males swarm low over the ground above the nest holes, awaiting the emergence of new females. When one emerges, several males will fall upon her, creating a mating ball of several males (a dozen or two), all desperate to mate with the single female at the centre.

The well-known bumblebees are the social bees. Most of them nest in old mouse nests, under vegetation or in banks. *Bombus terrestris* is probably one of our best-known bumblebees. The huge queens are out of hibernation on the first warm days of the year, taking nectar from early flowers or buzzing about low over the ground searching for a suitable nest site. *Bombus pascuorum* is one of the commonest and most widespread, certainly where I live. It is a rather variable species but always has some black hairs on its abdomen that help distinguish it from other brown bumblebees.

Many of our bumblebees have suffered dramatic declines, with at least two species now extinct. A third, *Bombus subterraneus*, disappeared completely in the 1980s but has been successfully re-introduced from Sweden and is slowly re-establishing. *Bombus muscorum* only survives in numbers in coastal locations, with a stronghold on the Scottish islands; on Shetland, it has evolved into a separate subspecies (*Bombus muscorum* ssp. *agricolae*). At the other extreme end of Britain, another subspecies was on the Isles of Scilly, but sadly the 'Scilly Bee' is probably extinct now.

One bumblebee is bucking the trend. In 2001 *Bombus hypnorum* was recorded in Britain for

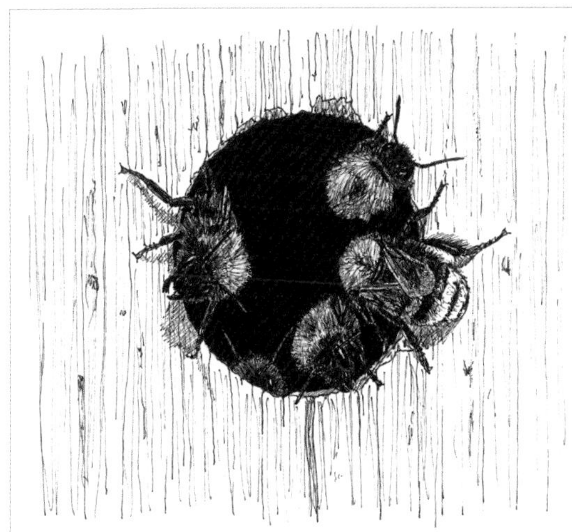

The aptly named Tree Bumblebee (Bombus hypnorum) nesting in a bird box in our back garden. In hot weather several workers would sit in the entrance hole rapidly fanning their wings to cool down the nest. They worked in shifts, taking it in turns for up to a minute, sometimes longer, while other workers came and went bringing in pollen loads.

the first time in Wiltshire, having arrived from continental Europe. By 2013 it was found in most English counties and had spread into Scotland. It is sometimes called the Tree Bumblebee as it nests in cavities in trees. It has happily taken to nesting in bird boxes, exploiting a niche not used by our native species, and so far is doing very well. It has nested in our garden in an old Blue Tit nest box that I deliberately put up on a west-facing fence about four feet off the ground in the hope that they would use it. It is one of our most distinctive and easily recognised bumblebees, having a deep gingery thorax and black abdomen with a white 'tail'. None of our other species have this combination.

C is for... COLEOPTERA

1 Cantharis rustica
2 Small Bloody-nosed Beetle
3 Agapanthia villosoviridescens
4 Wasp Beetle
5 Adonis Ladybird
6 Nicrophorus investigator
7 Cryptocephalus bipunctatus
8 Green Tortoise Beetle
9 Violet Ground Beetle
10 7-spot Ladybird
11 Cockchafer adult beetle
12 14-spot Ladybird
13 Rose Chafer
14 Common Malachite
15 Devil's Coach-horse
16 Cockchafer larva
17 Asparagus Beetle
18 Thick-thighed Beetle

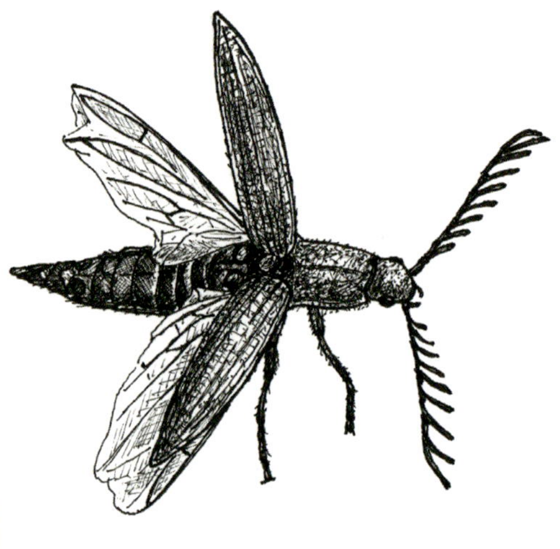

A click beetle (Ctenicera pectinicornis) launching into flight, elytra spread and wings unfurled.

Coleoptera means 'sheath-winged', and describes the hardened outer wings that form the elytra or wing cases that characterise the beetles. Although it is the largest order of insects in the world, containing the greatest number of species, in Britain it is a lowly third, behind flies (Diptera) and wasps (Hymenoptera). Beetles come in an amazing array of shapes, sizes and colours, and have many fans.

Collecting and studying beetles was extremely popular amongst Victorian gentlemen, along with butterfly collecting. Charles Darwin was a great lover of beetles. When it came to the vast number of beetle species in the world, the eminent evolutionist J. B. Haldane famously said that the Creator (if there was one) must have been inordinately fond of beetles.

I have tried to do justice to beetles and showcase their diversity and beauty within the space available, but there are just so many of them. Luckily, I was limited by the number of species that I'd encountered and then been able to identify.

The Cockchafer (*Melolontha melolontha*) is a firm favourite of mine. I love these huge blundering beetles with their shiny brown elytra making them resemble a juicy date and their fabulous fringed antennae like moose antlers. We often get them in the moth trap, and if you put out your finger they automatically cling on to it. They are difficult to prise off sometimes, their clawed tarsi (feet) tickling. The adults feed on leaves whereas the larvae feed on the roots of various plants. The larvae are large, white, alien-looking grubs, sometimes dug up when gardening. Apparently badgers are rather fond of them, and have been known to dig up a lawn overnight to feast on them.

We encountered the Rose Chafer *(Cetonia aurata)* on a visit to the Isles of Scilly, finding several of them together on Wild Carrot flowers. They are a beautiful, iridescent green with white markings, a bright shiny jewel of a beetle.

Both the Violet Ground Beetle (*Carabus violaceus*) and Devil's Coach-horse (*Ocypus olens*) are generally considered welcome in the garden as they are voracious predators, chomping their way through countless slugs. They are best searched for at night on a damp evening when the molluscs are out and about.

Nicrophorus investigator is one of the burying beetles, also known as sexton beetles after the old name for a church official in charge of grave digging. They are found around small bird and mammal corpses which they bury and then lay their eggs under in order to provide a safe larder for their larvae. They sometimes turn up in moth traps, attracted by the light. The black and orange colour is to warn would-be predators that they are distasteful. They don't smell too good, either – I made the mistake of picking one up once and they

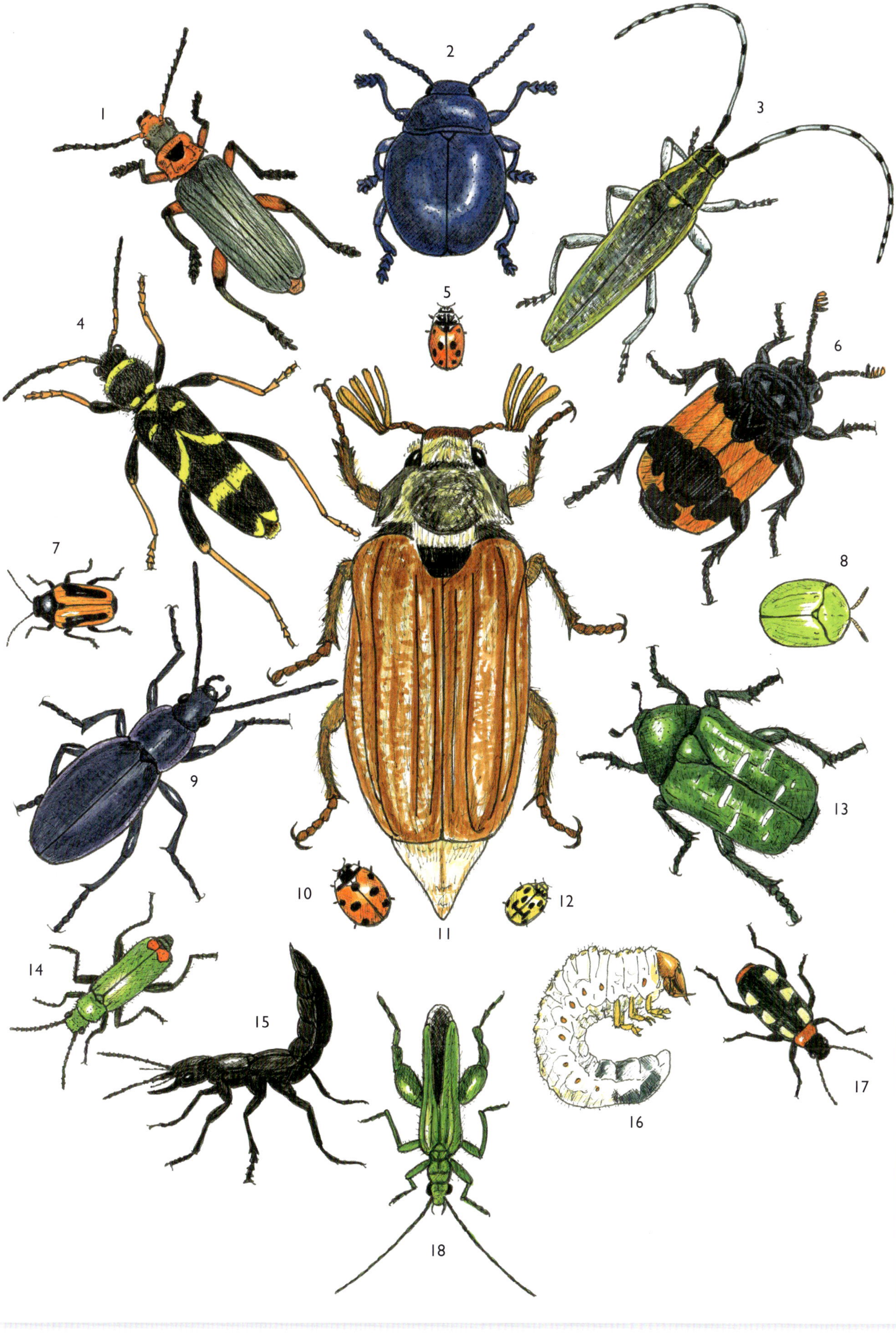
1
2
3
4
5
6
7
8
9
10
11
12
13
14
15
16
17
18

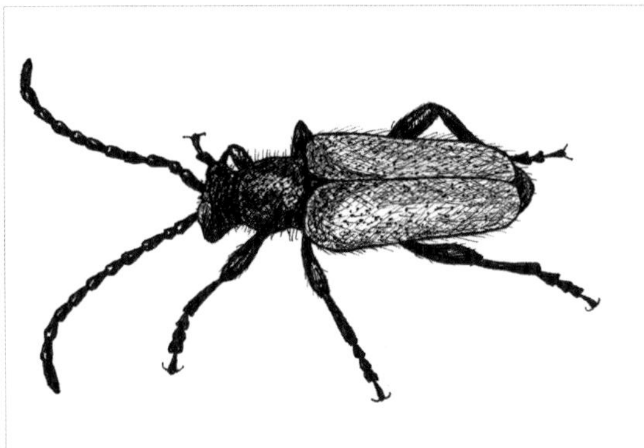

The Fairy-ring Longhorn Beetle (Pseudovadonia livida) is relatively small compared with many of the other longhorn species. They can be found visiting various flowers including Oxeye Daisies and Hawthorn blossom. Their light brown elytra are heavily pitted and covered in fine golden hairs which make them rather good at pollinating open flowers. Unusually for longhorns, their larvae develop in the humus layer of soil, feeding on the mycelium of Fairy-ring mushrooms (Marasmius oreades), hence the English name.

absolutely stink. My fingers still smelt after washing them several times.

Longhorn beetles are another favourite. There are more than 60 species in the UK, many of which are quite large. They are all endowed with impressively long antennae. The larvae of most species develop in dead wood, some taking several years to mature; while several are nocturnal, quite a lot can be found on flowers during the day. The Wasp Beetle (*Clytus arietis*) is a striking example and is perfectly harmless despite its name. *Agapanthia villosoviridescens* has lovely alternate light- and dark-striped antennae, and its greyish abdomen is covered in a bloom of downy golden hairs. It can often be found on Hogweed flowers.

A small group of beetles are known as soft-winged flower beetles, in the family Malachiidae. One of the most frequently encountered is the Common Malachite (*Malachius bipustulatus*). I watched a couple of these small, pretty, metallic-green beetles sparring in our meadow one summer. They faced off against each other and then slammed heads, locking antennae and thrusting back and forth like a pair of miniature stags at the rut. Eventually one was pushed over the edge and retreated. I presume that they were males having a territorial tiff.

The soldier beetles are mostly brightly coloured species that can be abundant on flower heads of umbellifers such as hogweed and angelica in summer. Most feed on pollen and other plant matter, but some will also eat other insects. Their larvae are predators living in soil and leaf litter. *Cantharis rustica* is common in grassland, being encountered in meadows, roadside verges and woodland rides.

The aptly named Thick-thighed Beetle (*Oedemera nobilis*) feeds on pollen and is commonly found on the flowers of Oxeye Daisy in the summer. Only the male has the distinctive enlarged hind legs.

Of the many lovely ladybirds, I have depicted three: the common and widespread 7-spot (*Coccinella septempunctata*) and 14-spot (*Propylea quattuordecimpunctata*) – known as the Smiley Face Ladybird from the often fused pattern of the black spots; and the Adonis Ladybird (*Hippodamia variegata*). This last one is more local and favours dry, sandy habitats, turning up on our allotment most years and occasionally in the garden.

The Small Bloody-nosed Beetle (*Timarcha goettingensis*) is a lovely shiny blue beetle that has a slow, methodical gait with its outsize feet and is lovely to watch as it saunters along. The ordinary Bloody-nosed Beetle (*Timarcha tenebricosa*) is the largest of the Chrysomelidae or leaf beetles. Apparently, as a defence, they exude a reddish liquid from their mouth if handled, hence the name. I have picked them up on several occasions for a closer look and they have never bled on me, I am happy to say.

Cryptocephalus bipunctatus is another of the leaf beetles and can sometimes be found on the foliage of various trees. The Green Tortoise Beetle (*Cassida viridis*) is also in the same family. There are about a dozen species of these odd-looking beetles, most of which are varying shades of green. The flattened extensions to the elytra and the pronotum (the plate covering the top of the thorax) completely cover the head and the legs, giving them their characteristic appearance. When disturbed, they tuck in their antennae and legs much like a tortoise, and clamp down on to a leaf.

Asparagus Beetles (*Crioceris asparagi*) occur on our allotment. When we first took on the plot we were a bit concerned about the asparagus crop, but the beetles haven't proved much of a pest. We leave a few spindly bits of asparagus to develop while we pick the larger spears. The beetles then generally lay their eggs on this sprue, and the larvae can chomp away while we get a good harvest of the rest and the beetles continue to exist.

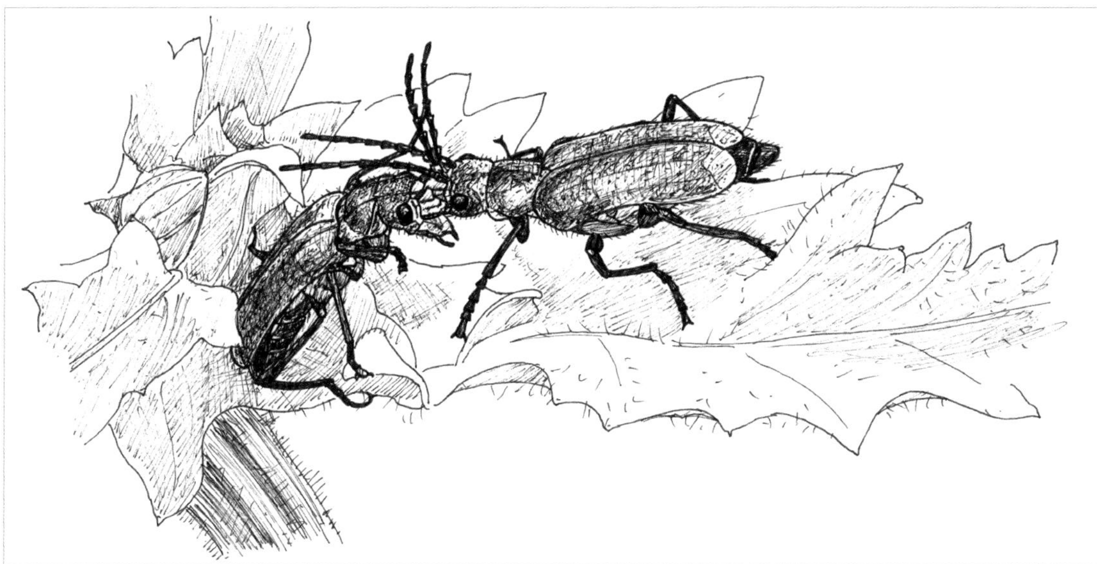

Common Malachite beetles (Malachius bipustulatus) sparring on Oxeye Daisy.

D is for... DRAGONS & DAMSELS

1 Keeled Skimmer
2 Large Red Damselfly
3 Blue-tailed Damselfly
4 Migrant Hawker
5 Broad-bodied Chaser
6 Norfolk Hawker
7 Willow Emerald
8 Black Darter
9 Banded Demoiselle

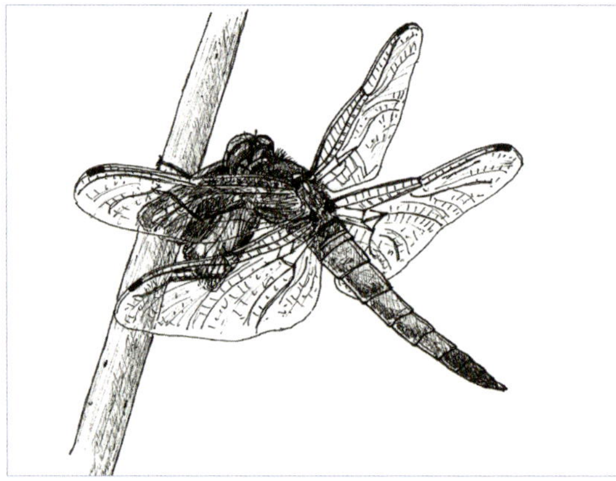

A Black-tailed Skimmer (Orthetrum cancellatum) alights on a reed stem at Strumpshaw Fen in Norfolk to devour its prey, a Large Skipper butterfly (Ochlodes sylvanus). Dragonflies are true masters of aerial manoeuvring, catching their prey on the wing. I have seen Brown Hawkers (Aeshna grandis) catch bumblebees, and the largest hawkers will catch and eat smaller species of dragonfly.

Dragonflies and Damselflies belong to the order Odonata, which is divided into two sub-orders: Zygoptera, meaning equal wings, contains the damselflies; and Anisoptera (uneven wings) contains the dragonflies. Damselflies are rather dainty looking and have delicate wings that are generally held back along their bodies when at rest, although the emerald damselflies rest with wings held out and are hence often called spreadwings.

The dragonflies far outnumber the damsels in Britain. They are characterised by much more robust wings that are always held out from the body, usually at right angles but often pointing somewhat forward. They have very large compound eyes and are fast, agile fliers. The dragonflies are split into various groups, descriptive of their hunting styles: darters, chasers, hawkers, skimmers and so on.

The hawkers are represented by the Migrant (*Aeshna mixta*) and the Norfolk (*Aeshna isosceles*); the latter is also called the Green-eyed Hawker. The Migrant Hawker is common in the south of Britain; unlike many hawkers, it isn't particularly territorial and can often be found in large numbers. We used to regularly get a dozen or so hanging about together on the stems of an old honeysuckle at the end of the garden.

The Norfolk Hawker is confined to East Anglia where it is restricted to grazing marshes with unpolluted water in dykes that support colonies of Water Soldier. These spiky aquatic plants are where the Norfolk Hawker prefers to lay its eggs. Males can be seen patrolling up and down the dykes, chasing off other males and searching for females. Their green eyes are obvious even as they flash past.

I love Broad-bodied Chasers (*Libellula depressa*), especially the males with their blue abdomens with contrasting yellow flashes on the sides. The female is brown but still has the yellow sides. They like small lakes and ponds and have occasionally emerged from our own pond, usually after someone has donated waterweed and probably, inadvertently, a larva or two.

Keeled Skimmers (*Orthetrum coerulescens*) are dragonflies of heath and valley mire. They rest with their wings held characteristically forward. The male's blue coloration becomes dulled by age by a waxy bloom known as pruinescence.

The Black Darter (*Sympetrum danae*) is our smallest dragonfly. I've only ever seen one, a female, as she sat on vegetation by the side of a boardwalk on Meathop Moss in Cumbria. It is the males that are largely black but they spend their time darting about patrolling moorland bog pools rather than posing in front of would-be wildlife artists like me.

The Large Red Damselfly (*Pyrrhosoma nymphula*) is very common, and we have them in our garden pond. Every year I watch the aquatic larvae in their struggle to break the surface film and emerge from their watery world, clinging on to a plant stem for several exhausted minutes then slowly clambering up. Then the skin splits and a new creature pulls itself

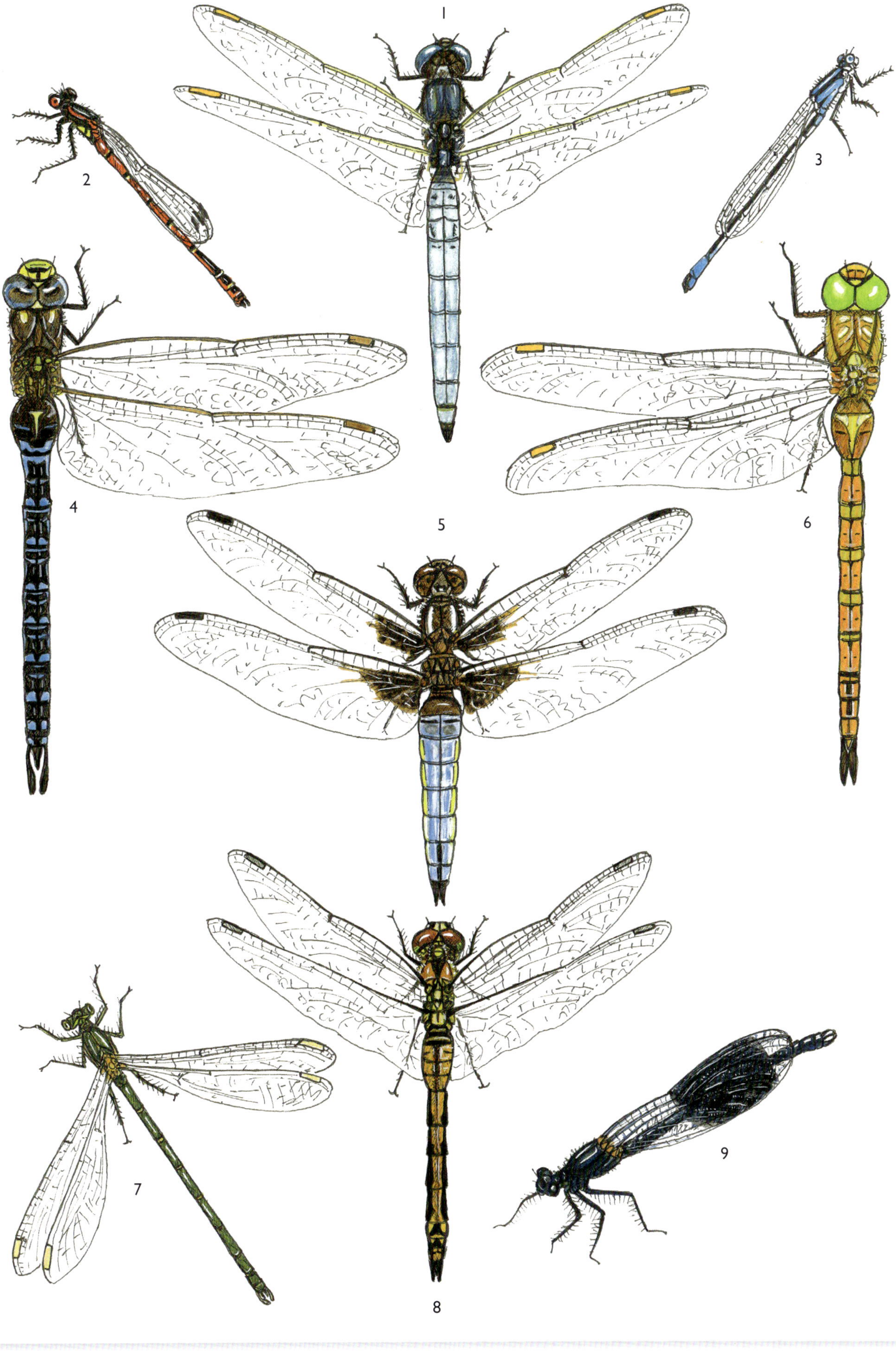
1
2
3
4
5
6
7
8
9

out of the old skin, colourless to start with, with tiny crumpled wings that unfurl and gradually inflate as fluid is pumped into them. And then, with wings tremblingly spread, it takes to the air and moves away from the pond to the safety of a flower border as the colour starts to form in the abdomen.

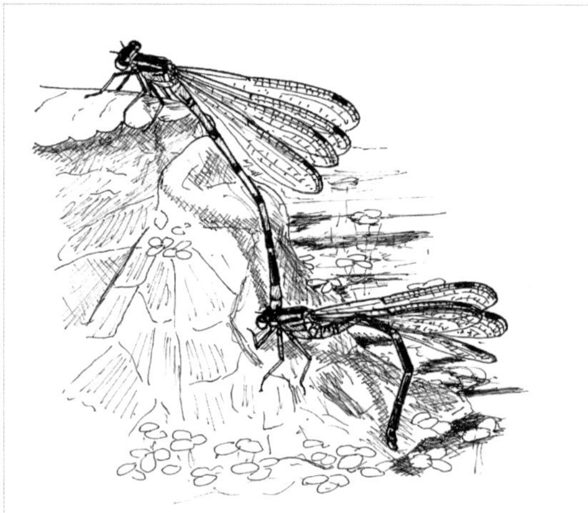

Typical damselfly egg-laying behaviour with paired Coenagrion puella (Azure Damselfly) attaching eggs to a submerged plant in our pond (Marsh Marigold in this instance).

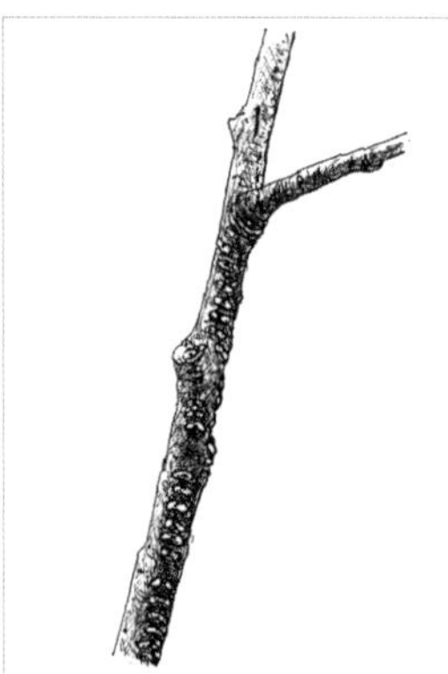

The distinctive paired scars (galls) where a Willow Emerald has inserted her eggs into a Salix (willow) twig.

The emerging damselflies have to run the gauntlet of the resident House Sparrows which seem to know unerringly when they start to emerge. One year I stationed myself by the pond for most of a day after I discovered that one of the resident Robins was picking off every newly emerged damselfly. We joked that this was how it kept its red breast! I don't mind the birds snaffling a few, but there are limits. Decimation (in the true sense of the word) is one thing, but genocide is another!

The Blue-tailed Damselfly has a black abdomen with a striking blue 'tail light'. It can tolerate relatively high levels of pollutants, and as such can sometimes be the only species of damselfly present where water quality is poor. This tolerance means they are able to colonise new ponds quite quickly, exploiting them before other species move in. The scientific name *Ischnura elegans* is much more poetic than the English one.

The Willow Emerald (*Lestes viridis*) is a fairly new arrival to Britain, found in the south-east but spreading, probably as a result of climate change. They can be distinguished from other emerald damselflies by the pale wing-spots (*pterostigmas*). They are generally seen in trees or bushes, as they have the unusual habit of laying their eggs into small branches overhanging water. This leaves characteristic scars in the twigs in the form of small oval-shaped galls. These galls are often found in winter when they can be quite obvious on bare branches. Sometimes it is the galls that are detected before the damselflies themselves.

The Banded Demoiselle (*Calopteryx splendens*) is a beautiful creature of slow-flowing rivers where it can be very abundant. The males can be spotted flicking low over the water or sitting on bankside vegetation. We were lucky enough to encounter a mass emergence of these beautiful iridescent damselflies one year on a walk beside the River Little Ouse near Brandon in Suffolk (staying on the Norfolk side of the river, of course!).

Conditions were obviously perfect, for as we walked along the narrow path the head-high vegetation to either side was covered in countless brilliant blue-green bodies that flew up with an audible flick of the wings as we brushed by. There were dozens of them, probably a hundred or so, for more were flying over the river. Mostly they were males, but we also saw a few very fresh females.

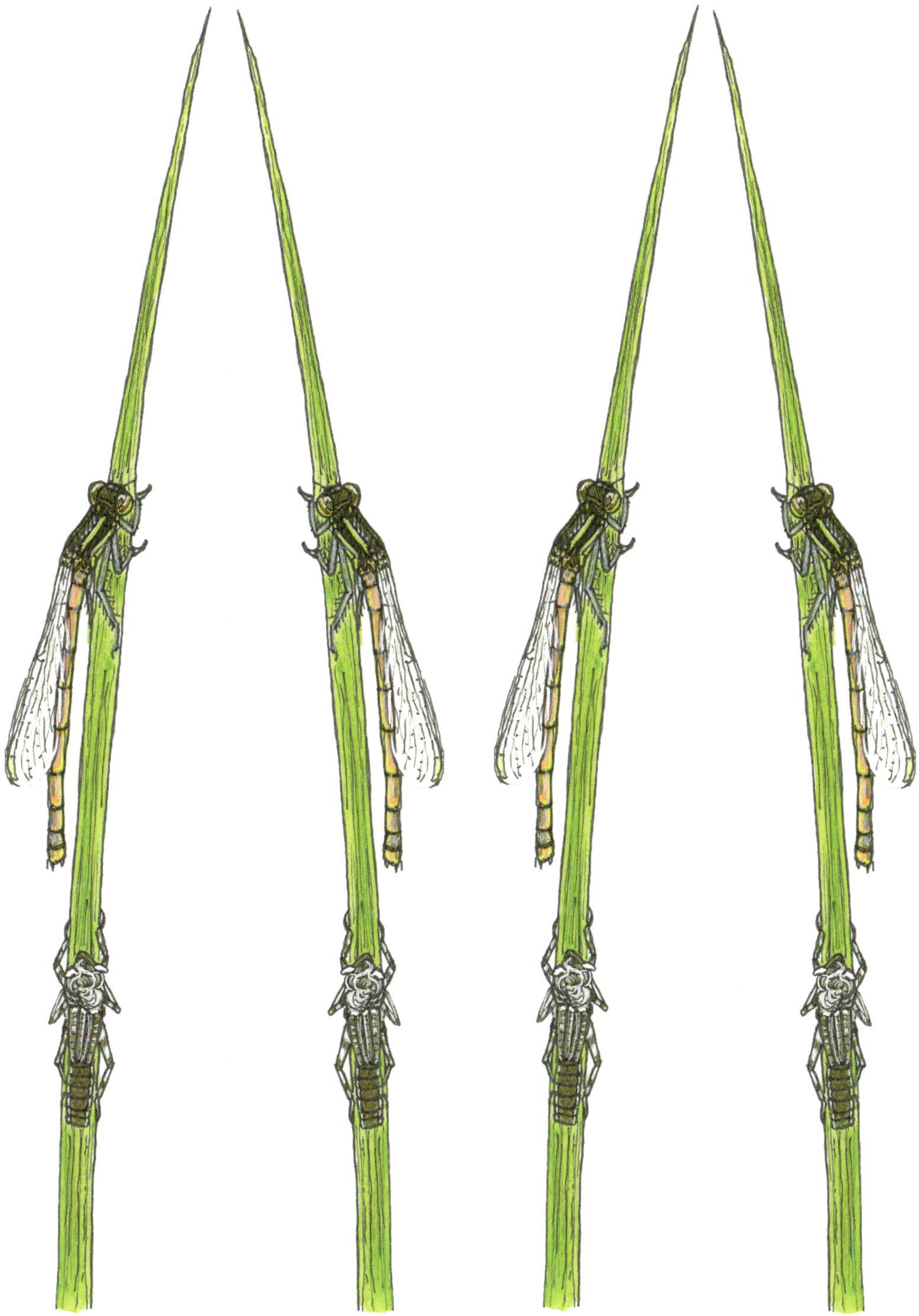

E is for... EMPERORS

1 Purple Emperor Butterfly
2 Emperor Moth (male)
3 Emperor Dragonfly (female)
4 Purple Emperor caterpillar
5 Emperor Moth caterpillar
6 Emperor Moth (female)
7 Purple Emperor Butterfly

The epithet Emperor is reserved for the most majestic of our insect fauna. The Purple Emperor (*Apatura iris*) is named after the imperial purple of the Roman emperors. This butterfly was known by Victorian lepidopterists as 'His Most Imperial Majesty' or 'The Most Majestic of Flies'. Largely a denizen of oak woodlands, even though the caterpillars actually feed on sallows, the males of this gorgeous butterfly seek out the tallest of oak trees to patrol around. The butterflies do not visit flowers for nectar. Instead, they derive their sustenance from aphid honeydew, hence the attraction of oak trees whose leaves are often coated in the sticky substance.

In order to catch these beauties for their collections, 18th-century collectors used 15-foot handles on their nets. The Victorians doubled this to 30, and there is even one account of a 50-foot net being employed! An easier way to catch them was to seek out the local gamekeeper's gibbet, where they could be caught with ease as they supped the juices of fresh corpses.

On hot summer days male Purple Emperors can be seen soaring above the treetops or flying up and down woodland rides seeking out the elusive females. They are very territorial, and will see off anything that strays within sight; they have even been known to chase after small woodland birds that stray too near. They are lured down from their aerial splendour by the most unattractive delights such as fresh fox scats (droppings) or horse dung which they probe with their pale lemon-yellow proboscis, sucking up vital minerals. It is then that the beautiful purple sheen present only on the males can be fully appreciated.

The tiny young caterpillars of the Purple Emperor spend the winter hibernating exposed on a twig. At this stage they are brownish in colour to blend in with the bare branches. By contrast, the fully grown caterpillar is a lovely pale green with diagonal yellow stripes. This gives them perfect camouflage as they feed on the upper surface of a leaf.

Male Emperor Moths (*Saturnia pavonia*) fly fast and erratically in spring sunshine, a blur of orange like a Small Tortoiseshell butterfly on speed. Close up, the eye spots on the hindwings are a stunning sight. In males, the forewings are a warmer, browner shade; and the hindwings, when revealed, are orange. Females are much larger, a lovely soft grey all over but still with those beautiful big eyes. Although the males are active during the day, the females generally fly at dusk. Newly emerged, unmated females give off a strong pheromone to attract the males whose large feathery antennae enable them to pick up their scent from up to a kilometre away.

Emperor Moth larvae are rather lovely, too. The mature fat green caterpillars have a line of either purple or yellow spots around each segment, often surrounded with a black ring and topped with stout black bristles. The earlier instars are quite different, being black and orange. They feed on a variety of woody plants, most commonly Bramble and Heather, and can be found in a variety of habitats from heathland and moorland to woodland rides and hedgerows and even fens. The caterpillar spins a tough silken cocoon in which to pupate, and these can sometimes be seen on Heather, quite high up on the stems. I have always found them after the moth has already emerged in spring.

Our largest dragonfly has been ennobled with the name of Emperor Dragonfly – *Anax imperator*. The males have a brilliant blue abdomen whereas the female's is green. Both have a darker green thorax and yellow front of the wings (the costa), with eyes that are blue in males or greenish in females. A distinctive dark line runs dorsally (on the top) down the centre of the abdomen. With experience, both sexes can be recognised in flight by the characteristically down-curved abdomen. They are powerful fliers, and will chase and hunt down a variety of other insects from butterflies to other dragonflies. The nymphs, which grow to more than two inches long, are voracious predators that eat anything from other aquatic invertebrates to tadpoles and small fish. They live for about two years in their watery, weed-filled world before they emerge and take to the skies for a single splendid summer of aerial manoeuvring.

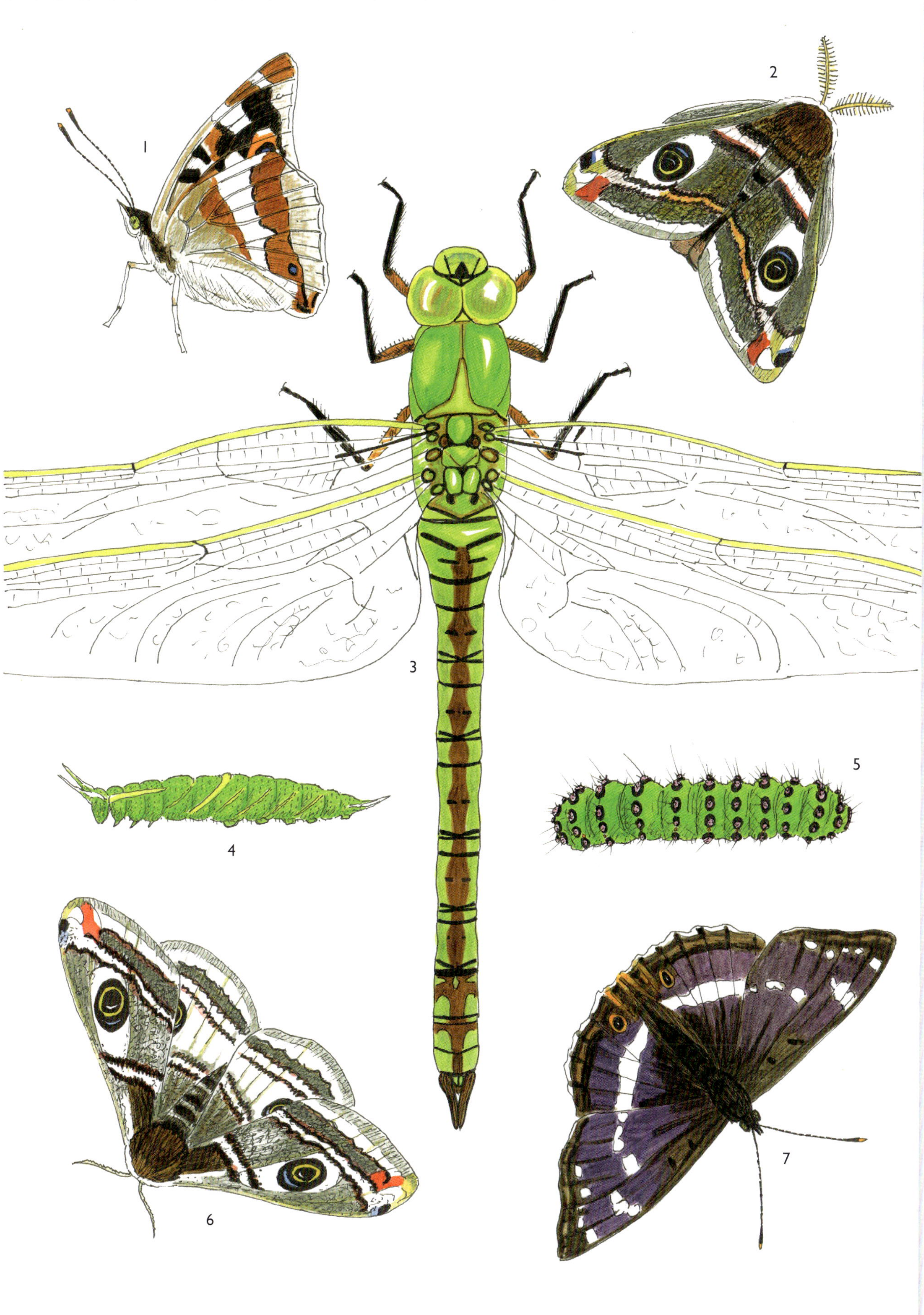
1
2
3
4
5
6
7

F is for... FLIES

1 Mesembrina meridiana
2 Anthomyia pluvialis
3 Eriothrix rufomaculata
4 Sicus ferrugineus
5 Physocephala rufipes
6 Nemotelus pantherinus
7 Bombylius major
8 Stomorhina lunata
9 Nephrotoma flavescens
10 Chloromyia formosa
11 Neoitamus cyanurus
12 Calliphora vicina
13 Tachina grossa
14 Lucilia sp.
15 Palloptera muliebris

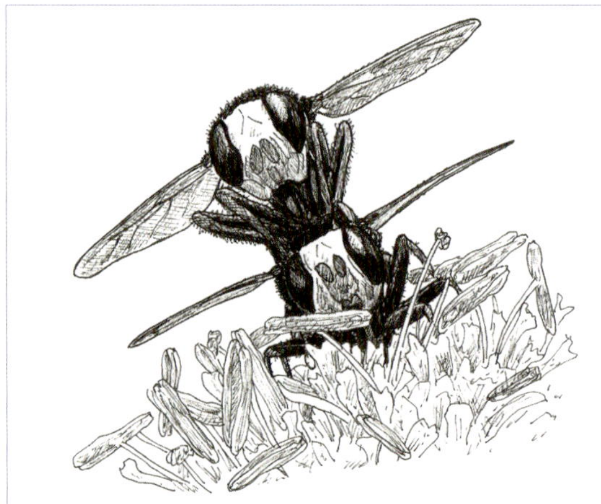

Stacked-up Sicus. I often come across paired-up Sicus ferrugineus on flowers when I'm out looking for solitary bees. These two were on a Field Scabious flower in my local cemetery. I think they look rather sweet and somewhat comical.

Flies seem to be universally loathed, yet their importance should not be underestimated. They pollinate flowers (not least Cocoa, which gives us chocolate). Many of their larvae are important for breaking down organic matter, from vegetation and animal dung to corpses, and let's not forget their role in forensic science when times of death can be established from the development of fly larvae. In medicine, even today, maggots are used to clean up wounds, eating the dead flesh to prevent gangrene.

Flies also make up a vast proportion of the food chain. Swifts eat insects on the wing; each bolus of food collected by a Swift contains around 300 insects, and each nest of young may receive 3,000 food-balls per day. (They won't all be flies or even insects – surprisingly, perhaps, tiny spiders can make up some of the catch, too.)

'True Flies' belong to the order Diptera, having only one pair of wings (*di* meaning two, and *ptera* meaning wing), unlike other winged insects which have two pairs. The hind wings are modified into a pair of halteres that act as balancers when they fly. These are most readily seen on the craneflies and some of the larger hoverflies.

Take a close look at a fly – there is a lot more to it than meets the eye. They can be beautiful, terrifying, macabre, sinister, bizarre, even comical. They have remarkable life stories.

The Dark-edged Bee-fly (*Bombylius major*) is probably my favourite. They emerge in late March or early April, and I look eagerly for the first ones in spring sunshine around Forget-me-not flowers in the garden. They are fantastic furry little things, hovering with incredibly fast wings, a blur that suddenly stops to reveal the dark edge that gives them their English name. They hover with their long proboscis probing the depths of a flower's corolla, supping nectar. And yet all this fluffy loveliness hides a sinister side, for the Bee-fly is a parasite of various solitary bees and wasps. Before it lays its eggs the Bee-fly dips its abdomen in sand, priming its eggs with a heavy load of sand grains so it can then fire them into the vicinity of a bee's nest by flicking its abdomen. The larvae feast on the stored food supply and the host's larvae.

The Conopidae (thick-headed flies) are a strange-looking bunch. They are either long and thin, rather wasp-like, often black and yellow, or short and thick-set. They are all parasitoids, laying eggs directly on an adult wasp or bumblebee. The larva develops inside the host, pupating when the host dies. How lovely.

One of the commonest is *Sicus ferrugineus*, sometimes called the Brown Bee Jumper. It is often seen visiting various flowers for nectar but it is also on the lookout for bumblebees. It will literally jump on a bee's back and lay an egg on it. I'm rather fond of *Sicus*, even though it looks rather sinister with its hunched back and deformed-looking curled abdomen – it would be a good candidate for Shakespeare's Richard the Third. A rather more elegant and attractive-looking conopid is

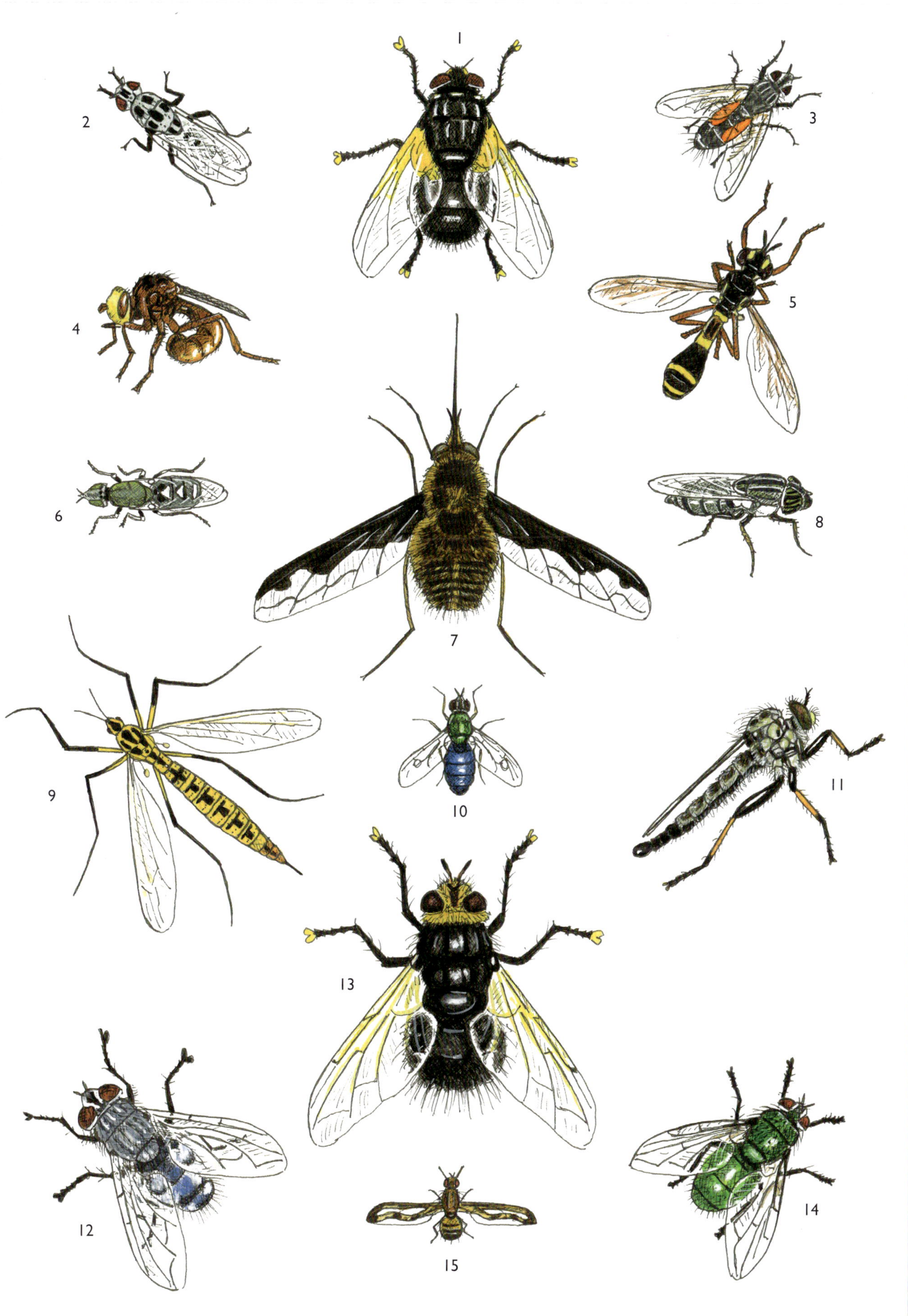
1
2
3
4
5
6
7
8
9
10
11
12
13
14
15

Physocephala rufipes, which also parasitises bumblebees.

The well-known Bluebottles (*Calliphora vicina*) and Greenbottles (*Lucilia* sp.) are members of the Calliphoridae or blowflies. Bright and shining, they are beautiful jewel-like flies often seen basking on walls or trees in sunshine or visiting flowers. Like most of their family, they lay their eggs in carrion, and it is these larvae that are used in forensic science to determine time of death in some murder cases.

Stomorhina lunata is a very striking species. The female (pictured) is a lovely silvery-grey colour,

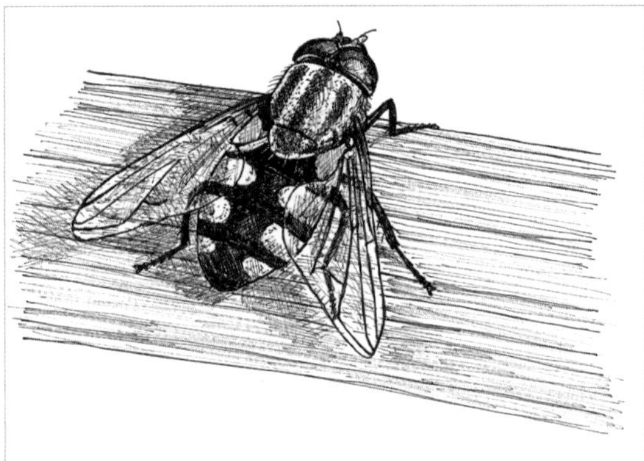

The boldly marked black and yellow abdomen of male Stomorhina lunata makes it easy to mistake for a hoverfly.

with the most amazing eyes – greenish-grey with horizontal purple stripes. The male is equally attractive, having a black and yellow abdomen, grey striped thorax and reddish eyes with similar stripes to those of the female. Both sexes are often mistaken for hoverflies when first encountered. It is known as the Locust Blowfly as its larvae develop in locust nymphs. It has only recently been recorded in Britain, and if it has been breeding here then presumably it is using grasshopper or cricket nymphs as we don't have locusts over here (yet!).

Muscidae is a large family that includes some of our most abundant flies. My favourite by far is *Mesembrina meridiana*, often called the Noon Fly from its habit of sunning itself on tree trunks at midday. It is a rather handsome fly – large, shiny black with deep yellow wing bases and a yellow face. In late summer and early autumn it can be found on brambles, feasting on the juices of ripe fruit. But it is best searched for on nice fresh cowpats, an entomologist's favourite hunting ground, where it lays its eggs.

The tachinids comprise a large family of parasitic flies whose larvae develop in other insects, mostly the caterpillars of moths and butterflies. These generally bristly flies range in size from the

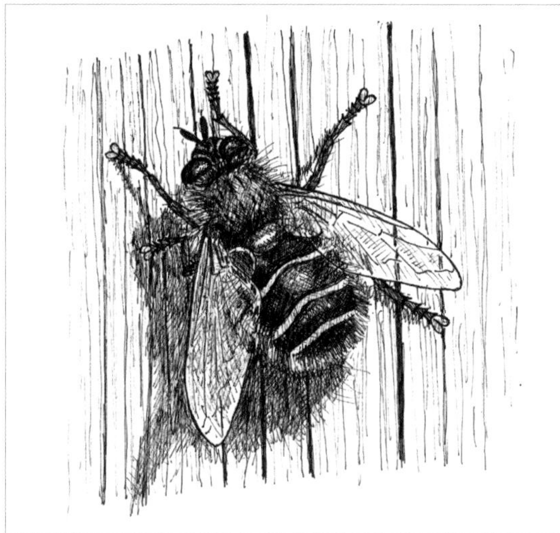

The tachinid fly Tachina ursina casting its bristly shadow on a fence post. This is one of my favourite flies, and I make a special trip to the Norfolk Brecks each spring to see one.

smallest (around 2mm) to the largest (20mm), *Tachina grossa*. This is a truly fabulous fly with black body and yellow head like a huge wiry-coated punk bumblebee. It also sports a bright yellow Elizabethan ruff. It can be found visiting various flowers in July or August. We found ours on Hemp Agrimony flowers along the edge of woodland. On a smaller, neater scale is *Eriothrix rufomaculata*, easily recognised by the red sides to the abdomen. It is common and widespread in unimproved grasslands, and is a regular visitor in our garden, often seen sitting on Wild Carrot flowers in our mini-meadow.

Picture-winged flies are a group of smallish flies usually with strikingly patterned wings. The males waggle their wings to impress females or to drive away other males from their territory. *Palloptera muliebris* has relatively long, narrow wings that it holds out at right angles and parades up and down like a miniature aeroplane taxiing for take-off, manoeuvring back and forth, twirling its wings like ailerons. It is rather comical to watch.

The Anthomyiid flies are often small, rather slender species that can be difficult to identify. The numerous species include those whose larvae feed in plant roots, including ones that can be pests in crops from onions to cabbages, a bane of many

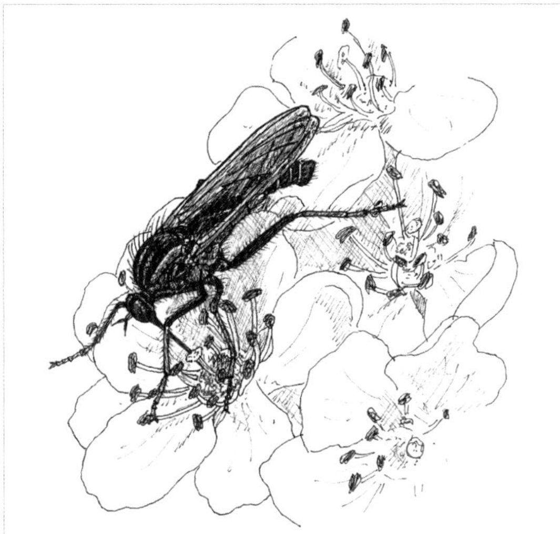

Empis tessellata feeding on nectar on Hawthorn blossom. Clouds of males are often seen 'dancing' in the air above blossom in spring, and are sometimes known as dance flies. The males congregate in this way in order to attract females. During courtship a male will present a female with a dead insect as a pre-nuptial gift. While she is distracted by a free meal he hops on her back and mates with her. Sometimes the male will then take back the gift and either eat it himself or give it to another female – what a cad!

an allotment owner. Others mine leaves or feed in decomposing vegetation, including strandline seaweed, and some adult flies eat bird droppings, so not all are 'bad'. Many are rather drab and inconspicuous but a few are rather strikingly marked, such as *Anthomyia pluvialis*.

Many of the robberflies, including *Neoitamus cyanurus*, are large and conspicuous. Their long, stout, bristly legs enable them to tackle prey larger than themselves, clasping them tightly as they deliver a killer 'blow' with their highly toxic saliva. Their relatively small heads are dominated by huge eyes that give them superb vision, allowing them to pounce accurately on their chosen prey. They are generally seen lounging about on vegetation but quickly spring into action. The males treat the females rather like prey items, too – pouncing on them to mate without preamble.

Some of our prettiest flies are members of the Stratiomyidae, commonly called soldierflies after the colourful ceremonial uniforms of some regiments. The smaller species are the soldiers and centurions such as *Chloromyia formosa* (Broad Centurion). Then there are generals (see plate K), colonels and majors. A few are known as snouts, including *Nemotelus pantherinus*, the Fen Snout, presumably after their elongated 'face'.

There are more than 300 species of cranefly in Britain, which I find quite a staggering number. The larger, commoner species are often known as 'Daddy-long-legs', and are familiar to many people as they sometimes come indoors at night attracted to light or are found in gardens. But there are a lot of less conspicuous species, many of which are extremely rare and known only from ancient woodland where there are veteran trees and lots of dead timber in which the larvae develop.

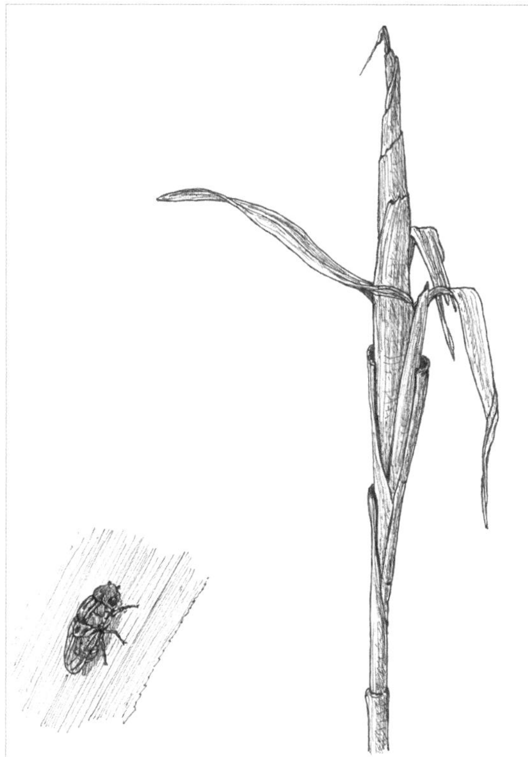

The strange-looking fly Lipara lucens (above left) lays its eggs in Common Reed where it causes distinctive Cigar Galls (above right). There is only one fly larva per gall. The adults emerge in June but the galls are most easily seen during the winter. The vacated galls are sometimes used as a nest site for the Reed Yellow-face Bee (Hylaeus pectoralis).

Many of the adults have reduced mouthparts, and barely feed. In some species the larvae develop in the soil, some feeding on roots, and are known as leatherjackets and resemble caterpillars. Other larvae develop in dead wood or fungi. The *Nephrotoma* craneflies are attractive black and orange species. *Nephrotoma flavescens* occurs in our garden, and is known as the Tiger Cranefly.

G is for... GEOMETERS

1 Brimstone
2 V-Pug
3 Speckled Yellow
4 Lime-speck Pug
5 Clouded Magpie
6 Small Dusty Wave
7 Latticed Heath
8 Yellow-barred Brindle
9 Purple-bordered Gold
10 Green Carpet
11 Clouded Border
12 Swallow-tailed Moth
13 Waved Umber
14 Riband Wave
15 Oak Beauty
16 Scalloped Oak
17 Scalloped Hazel
18 Common Emerald

The major division of moths in the UK is into either macro or micro moths. The macros, as the name suggests, tend to be large; and the micros tend to be on the small to very small size – although there are plenty of exceptions in both camps. The macro moths tend to have been better studied over the years and were given English names by the earliest collectors.

The Geometridae is the second-largest family of macro moths in Britain (the largest is the Noctuidae). Most geometers are characterised by having rather broad, triangular wings and slender bodies. With a few exceptions, they sit at rest with their wings spread flat, the forewings held forward and partly exposing the hindwings, rather like butterflies. The pattern on the forewings, often a series of wavy lines, continues on to the hindwings, helping to break up the outline and camouflage them at rest during the day.

The caterpillars are also characteristic. They only have two pairs of prolegs, also known as false legs, comprising a pair of claspers at the end of the abdomen and a second pair just in front. This leaves nothing in between before the three pairs of true legs (or thoracic legs) at the front. This gives rise to a characteristic looping movement (see Brimstone caterpillar on plate L), which gives them their common English name loopers (inchworms in the USA). The word Geometrid is from the Greek meaning 'ground measurer', and relates to the larva's characteristic movement.

It never ceases to amaze me when I open a moth trap to see dozens of specimens. I wonder where they hide during the day, especially the more brightly coloured ones. I love the great reveal, lifting out the egg boxes to find treasures lurking beneath, never knowing just what will be there. Even the drabber species exhibit subtle beauty when looked at closely.

Except for Speckled Yellow (*Pseudopanthera macularia*) and Purple-bordered Gold (*Idaea muricata*), all the species on the plate have been seen in my garden, although these two do occur elsewhere in Norfolk. The Speckled Yellow is a Breckland speciality, flying during the day along open woodland rides, its larvae feeding on Wood Sage. Purple-bordered Gold is a scarce species of wet heaths and bogs. I haven't yet seen one in Norfolk, but did find them on a trip to Cumbria while looking for Large Heath butterflies (*Coenonympha tullia*) on Meathop Moss. They can be disturbed from low vegetation during the day, when they like to play hide and seek, disappearing into heather where they hang upside down – making them difficult to sketch.

Latticed Heath (*Chiasmia clathrata*) is another day-flier and could be mistaken for a butterfly, especially as they sometimes sit with their wings held upright. Indeed, one well-known nature writer freely admits to having mistaken them for Dingy Skippers (*Erynnis tages*). They are a fairly common grassland species, and I've even had a couple turn up in the garden moth trap – day-flying moths do come to light sometimes.

Swallow-tailed (*Ourapteryx sambucaria*) and Brimstone (*Opisthograptis luteolata*) are old favourites, occurring regularly in our moth trap but still always nice to see. The bright green colours of V-Pug (*Chloroclystis v-ata*), Green Carpet (*Colostygia pectinataria*) and Yellow-barred Brindle (*Acasis viretata*) fade as they age, and the pinned specimens in old collections don't retain any green colour at all and look like completely different species.

Of the various emerald moths, which all share the same shimmering green colour, the Common Emerald (*Hemithea aestivaria*) is distinguished by its wavy cross lines and chequered border. A number of our moths, and some butterflies, have had various English names in the past, coined by different collectors. In the mid-18th century the Common Emerald was known as the Small Green Housewife for some strange reason.

The Riband Wave (*Idaea aversata*) is one of the plainer geometers but shows a lot of variation in the subtle shading across its wings, while the Waved Umber's (*Menophra abruptaria*) dark and light broken bands offer superb camouflage when the moth is at rest on a tree trunk. The Clouded Border (*Lomaspilis marginata*) is very striking in its black and white simplicity, while the Clouded Magpie (*Abraxas sylvata*) adds a warm palate of ochre and grey with iridescent blue to the white canvas of its wings.

Scalloped Oak (*Crocallis elinguaria*) and Scalloped Hazel (*Odontopera bidentata*), along with Oak Beauty (*Biston strataria*), are the atypical, rather hefty geometers, broad bodied and holding their wings over their abdomens. At the other end of the scale are the diminutive Lime-speck Pug (*Eupithecia centaureata*) and Small Dusty Wave (*Idaea seriata*).

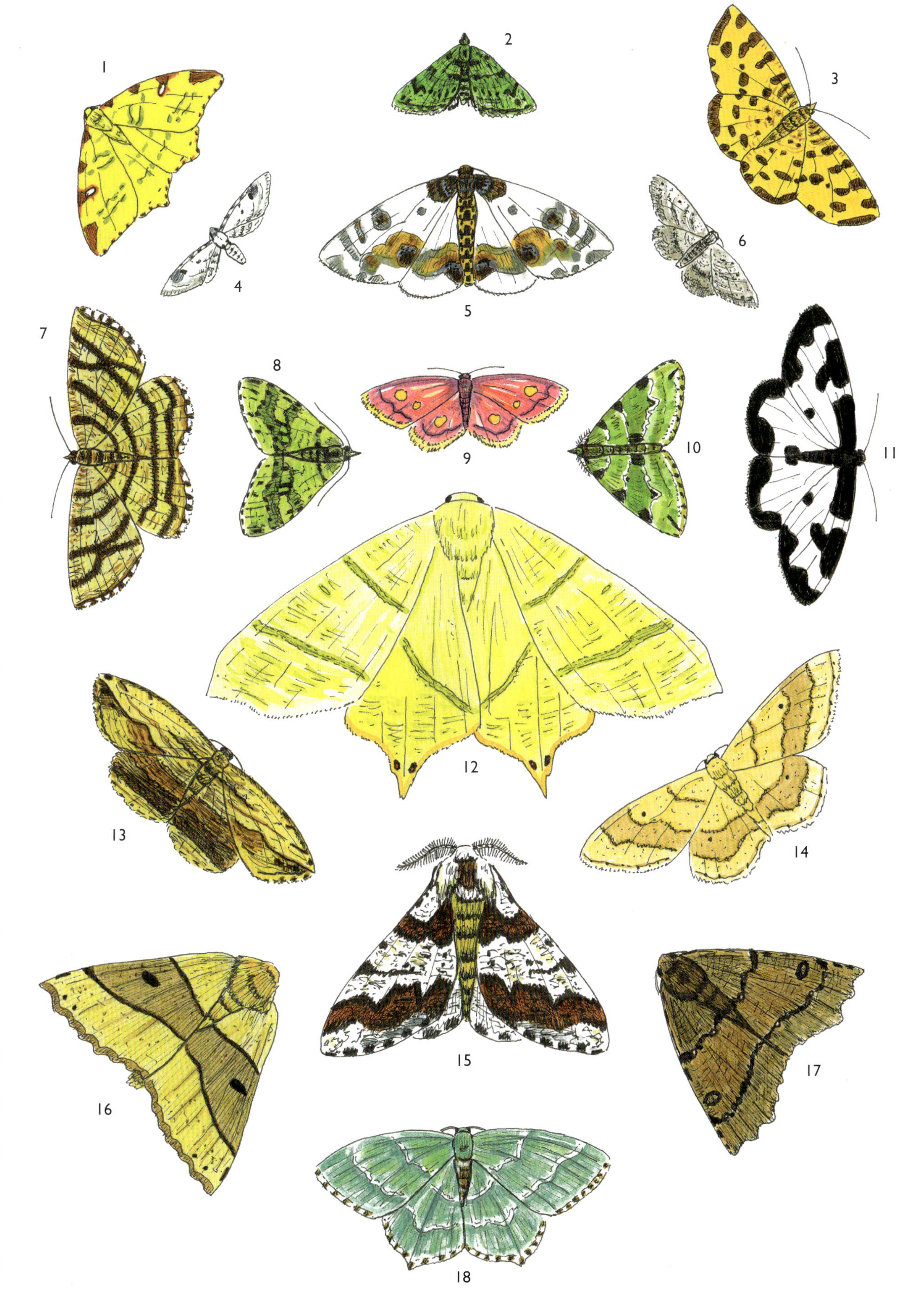
1
2
3
4
5
6
7
8
9
10
11
12
13
14
15
16
17
18

H is for... HOVERFLIES

1 Portevinia maculata
2 Rhingia campestris
3 Eristalinus sepulchralis
4 Chrysotoxum festivum
5 Pipiza noctiluca
6 Sericomyia silentis
7 Episyrphus balteatus
8 Helophilus pendulus
9 Eupeodes luniger
10 Eristalis intricaria
11 Cheilosia impressa
12 Leucozona lucorum
13 Myathropa florea

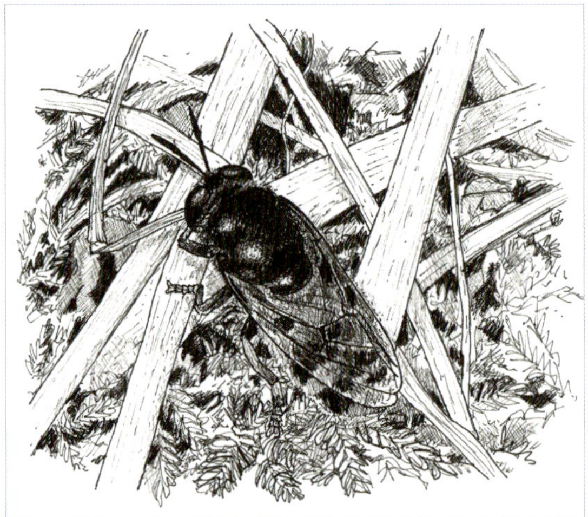

One of my best finds – the scarce and rarely seen Microdon analis put in an all too brief appearance when I was looking for Chequered Skipper butterflies (Carterocephalus palaemon) in Scotland. They don't visit flowers, spending a lot of time sitting about on the ground. Their larvae are odd dome-shaped creatures that were once thought to be molluscs (they look like tiny scrunched-up slugs but without the horns) and live in ant nests. It is generally easier to find the larvae than the adult.

Hoverflies are True Flies, members of the Diptera, having one pair of wings. They make up a large family called the Syrphidae, and are distinguished from other flies by the presence of a false vein called the vena spuria in their wings. This modification enables them to flex their wings and hover with relative ease.

Many hoverflies are characteristically black and yellow, and some are rather good wasp or bee mimics. This makes them less likely to be attacked by birds, which think they are armed with a nasty sting. While a lot of species are large and obvious, others are small, dark and inconspicuous. As most species of hoverfly spend a lot of time visiting flowers, they are extremely important pollinators. This also means they are easy to observe, and probably one of the reasons many people choose hoverflies as their first group of invertebrates to try and identify.

Although the majority of adults visit flowers and have similar habits, their larvae have very diverse lifestyles. Some larvae live openly on leaves, eating greenfly; others hoover up debris in wasp or hornet nests; while some feed inside plant stems. Others lead aquatic lives in rot holes and in dingy, stagnant water, breathing through a telescopic tube at their rear end; these are known as rat-tailed maggots. There are even some that live in ant nests.

Of the large, conspicuous hoverflies, one of my favourites is *Helophilus pendulus*, a handsome 'hover', black and yellow with a striped thorax. This was probably the first hoverfly I identified. They can be seen anytime between April and October, and are generally associated with water. I see them regularly around our pond margins during the summer, and they linger on through the autumn. *Sericomyia silentis* and *Myathropa florea* are two other bold black and yellow hovers. The latter is sometimes called the Batman Hoverfly from the black pattern on the thorax. All three have aquatic larvae.

Rhingia campestris is one of our most distinctive hoverflies, with its elongated 'snout' or rostrum making it the English Electric Lightning of the hoverfly world (for those who remember early jet planes). The rostrum houses a rather long proboscis that the hoverfly unfolds to feed on nectar in flowers with a very deep corolla that other hovers cannot reach. I have seen them on Green Alkanet flowers in spring and on Buddleia in summer. Their larvae develop in cow dung.

There are several very good wasp mimics including *Chrysotoxum festivum*, one of a group of boldly marked black and yellow hoverflies with

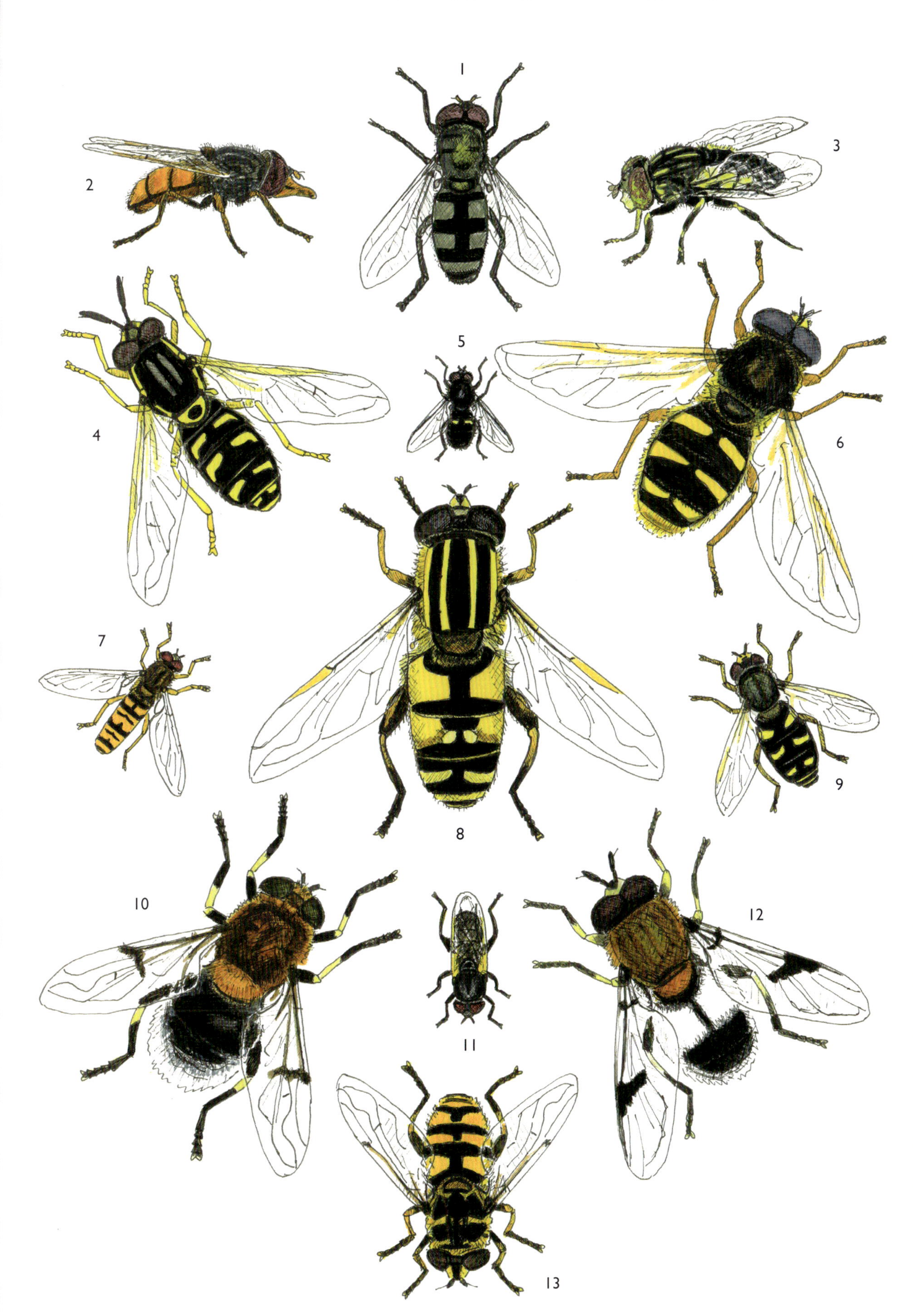
1
2
3
4
5
6
7
8
9
10
11
12
13

characteristically long antennae. Considering their large size and conspicuous coloration, not much is known about their larval stages. It is thought that they develop in ant nests, feeding on root aphids. I have found them wary and often difficult to approach. They tend to skulk about in our meadow, close to the ground amongst the grass clumps where there are ant nest mounds, so they may well be ovipositing (egg laying), but I haven't been able to observe it for certain.

Eristalis intricaria is a fairly convincing bumblebee mimic, especially the more strikingly coloured, slightly larger females. In spring they can often be seen visiting sallows for nectar, but later in the year thistles and knapweeds are favoured along with bramble flowers.

Another bumblebee mimic is *Leucozona lucorum*. This is mostly on the wing in spring with a peak in May. Although associated with woodland, we occasionally see one in our garden where it seems rather partial to forget-me-not flowers. It is a particularly striking species with its black and white abdomen and dark wing cloud.

Of all the hovers, *Eristalinus sepulchralis* is one I try and seek out every year. Look for them on flowers in areas with pools and ditches, for the larvae develop in submerged rotting vegetation and are one of the rat-tailed maggots. The adults are not especially large or conspicuous and can easily be overlooked, but when you take the trouble to peer closely at them they are really rather lovely. There is definitely something of the crypt about them, from the wonderful name to their gorgeous motley green and purple eyes. It is always a treat to find one.

Portevinia maculata is a bit of a specialist. Its larvae feed in the bulbs and stems of Ramsons (Wild Garlic). Males can be found sitting around patches of flowering Ramsons but the females tend to skulk around the base out of sight. If you're around Wild Garlic in spring just as the flowers are coming out, have a look for this unprepossessing hoverfly. In sunlight the grey shimmers with a subtle pewter beauty.

Episyrphus balteatus is probably our commonest and most widespread hoverfly, and is instantly recognised by its orange abdomen with double black stripes per segment. As with several other species, the background colour of the abdomen can vary greatly, in this case from more yellowy orange with thin black stripes to very dark with thicker black bands. This is a result of the ambient temperature at which the larva develops, cooler conditions giving rise to the much darker individuals. It is one of the few hovers with a regularly used English name, the Marmalade Hoverfly. The resident population is augmented by migrants in the summer, and in good years you can get huge numbers of them.

Another common and widespread species is *Eupeodes luniger*. It occurs regularly in our garden, visiting a variety of flowers. The nine British species of *Eupeodes* can be difficult to distinguish, especially as, like *Episyrphus balteatus*, they can vary in the depth of colour and strength of markings on the abdomen. Female *luniger*, though, has an obvious dark Y-shaped mark on the frons (the top of the head between the eyes) so shouldn't cause confusion.

Not all hoverflies are big or boldly marked. At the smaller end of the scale are diminutive dark species such as *Pipiza noctiluca*, although in this species the female is at least distinguished by twin pale spots on the abdomen. *Cheilosia* species are also mostly dark, although somewhat larger. Many are similar in appearance, but several are fairly distinctive – including *Cheilosia impressa*, which has obvious yellow wing bases, most notable in the female as depicted.

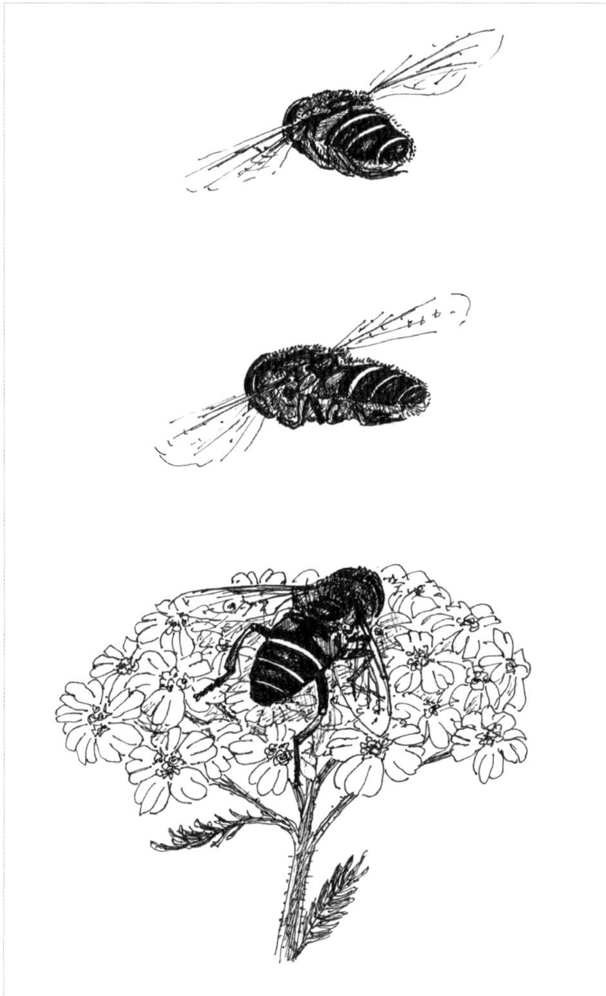

The characteristic behaviour of Eristalis nemorum where males hover above females as part of their courtship. Here, two males vie for a female as she feeds on Yarrow flowers, stacked up much like the holding patterns of aeroplanes as they wait to land at a busy airport.

I is for... ISOPODS

1 Platyarthrus hoffmannseggi
(Ant Woodlouse)
2 Trichoniscus pusillus
(Common Pygmy Woodlouse)
3 Porcellio scaber
(Common Rough Woodlouse)
4 Ligia oceanica
(Sea Slater)
5 Philoscia muscorum
(Common Striped Woodlouse)
6 and 7 Armadillidium vulgare
(Common Pill Woodlouse)
8 Porcellio spinicornis
9 Oniscus asellus
(Common Shiny Woodlouse)
10 Asellus aquaticus

Welcome to the wonderful world of woodlice, the terrestrial crustaceans related to crabs, shrimps and lobsters. Most organisms belonging to the Crustacea are aquatic. The isopods, on the other hand, include creatures that are wholly terrestrial. The most familiar of these are the woodlice.

In common with other crustaceans, woodlice have a hard external skeleton containing calcium carbonate. When they shed this exoskeleton to grow, they start with the rear half and eat it in order to obtain the all-important calcium. Then they shed the front half. Sometimes this is consumed, too, but they have to wait for their mouthparts to harden first.

The structure of a woodlouse is very different to that of an insect or a spider (see diagram, page 45). After the head, the body is divided into seven segments (the pereon), each with a pair of legs, a further five smaller segments (the pleon) then the telson and uropods forming the tail end.

They are terrestrial animals although *Ligia oceanica* (the Sea Slater, our largest woodlouse, a whopper at up to 3cm long) is confined to the coast. It is largely nocturnal and can be found on the upper strand line, usually around rocks where it scavenges on all manner of detritus.

I included *Asellus aquaticus* (sometimes called the Water Hog-louse) on the plate as it, too, is an Isopod, closely related to the woodlice but in a different family. *Asellus* species have a totally aquatic existence, living in fresh water. They have the same number of legs as the woodlice (seven pairs) but these differ in being of unequal size, the ones towards the back becoming increasingly longer. They are likely to be found in any garden pond (there are literally dozens in ours) but are generally active at night so it is best to look for them after dark with the aid of a torch. The ones in our pond particularly like grazing on decaying water lily leaves.

For crustaceans, woodlice are extremely well adapted for life on land. Because they have evolved from aquatic ancestors there is a danger that they could dry out, so they tend to live in moist conditions away from bright sunlight, under bark and stones or in deep leaf litter. They have evolved ways to prevent desiccation and to conserve moisture by excreting waste products in the form of ammonia gas rather than liquid urine. The smell of ammonia that they give off led to the Dutch name *pissebed*. Also, their young are protected for the first few weeks of their life by being retained in a special fluid-filled brood pouch. Some species have developed special book lungs (air-filled cavities comprised of thin plates arranged like book pages) so they can breathe without losing too much moisture. These are visible as small white areas on the underside of the woodlouse (eg, in the Common Rough Woodlouse).

Woodlice have a long history of association with people. They were once used in various medical cures, and were often carried around in little bags and used to treat stomach upsets. (Presumably the calcium carbonate in the exoskeleton acted as a mediaeval indigestion tablet.) Due to their long familiarity they have accrued a greater number of vernacular names than any other creature in Britain. These include such delights as Chiselbob or Cheesebob, Slater, Sour-bug, Sow-pig and the rather ghoulish Coffin-cutter.

There are more than 30 species of woodlice native to Britain, and a few other imported species

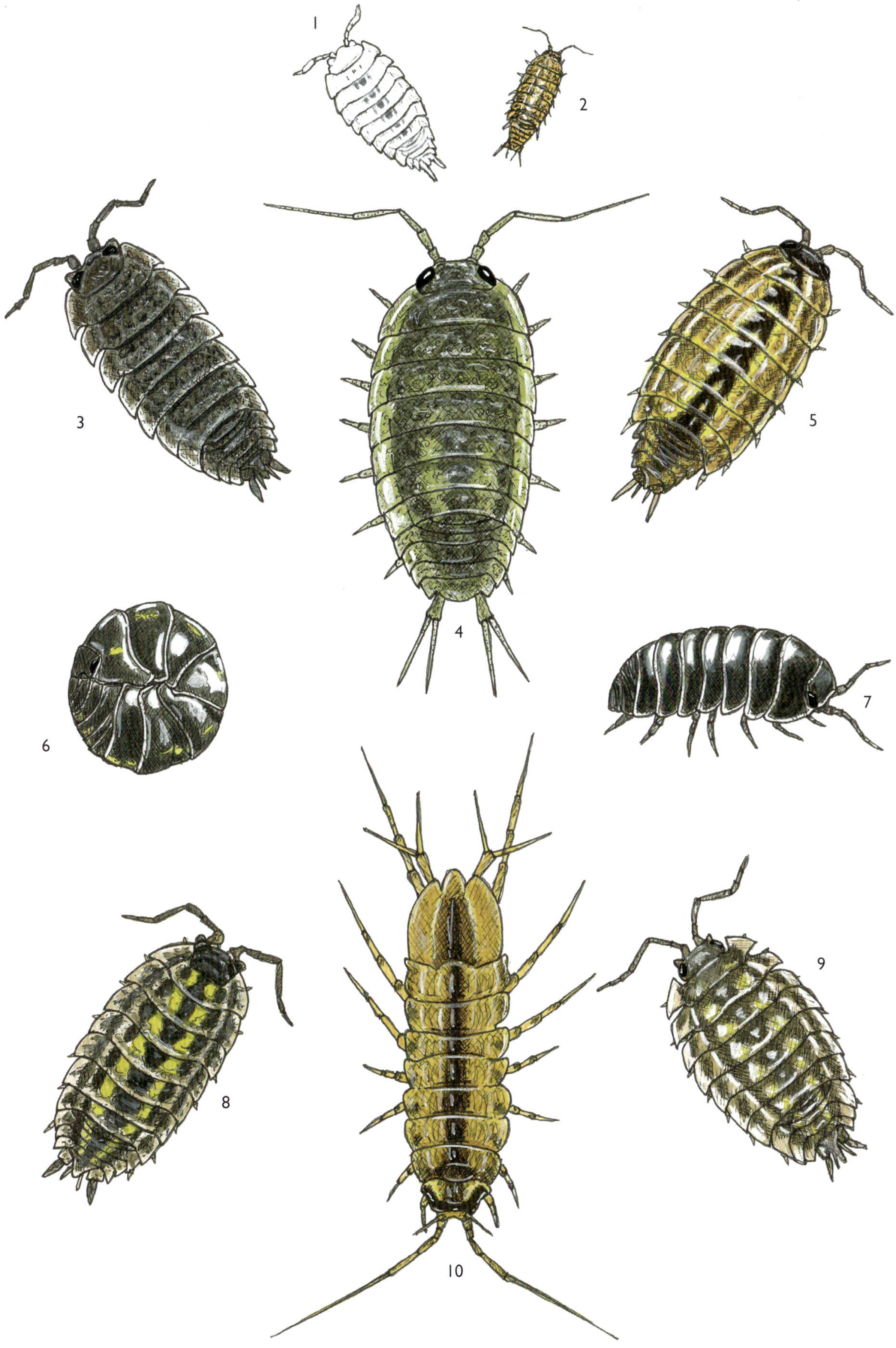
1
2
3
4
5
6
7
8
9
10

that survive in commercial greenhouses. Many are far from common and live in specialist habitats, such as within shingle above the high tide line on beaches. Most gardens should support more than one species, and they can easily be found by looking under flower pots, stones, logs or amongst fallen leaves where they eat decaying plant matter. Compost heaps are also good places to look for them as they provide food and shelter and somewhere moist to thrive.

The Common Pill Woodlouse (*Armadillidium vulgare*) is well known, the classic roll-up-into-a-neat-little-ball creature often found in gardens under stones and flower pots or at the bases of plants. It was doubtless these little 'pills' that were carried around and used medicinally in days gone by.

Common Pygmy Woodlice (*Trichoniscus pusillus*) are very small and active and require a bit of searching to find – they like it pretty damp, and are in fact abundant in leaf litter in woodland. The ones in our garden are in the shadiest spot where a water butt leaks and keeps the ground moist.

I rather like the Common Rough Woodlouse (*Porcellio scaber*), mainly because its scientific name translates as Rough Little Pig, *Porcellio* meaning little pig and *scaber* rough or scabrous. Although superficially similar, the Common Shiny Woodlouse (*Oniscus asellus*) is in a different genus. This is clear when you count the number of segments making up the antennal flagella – three for the Shiny and two for the Rough. The Common Rough Woodlouse is further distinguished by having two pairs of book lungs, which the Common Shiny Woodlouse lacks.

The Common Striped Woodlouse (*Philoscia muscorum*) has a distinctive stepped outline to its body where the pereon and pleon join, making it instantly recognisable compared with the other commonly seen species.

All of the Common Rough, Shiny, Pygmy, Striped and Pill Woodlice are likely to be found in gardens. They are sometimes known as the Famous Five or the Big Five. It is said that the benchmark for a good invertebrate site is one that has the Big Five plus one (plus two being even better). I thought that our garden was a pretty good place for invertebrates, but I had somewhat neglected the woodlice and didn't even know if we had the entire Big Five. So I spent a cold winter day hunting through dead leaves, under stones and through piles of decaying wood and bark and managed to find all of them. Eventually our very own 'plus one' – *Porcellio spinicornis* – turned up on the wall by the kitchen door, so the garden was officially good for invertebrates! Now I just had to locate a 'plus two'...

I really wanted to find an Ant Woodlouse (*Platyarthrus hoffmannseggi*) to complete the plate, so I spent a lot of time turning over stones in places I probably shouldn't have, though I did always carefully put them back, as you should. Tiny, white and blind, Ant Woodlice live almost exclusively in ant nests, feeding on the detritus of the colony. Finally, I found a few. They may be blind but they are certainly light-sensitive, and scurried off as fast as their 14 little legs could carry them, antennae twitching rapidly all the while. I found them under a stone along with Black Garden Ants (*Lasius niger*) which hurriedly started moving their vulnerable larvae as I lifted the stone. Five feet away under another stone were more Ant Woodlice but this time with Yellow Meadow Ants (*Lasius flavus*).

As is the way, I later found them in my own garden. Clearing up a 'calling card' left by one of the neighbourhood cats in the meadow, I accidentally pulled up a clump of turf. Underneath were a few Yellow Meadow Ants, and as I started replacing the turf two little white Ant Woodlice appeared waving their antennae at me. They say every cloud has a silver lining – so hooray for cat poo... I got my 'plus two'!

With their armour-plated bodies, woodlice don't have many enemies. Centipedes will attack them, as will shrews, and I have watched Wall Lizards on the Isle of Wight snaffling them up. But their most fearsome predator is the Woodlouse Spider (*Dysdera crocata*), which has massive jaws (chelicerae) specially adapted for tackling them. We used to find these amazing spiders in our previous garden but I hadn't seen one for years. They tend to be nocturnal so I undertook some evening searches and eventually turned one up.

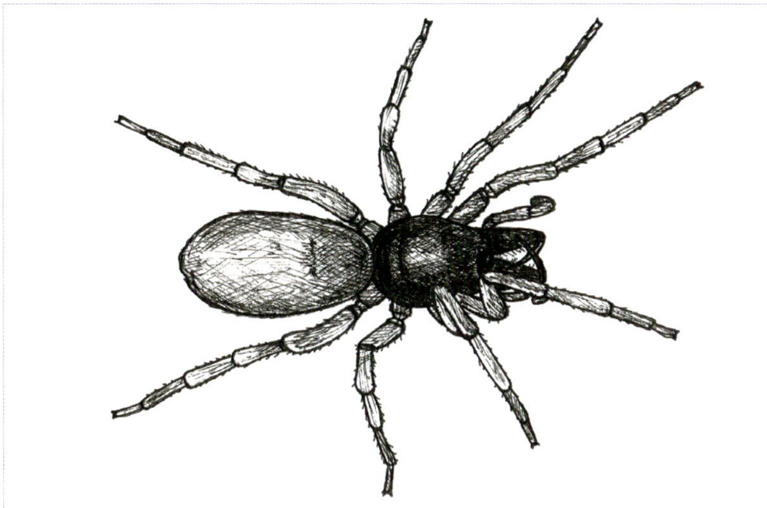

Dysdera crocata (Woodlouse Spider) – a fearsome-looking beast with enlarged chelicerae perfect for tackling the tough exoskeleton of woodlice. After some searching, I finally found this one under a bit of old railway sleeper left over from making raised beds in the garden. She was carefully returned to her hideaway once she had been sketched and photographed. So pleased to know they are about, but not sure the woodlice agree...

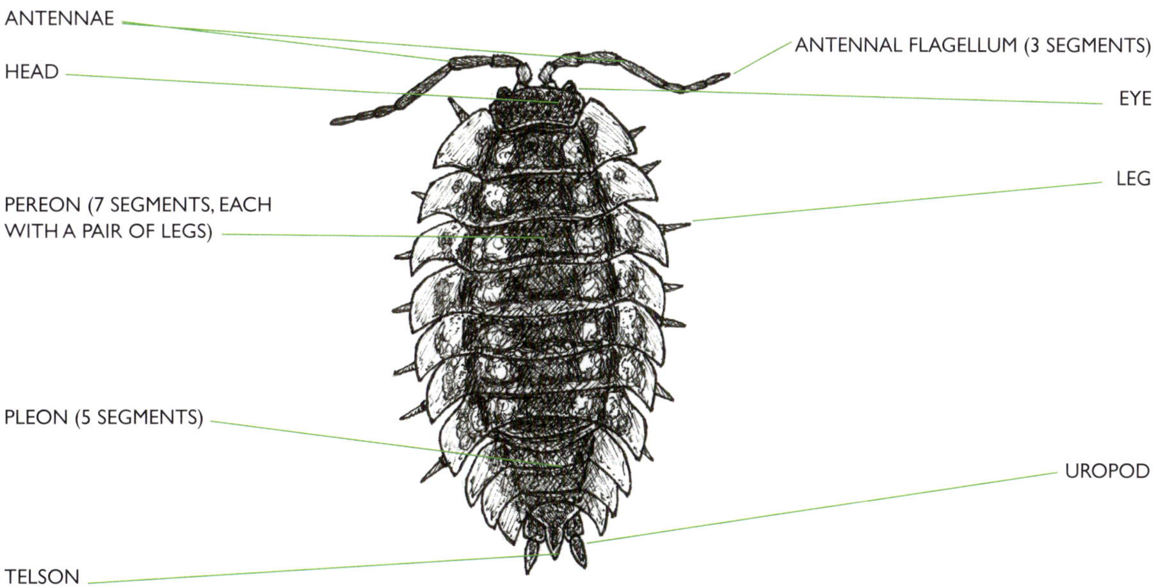

A typical woodlouse (Oniscus asellus) showing the arrangement of the different body segments and the seven pairs of legs.

J is for... JUMPERS and JEWELS

1 Trichrysis cyanea
2 Chrysura radians
3 Sittipub pubescens
4 Evarcha falcata
5 Heliophanus sp.
6 Salticus scenicus
7 Chrysis sp.
8 Hedychrum niemelai

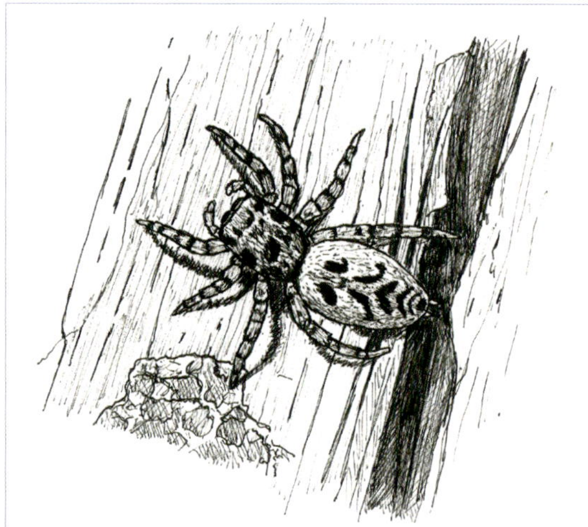

Salticus cingulatus is generally found on old trees in a variety of habitats. This one was on a dead tree stump beside the river at Strumpshaw Fen in Norfolk.

In this case, Jumping Spiders and Jewel Wasps... The jumping spiders all belong to the family Salticidae. They share the same morphological characteristics, a rather square-fronted cephalothorax with four large forward-pointing eyes (the other four eyes are much smaller and set farther back) and a compact abdomen with short, powerful legs for jumping. Rather than spinning a web and sitting about waiting for something to fly in, these spiders actively stalk their prey and jump on it. They have exceptional eyesight, and when you look closely at them they appear to look right back, sizing you up rather disconcertingly!

I have a soft spot for the jumping spiders. They include some of my all-time favourites. Perhaps it's their small size coupled with relatively short legs. Even when I was young and rather scared of spiders, I always found them fascinating and was far less wary of them. Many are attractively patterned when viewed up close and can look quite 'fluffy'. If you aren't comfortable around spiders, then maybe these little critters are a good place to start. They always look cute and cuddly to me and quite adorable, especially with those amazing eyes.

Probably the best-known 'jumper' is *Salticus scenicus*, the Common Zebra Spider. It is closely associated with people (synanthropic) and can regularly be seen on sunny fences and walls around houses. Black and white at first glance, up close the abdomen is warm shades of brown with white flecks, pretty as a Fair Isle knit, while the carapace is a polished black with a patch of shining white hairs.

Sittipub pubescens (formerly *Sitticus pubescens*) is also associated with houses and gardens, although it is not as common or widespread as *Salticus scenicus*. Rather small and drab, it too deserves closer inspection for then it is seen to comprise subtle shades of browns, oranges and greys.

Heliophanus species are known as the sun jumpers as they are generally active on hot, sunny days. The commonest two are *Heliophanus flavipes* and *Heliophanus cupreus*. Small and black with white hairs on the abdomen, the females have contrasting pale yellowish-green legs. They are both rather similar, especially juveniles like the one depicted on the plate, and can be found on flowers in a range of open habitats. On dull days they tend to skulk low down, but become increasingly active in warm weather when they can then be found hunting on flowers.

Evarcha falcata, on the other hand, is a woodland species, found in glades low down amongst vegetation where it can be difficult to spot until it moves. It is quite dark with subtle markings that help it blend in well with its surroundings, especially in dappled light.

The jewel wasps, also known as ruby-tailed wasps, are members of the family Chrysididae and are parasites on various species of solitary wasps and

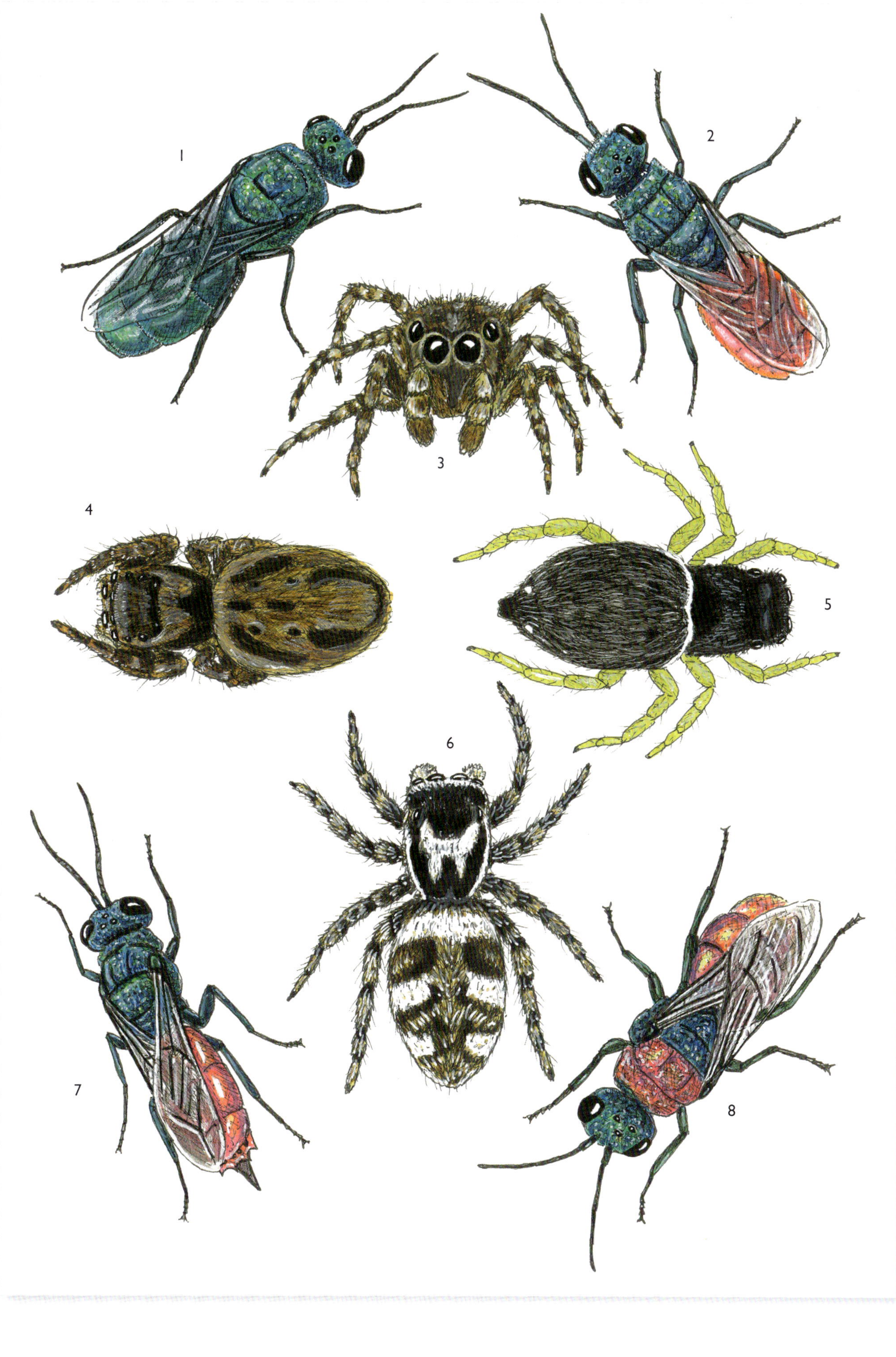
1
2
3
4
5
6
7
8

bees. There are around 30 species in Britain, and all share the same beautiful jewel-like colours which make them rather difficult to tell apart. Their bodies are well-armoured with a tough cuticle, and the curved shape of the abdomen enables them to roll up into a ball in defence if attacked when entering a host nest. They are small, very active and rarely pose to be sketched or photographed. Although they are very pretty and exotic-looking, they are sometimes overlooked due to their small size. They are often seen investigating holes in dead wood or nest entrances in sandy soil, but they also readily visit flowers.

Hedychrum niemelai is restricted to sandy areas of the south-east of Britain where it parasitises the digger wasp *Cerceris quinquefasciata*. Neither species is particularly common, but we are lucky to have recorded both in our small suburban back garden where they can be found on flowers such as Oxeye Daisy and Yarrow in our mini-meadow in summer. We have also had them visiting wildflowers on our nearby allotment, where we deliberately encourage so-called arable weeds to flower (much to the annoyance of certain unenlightened plot-holders who don't tolerate anything that isn't edible).

Trichrysis cyanea is one of the few that is relatively easy to identify, being the only totally turquoise/greenish-blue one that you are likely to come across. It is relatively slender and has 'teeth' at the end of the abdomen (similar to *Chrysis* species) that distinguish it from other blue-green species, although these are only visible at certain angles. It lays its eggs in the nests of *Trypoxylon* wasps, and is usually seen exploring holes in dead wood in search of the wasps' nest chambers.

Chrysura radians is a parasite of *Osmia* bees, especially *O. leaiana*. Having found several species of solitary bee in our garden, we put up some bee hotels. Soon we had several different species using them, and this attracted the parasitic bee and wasp species including *Chrysura radians*. You plant up a garden to attract bees, supply them with somewhere to nest, then watch as their parasites move in! This is one of the joys of entomology. You attract one species into the garden only to have another, equally interesting, species turn up to parasitise and/or eat it. I tend to agree with the theory that the presence of parasites shows that the host population is doing well enough to support them. If the host is rare then its parasite will almost certainly be rarer, so I sit back and enjoy them.

There are several *Chrysis* species, a distinctive genus because of the projections on the tip of the abdomen, but microscopic examination is required to determine species. Some are parasitoids on solitary wasps whilst others target solitary bees. *Chrysis ignita* is known to parasitise solitary bees including the widespread *Osmia bicornis* (the Red Mason Bee), so look for them around bee hotels if you have them. Once they find a host nest, the wasp nips inside and lays an egg. When her larva hatches out it kills and eats the host larva. If more than one wasp egg is laid in the host nest then the strongest larva to emerge will dispatch the others and probably eat them, too.

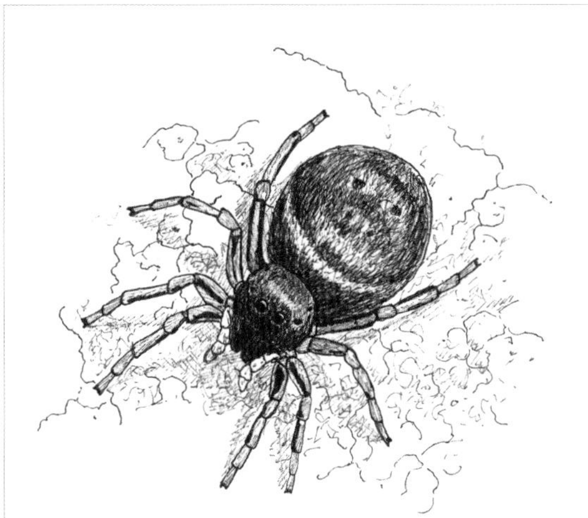

Seeing eye to eye. An adult female Heliophanus cupreus hunting on a lichen-encrusted wall in Ventnor Botanic Gardens, Isle of Wight. We were watching the resident population of Wall Lizards basking in the sunshine when this little beauty showed up. Hopefully she evaded the beady-eyed lizards that were busy hunting out woodlice from the Ivy-leaved Toadflax growing on the walls. The dark marks on the legs distinguish this species from H. flavipes.

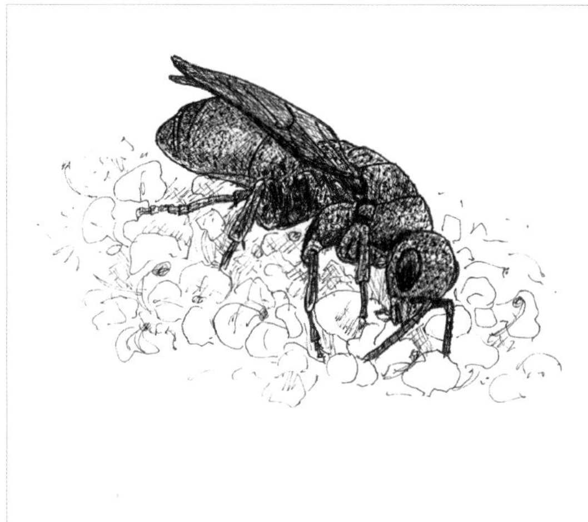

Hedychridium roseum is typical of the jewel wasps in having a deep cerise-pink abdomen with a contrasting blue-green head and thorax. It is a distinctive species, however, as the abdomen is dull rather than shiny. It is a parasite of the wonderfully named wasp Astata boops.

K is for... KALEIDOSCOPE

I have to admit that I struggled to find a theme for 'K' but then hit upon the idea of pushing the symmetrical style of the other plates to the extreme. So this plate has been designed as a kaleidoscopic pattern of colours and shapes portraying the diversity of the largest group of arthropods, the insects.

The plate is un-numbered and there is no key alongside. Instead, think of it as an identification challenge. I hope it will encourage readers to start looking at and enjoying identifying our amazing invertebrates for themselves. There is a list of the species on page 109; and, if you get really stuck, a numbered version of the plate can be found on the website that accompanies this book, https://arthropedia.co.uk/

There are 82 individual insects of 62 different species, from beetles and bugs to bees, wasps and butterflies with all sorts in between – sawflies, grasshoppers and crickets, micro and macro moths, and flies. Most of the species were encountered in Norfolk, with quite a few in my garden in Norwich. Others, notably some of the butterflies, are only to be found farther afield so required holidays to far-flung corners of the country to track them down and see them.

As with all the plates, I have tried to balance colour and form to give an overall artistic design. I have included species that I couldn't quite fit on to the other plates, some because I only saw my first one after the appropriate plate was finished. I am particularly fond of beetles and bugs, and this is reflected in the number depicted. I love the many species of capsid bug, and made the most of them being subtle variations on a theme. While everyone is familiar with ladybirds, I deliberately picked some of the more unusual ones and then replaced some with a few of my other favourite beetles, small specialist species that are attracted to dung.

While working on the design of this plate I came across the following quote from John Ray, 17th-century naturalist and clergyman, describing how he felt about butterflies:

> "To contemplate their exquisite beauty and variety is to experience the truest pleasure. To gaze enquiringly at such elegance of colour and form devised by the ingenuity of nature and painted by her artist's pencil is to acknowledge and adore the imprint of the art of God."

I may not share Ray's religious beliefs, but I can appreciate the sentiment, and it comes close to how I feel about the natural world in general and insects in particular.

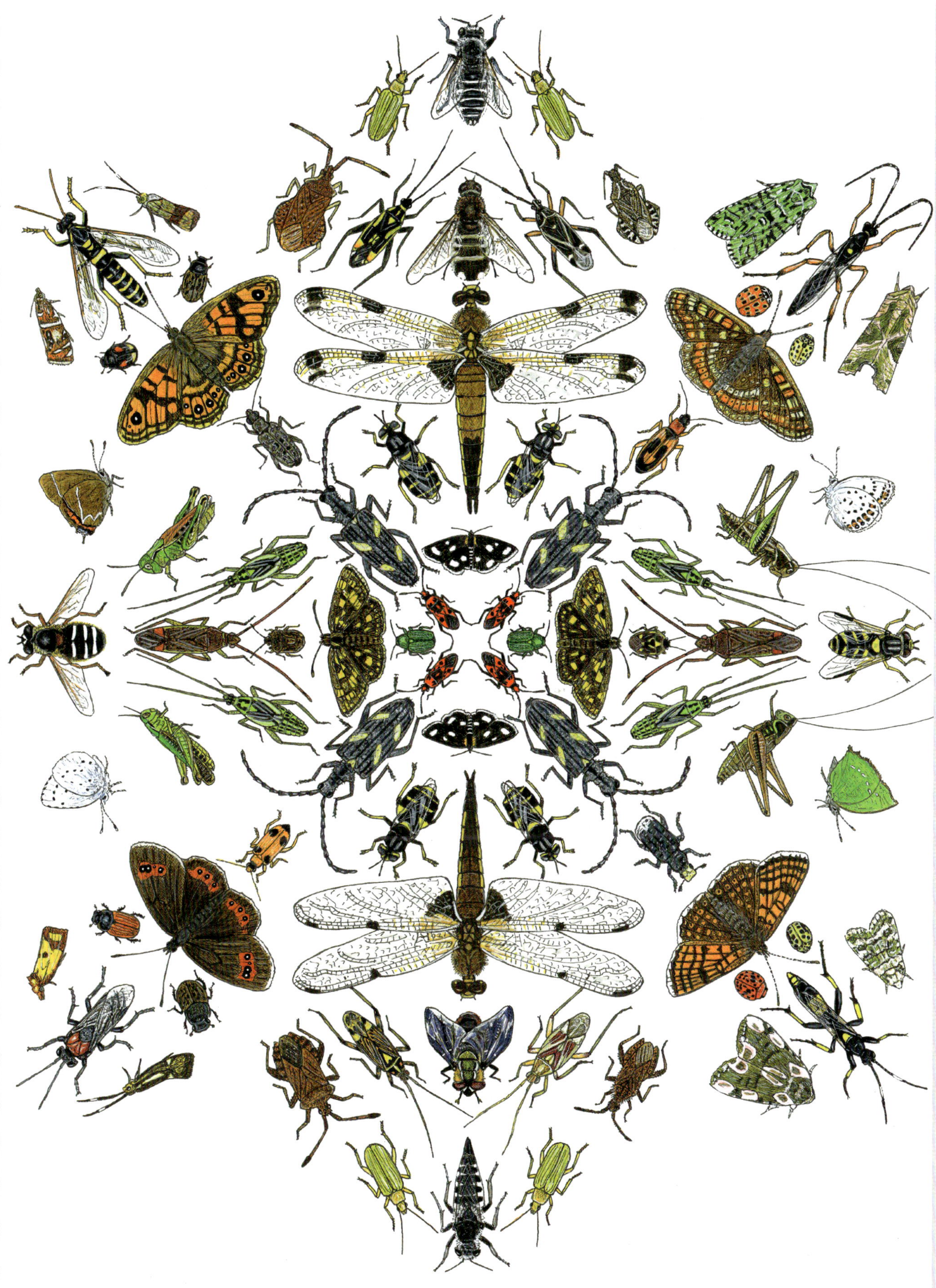

L is for... LEGS

1 Harvestman Dichranopalpus rasmosus
2 Woodland Dor Beetle
3 Sawfly Nematus pavidus larvae
4 Pond Skater
5 Common Earwig
6 Backswimmer
7 Spotted Snake Millipede
8 Centipede Stigmatogaster subterranea
9 Western Conifer Seedbug
10 Millipede Cylindroiulus caeruleocinctus
11 Large House Spider
12 Common Striped Woodlouse
13 Rhododendron Leafhopper
14 Mole Cricket
15 Centipede Lithobius forficatus
16 Black Oil Beetle
17 Red Velvet Mite
18 Downlooker Snipefly
19 Deer Tick
20 Brimstone Moth caterpillar

As arthropod means jointed foot or limb, I thought it only appropriate for plate L to represent Legs. That way I could showcase the diversity of forms that the insects have evolved in order to exploit different lifestyles and habitats. It also enabled me to shoehorn in a few more arachnids, including a large and handsome House Spider, and it was the only way I was ever going to accommodate the centipedes and millipedes.

The large House Spider (*Eratigena* sp. – previously *Tegenaria*) will be familiar to many people from encounters indoors when one of these moderately large, hairy beasts rushes unexpectedly across the living-room floor and makes you jump. These are usually males that have come indoors at the end of summer and beginning of autumn for a bit of shelter and, more importantly, on the hunt for a female to mate with. So feel a bit sorry for these amorous males; don't turf them out – they're only after a bit of cosy female company.

Harvestmen, properly called Opiliones, are also familiar to many people, but perhaps not *Dicranopalpus ramosus*. Its characteristic pose with legs spread out sideways and its two-pronged pedipalps (sensory organs that look like an extra pair of short legs) used to make it one of the most easily recognised Opiliones in Britain. Unfortunately, as is ever the case, it turns out that there is more than one species, so identification is not so straightforward after all.

As well as spiders and harvestmen, the arachnids include mites and ticks. Anyone who goes out looking for wildlife will soon become acquainted with Deer Ticks (*Ixodes ricinus*). They were already annoying little blood suckers that clung on to you persistently for a couple of days before dropping off, fully engorged, but then it was discovered that they can transmit Lyme Disease. Not all ticks carry the bacteria, but you wouldn't want to run the risk of getting it, so prevention is better than cure. I always wear long trousers and sleeves and try to avoid long grass and bracken when I'm out and about looking for invertebrates.

Red Velvet Mites (family Trombidiidae) are perfectly harmless but are sometimes mistaken for Red Spider Mites, which can be a problem on house or greenhouse plants. The velvet mites are usually found in really hot, sunny weather in summer, crawling over walls and roof tiles. They are tiny but worth a close look under a lens or microscope, when their velvety appearance can be properly appreciated.

The Common Striped Woodlouse (*Philoscia muscorum*) is the sole representative of this group of terrestrial crustaceans on the plate. Common in gardens, under stones and dead wood, these little

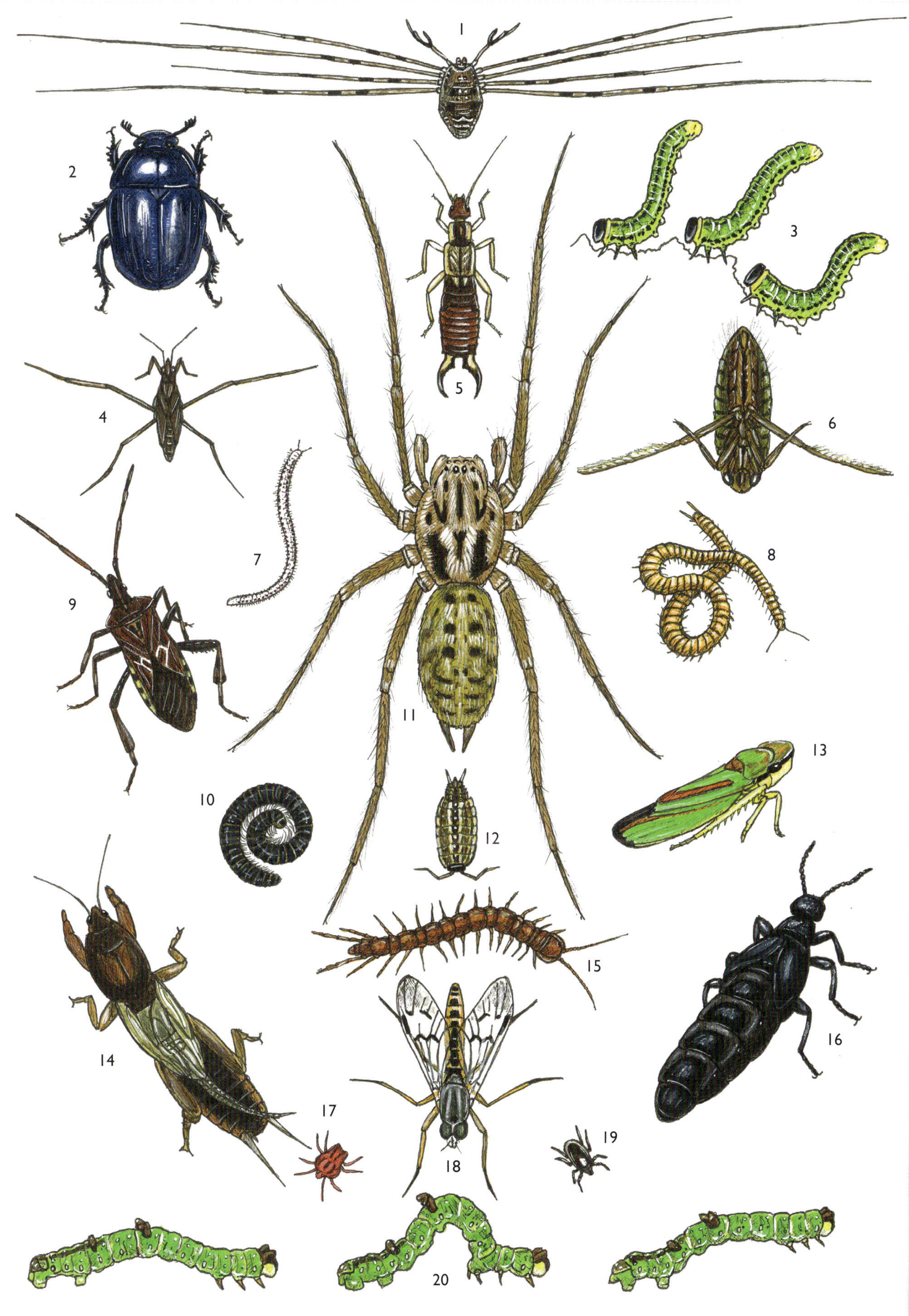
1
2
3
4
5
6
7
8
9
10
11
12
13
14
15
16
17
18
19
20

critters have been given a plate all of their own, I for Isopods, and you can find out more about them there in the accompanying text.

'Centipede' translates as one hundred legs. Although some do have more than this, none ever have exactly that many because they always have an odd number of pairs. Two species of centipede are illustrated. *Lithobius forficatus* is typical, one of the 'stone centipedes' and the species most likely to be found in gardens, being the commonest and most widespread. The long, thin bootlace centipede is one of the 'earth centipedes', *Stigmatogaster subterranea*. They are known as geophilomorphs, and are actually blind. I often disturb them as I'm digging out compost heaps or find them in the soil, when they writhe and twist themselves seemingly into knots. All our centipedes are carnivores and have a pair of strong, curving poison claws visible either side of the head.

By comparison, the millipedes are gentle, slow-moving herbivores. None has the 1,000 legs that milli- means. They are distinguished by having two pairs of legs per segment, and tend to be rather dome-shaped in cross section compared with the flattened bodies of centipedes, which have just one pair of legs per segment. The wonderfully named Spotted Snake Millipede (*Blaniulus guttulatus*) can be found under stones. Blind and seemingly helpless, the crimson spots along its sides are repugnatorial glands (or ozadenes) that emit a noxious concoction of hydrocyanic acid, iodine, quinine and chlorine (don't sniff too closely), so not so defenceless after all. The other millipede on the plate is *Cylindroiulus caeruleocinctus*, depicted coiled up in typical resting posture that resembles a fossil ammonite. The rest of the plate is taken up with insects. It's a celebration of the diversity of legs, which can be used for so many things, including jumping, skating across ponds, swimming through water and digging in soil or dung.

The Hemiptera or 'true' bugs are some of my favourite insects. Many are colourful and conspicuous while others are small, subtle and beautifully camouflaged. They are a diverse bunch, adapted to very different lifestyles, but all share the piercing rostrum with which they feed. Several have adapted to assume aquatic lifestyles. The Pond Skaters (*Gerris* sp.) stay above the surface; with their slender bodies and long, delicate legs, they skate about the surface film, detecting vibrations from other insects that fall in the water, moving in to feed on them as they detect their drowning struggles. By contrast, the Backswimmer (*Notonecta* sp.) spends its time upside down at or below the water surface, sculling along with its elongated oar-like hind legs. When threatened, it propels itself down into the depths out of harm's way, rising back up a few moments later, buoyed up by the air trapped around bristles on the underside of its body.

The Rhododendron Leafhopper (*Graphocephala fennahi*) is a really colourful bug that was accidentally introduced into Britain from the USA and has become well established in parts of the country where Rhododendrons have been planted and thrive. (I found them in Sheringham Park in Norfolk, which is known for its Rhododendrons and Azaleas.) About a centimetre long, they sit on top of the leaves, sometimes several together, but will soon hop off and glide away as you approach.

Another accidental import is the Western Conifer Seed Bug (*Leptoglossus occidentalis*), again from the good old US of A. It first arrived in continental Europe then spread to Britain. It is a large and distinctive species that feeds on the seeds of various conifers. Like most bugs it can fly, and one turned up in our garden. We don't have conifers ourselves, but there are plenty in the neighbourhood.

Mole Crickets (*Gryllotalpa gryllotalpa*) have sadly all but disappeared from Britain. Largely nocturnal, they have a distinctive song and tend to be heard but not seen. I was fortunate to see one in broad daylight in southern Spain, stopping me dead in my tracks in delighted surprise. They spend most of their lives underground and have enlarged front legs and tarsi (feet), rather like a mole (hence the vernacular name), enabling them to burrow through soil.

The Black Oil Beetle (*Meloe proscarabaeus*) is the biggest, most bizarre beetle I've ever come across, and I feel extremely privileged to have found one. It was at a campsite on the Isles of Scilly. While I was sitting outside our tent by a drystone wall I heard a scratchy rustling like a lizard, but there are no lizards on the islands. What could it be? I got up to investigate – and this huge, clumsy, beautiful thing appeared, a female Black Oil Beetle as long as my index finger.

Oil beetles are flightless parasites of bees. The female lays hundreds, if not thousands, of eggs in a burrow close to a colony of bees. When the larvae (known as triungulins) hatch they climb up on to a flower in the hope of hitching a ride on a bee back to her nest. Once there they feed on the pollen and nectar store meant for the bee larvae. We have five species of oil beetle in Britain, most of which are very rare, if not endangered, and three further species are already extinct here.

The Dor beetles (Woodland Dor, *Anoplotrupes stercorosus*) are some of our best-known dung beetles. They are sturdily built with a domed shape and stout, spined legs. They dig burrows below fresh animal dung, dragging some of it down to provision their nests. They are often encountered ambling along heathland paths or woodland tracks with a rather ponderous and clumsy gait. Often I find them lying on their backs with their legs waving in the air. This is quite convenient, as when I pick them up to right them I can check out whether or not they have pits and hairs on the underside, an aid to identification for some species.

The Brimstone Moth (*Opisthograptis luteolata*) caterpillar at the bottom of the plate is the classic 'looper' caterpillar (see plate G for the adult moth). These larvae have three pairs of true legs (the thoracic legs) at the front of their body, and just two pairs of false or prolegs at the back, which gives them their characteristic 'looping' gait. Other caterpillars not in the Geometridae have four more pairs of prolegs in the centre of the body.

At the top of the plate are the larvae of *Nematus pavidus*, a sawfly commonly found on willow. They are superficially similar to lepidoptera caterpillars but lack the final pair of prolegs (anal claspers). Sawfly larvae adopt a characteristic pose when threatened – flicking their bodies up into a curving s-shape.

There are just four native species of earwig in Britain, and only one of these is common and widespread; the other three have a southerly distribution and are not often found. They are odd-looking insects with pincers at their rear ends with which they can give you a nip if badly handled. The females tend their eggs, licking them to prevent the growth of mould, and look after their young until they can fend for themselves. The Common Earwig (*Forficula auricularia*) has fully formed hindwings, neatly folded and tucked away under the small, sheath-like forewings (a bit like the elytra of a beetle), and is capable of flight, though this is seldom observed. Male Common Earwigs can be distinguished from females by their more widely spaced curved pincers. In Scotland they are called 'Forky-tails'.

There are lots of insects with more evident wings that are well developed to make them masters of flight. Other plates have been dedicated to these brilliant aeronauts, from dragonflies to bees and hoverflies. I singled out the Downlooker Snipefly (*Rhagio scolopaceus*) as the sole obvious-winged representative. It is a rather elegant, long-legged species of fly that adopts a distinctive pose, head down, giving it its common name.

M is for... METAMORPHOSIS

1–4 Large Red Damselfly
1 Larva/ nymph
2 Exuvia
3 Teneral adult
4 Adult

5–8 Orange-tip Butterfly
5 Ovum/ egg
6 Larva/ caterpillar
7 Imago/ adult female
8 Imago/ adult male

9–13 Red Poplar Leaf Beetle
9 Ova/ eggs
10 and 11 Larvae
12 Pupa
13 Adult beetle

14–20 Green Shieldbug
14 Larvae/ nymphs 1st instars with empty egg cases
15 2nd instar
16 3rd instar
17 4th instar
18 5th instar
19 Adult
20 Adult female egg-laying

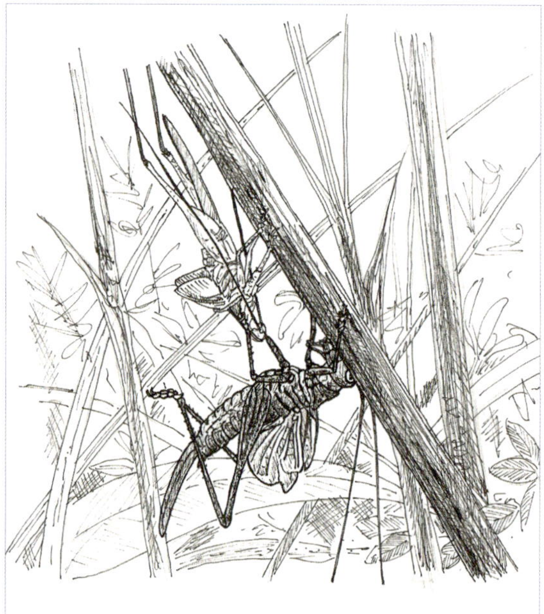

Incomplete metamorphosis: a female Long-winged Conehead (Conocephalus fuscus) undergoing her final moult pulls herself out of her last larval skin. She is vulnerable while she pumps fluid into her wings and waits for her cuticle (skin) to harden. Bush-crickets generally eat the shed skin but grasshoppers do not. I found this one in our mini-meadow in the early evening just before it got dark.

When it comes to metamorphosis, most people will be familiar with the concept of a caterpillar turning into a butterfly or a tadpole becoming a frog or toad.

Nearly all species of insect undergo metamorphosis of some kind during their lives. There are two main types, generally known as complete metamorphosis and incomplete metamorphosis. Complete metamorphosis is the one most of us are familiar with as it is the process by which a caterpillar transforms into a butterfly. Incomplete metamorphosis is the simpler of the two, with three stages of development. These are egg or ovum (plural ovum); a larva (or nymph), which goes through several growth stages, called instars, shedding its skin (known as moulting or ecdysis) to do so; and then the adult. The instars are essentially like smaller versions of the adult, differing mainly in that they lack wings although these can be seen developing in the form of wing buds in their later stages. The larva and adult often share a similar lifestyle and diet.

Complete metamorphosis has four stages: egg (ovum); larva (again, shedding its skin several times in order to grow); pupa (usually called a chrysalis in butterflies); and the adult (sometimes called an imago, especially in butterflies). The larva and adult insect couldn't be more different, and they are adapted to very different lifestyles. The larva is a perfect eating machine designed to maximise growth, while the adult is adapted to finding a mate and breeding. For example, a butterfly is a delicate winged creature that sups nectar from flowers with a long, thin proboscis – and its sole purpose in life is to reproduce, thus ensuring the survival of the species. Its caterpillar, on the other hand, has a long, thin, multi-legged body and is armed with sharp mandibles to chomp away through leaves or other vegetative material and grow as quickly as possible.

Insects that have complete metamorphosis include beetles (Coleoptera), flies and hoverflies (Diptera), butterflies and moths (Lepidoptera) and the bees, wasps, ants and sawflies (Hymenoptera).

In flies, the larvae are basically legless maggots with an eating hole at one end and an excreting hole at the other. They also have posterior breathing tubes. These larvae feed in or on a variety of substances, from rotting vegetation through dung to animal carcases. The larvae of the large family Tachinidae are parasitoids of other insects,

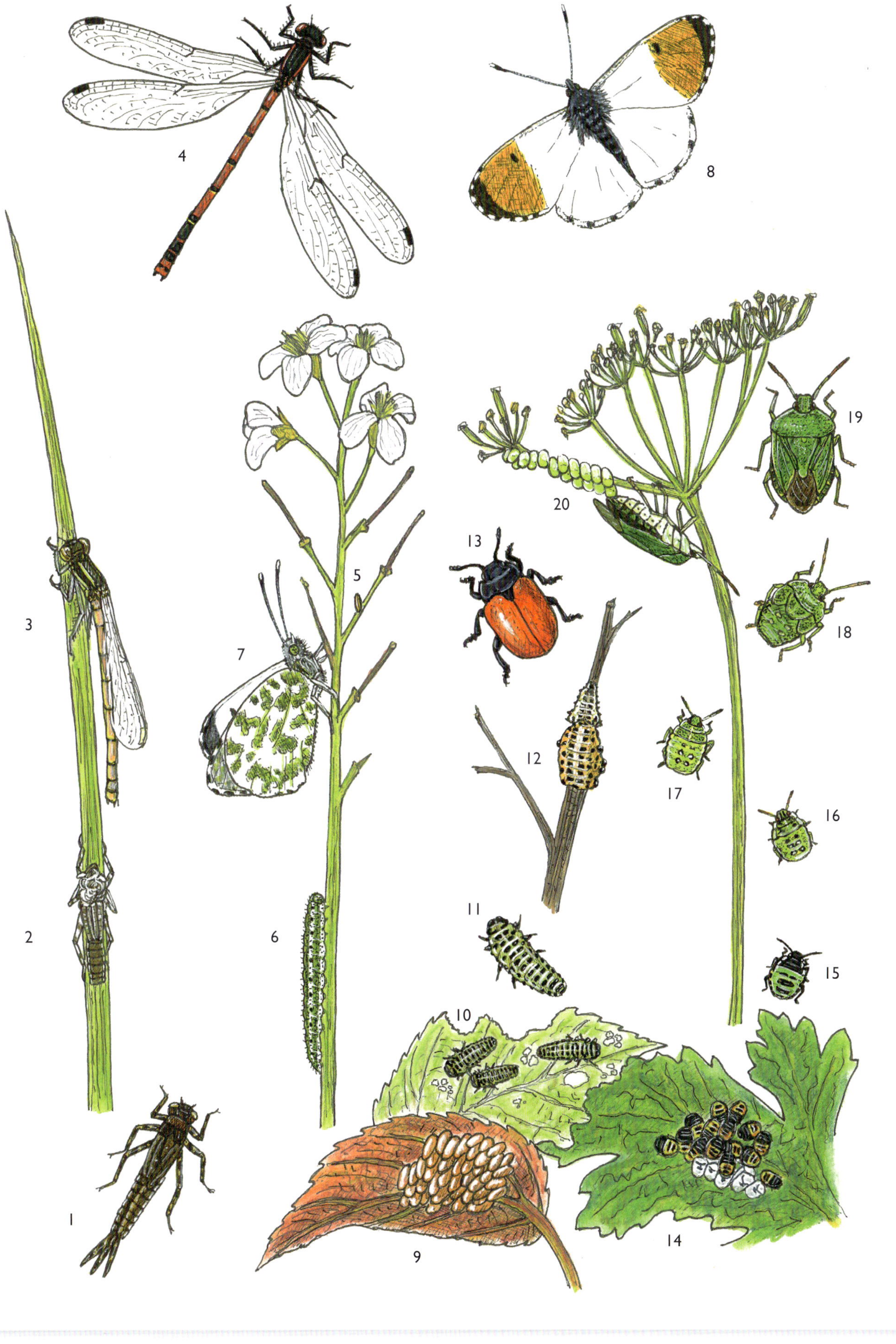
4
8
19
20
13
5
3
18
7
12
17
16
2
6
11
15
10
1
9
14

especially on moth caterpillars. These include *Eriothrix rufomaculata* and *Tachina grossa* (both plate F), whereas *Phasia hemiptera* (plate K) parasitises shieldbug nymphs.

Butterfly and moth larvae are the classic caterpillars – long, soft-bodied creatures with three pairs of jointed thoracic legs (called true legs) and a number of simple prolegs or false legs, including a pair at the end of the abdomen called anal claspers. Most caterpillars have four pairs of prolegs in the middle segments of the abdomen, although these are reduced to one pair towards the back in the geometers (see Brimstone moth caterpillar on plate L). The caterpillar sheds its skin several times as it grows.

The pupal stage, to all outward appearances, is one of inactivity, but this couldn't be further from the truth; it is during this period that the greatest transformation from larva to adult is taking place. It is a complex procedure, driven by hormones. Inside the hard protective pupal case, the larva's tissues and organs are broken down and then reorganised into the new form of the adult insect that eventually emerges.

Butterflies lay their eggs either singly or in batches on the larva's preferred foodplant. The female Orange-tip (*Anthocharis cardamines*) is usually careful to lay only one egg on each plant as her larvae can be cannibalistic, turning to their own siblings for sustenance when the developing seedpods that they feed on have been consumed (although, amazingly, one year I found nine fully grown caterpillars on a single large Field Pennycress plant in our garden – it was a very large specimen, with plentiful succulent seedpods to support them all). Cuckooflower or Lady's-smock is a favourite food plant of the caterpillar, and the butterflies also feed on nectar from the flowers. In our garden we grow their alternative food plant, Garlic Mustard, and with a little searching I usually manage to find one or two of the pale orange eggs each year, laid on the developing seedpods. The caterpillar grows to about an inch long and is well camouflaged at rest along the plant stem or seedpod. When fully grown, it turns into a chrysalis low down in vegetation, so well hidden that I have yet to discover one. Both sexes of the adult butterfly have blackish tips to the forewings, but only the male butterfly has the bright orange patches. Both have the beautiful green mottling on the underside of the hindwings that Jeremy Thomas, in his book *The Butterflies of Britain and Ireland*, rather beautifully describes as being "mossed".

Beetles, like the Red Poplar Leaf Beetle (*Chrysomela populi*), also undergo complete metamorphosis. The adult beetle lays its eggs in batches on the underside of fresh new poplar leaves. When the larvae hatch they often feed together for the first couple of stages and can be found in little groups on the surface of a leaf. They look nothing like the adult beetles, being short, soft-bodied squat little things but sharing the adult's strong mandibles and three pairs of jointed legs. When the larva is fully grown it finds a suitable plant stem to rest on then sheds its skin one last time to reveal the tough pupa. Inside, metamorphosis takes place and eventually the adult beetle emerges, complete with toughened elytra covering and protecting the membranous wings.

By comparison, in incomplete metamorphosis the change between larva and adult is much more gradual, although the earliest stages of development can look somewhat different. Insects that undergo incomplete metamorphosis include the 'true' bugs (Hemiptera), grasshoppers and crickets (the Orthoptera) and the dragonflies and damselflies (Odonata).

The Green Shieldbug (*Palomena prasina*) lays its eggs in batches on suitable vegetation, in this instance a flowerhead of Cow Parsley. When the young hatch, their first meal is often the empty egg case, and they stay together until their first moult. These young instars look rather different to the adults although the general shape is largely the same. The next instars start to look more like the adult, especially as the wing buds develop, becoming very obvious by the fifth and final instar. With the last moult, the fully winged adult insect emerges with its characteristic shield shape. Most of our shieldbugs over-winter as adults, emerging in spring when they mate.

Dragonflies and damselflies, perhaps surprisingly, also go through incomplete metamorphosis. You would think moving from a skulking aquatic larva to a splendid winged creature would involve a much greater change. But the larva is in fact very similar to the adult, albeit without wings (the wing buds can clearly be seen in the late instar nymph depicted).

The larva or nymph of the Large Red Damselfly (*Pyrrhosoma nymphula*), and all other damselflies and dragonflies for that matter, sheds its skin periodically as it grows. After it has reached its final larval stage, it hauls itself out of the water and climbs up the stem of a plant – and, with one last shedding of its skin, it emerges as an adult damselfly. Known as a teneral adult, it is almost colourless to start with, and its wings are tiny and crumpled, but fluid is pumped into the veins and the wings gradually fill out. The wings soon harden, and the colour of the adult insect becomes apparent. You can often find the empty shed skins of damselflies and dragonflies on vegetation around pond margins – these are called exuviae (singular, exuvia).

An insect often lives in the larval stage for a much greater period than it does as an adult. Some dragonflies can remain as a larva for two years or more, with the adult being on the wing for only a few weeks. Similarly, adult mayflies, which also undergo incomplete metamorphosis, live for only a few days as adults, having spent as long as two years as aquatic larvae. They are in the family Ephemeroptera, aptly named after ephemeral, meaning short-lived.

N is for... NETTLES

1 Peacock Butterfly
2 Small Magpie
3 Heterotoma planicornis
4 Nettle-tap
5 14-spot Ladybird
6 Deraeocoris ruber
7 Dark Bush-cricket
8 Nettle Groundbug
9 Peacock Butterfly caterpillar
10 Himacerus mirmicoides nymph
11 Small Nettle Weevil
12 Scorpionfly
13 Mother of Pearl
14 Snout moth
15 Liocoris tripustulatus
16 7-spot Ladybird
17 Large Nettle Weevil
18 Green Lacewing

As a child, the Stinging Nettle (*Urtica dioica*) was probably the first plant I learnt to identify, mainly to avoid getting stung. (The second was the humble dock – a pernicious weed to some gardeners but a vital salve to the sting of said nettles.) Nettles were also the place to look for the spiky black caterpillars of Peacock butterflies and their less flamboyant cousins, the Small Tortoiseshells.

All sorts of critters abound around a nettle bed, but it was years before I appreciated them and learnt to identify them. A stand of Stinging Nettles is a teeming metropolis of stems and leaves. Here you will find sap suckers, seed eaters, pollen pickers, leaf munchers and rollers, nursery web spinners, predators and prey. There are at least 30 species of insect that rely almost totally on nettles for food, and many more that will eat their leaves, seeds or pollen as well as that of other plants. Various creatures will shelter in nettles, and of course there are lots of insects that hang around nettles to prey on the ones that live there.

One example is the amazing-looking Scorpionfly (*Panorpa communis*) with its elongated beak-like head and the male's swollen claspers resembling the tail of a scorpion. They scavenge on dead insects, and aren't above stealing the odd morsel from a spider's web. The delicate Green Lacewing (*Chrysoperla* sp.), on the other hand, is an active predator that feasts on aphids, sucking them dry. It has voracious larvae that often camouflage themselves with the corpses of their victims.

Large Nettle Weevils (*Phyllobius pomaceus*) tend to sit about on the top of nettle leaves but quickly drop off and disappear as soon as you get anywhere near. This is typical beetle behaviour. Peer underneath the leaves or between the stems to find Small Nettle Weevils (*Nedyus quadrimaculatus*) and various bugs. *Deraeocoris ruber* and *Liocoris tripustulatus* are two of the mirid or capsid bugs commonly found on nettles. While *Liocoris* feeds on the actual nettles, *Deraeocoris* is a predator on small insects. Another capsid bug is *Heterotoma planicornis*, one of the strangest-looking bugs to be found on nettles. It is very small but is endowed with unwieldy-looking antennae that have a broad and flattened second segment, making them look rather like the semaphore bats used to

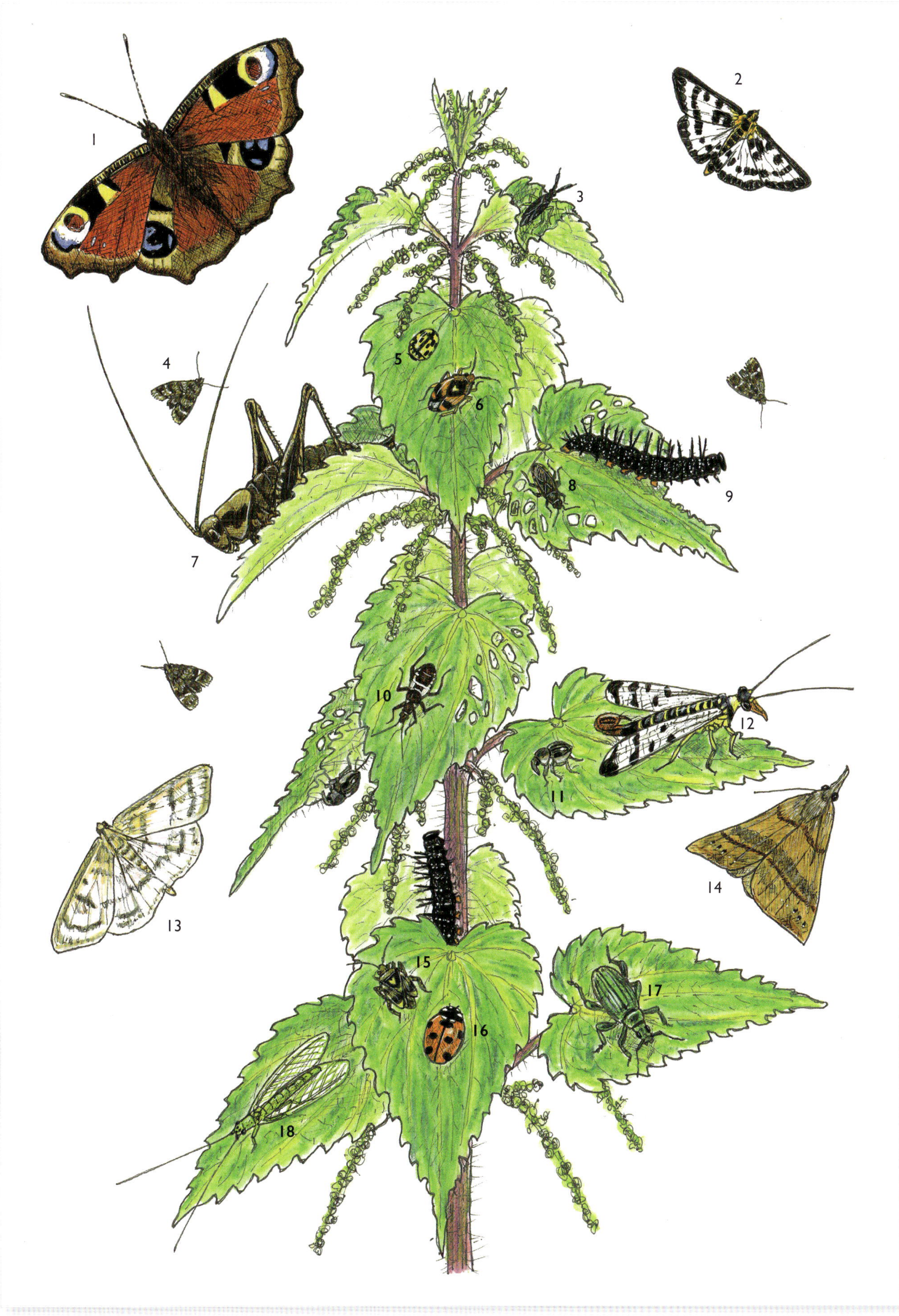
1
2
3
4
5
6
7
8
9
10
11
12
13
14
15
16
17
18

signal to landing helicopters. The males waggle them about, too, presumably to attract females.

The Nettle Groundbug (*Heterogaster urticae*) can be very numerous in a nettle patch, especially in spring when it emerges from hibernation. The Ant Damsel Bug (*Himacerus mirmicoides*) is a predatory bug often found on nettles. The early instar nymphs are very ant-like (*mirmicoides* means of or resembling an ant) but it is generally the late instar nymphs (depicted on the plate) that I find in our garden.

Several species of ladybird can be found by searching nettles, attracted by aphids that feed on the plants. In spring, a sunny patch of nettles can swarm with 7-spot Ladybirds (*Coccinella septempunctata*) that have spent the winter hibernating in the deep litter underneath. The 14-spot Ladybird (*Propylea quattuordecimpunctata*) is one of the last species to emerge from hibernation, and tends to be seen in much smaller numbers than the 7-spot.

Peacock (*Aglais io*), Comma (*Polygonia c-album*), Red Admiral (*Vanessa atalanta*) and Small Tortoiseshell (*Aglais urticae*) caterpillars munch their way through loads of nettle leaves, as do those of various moths such as Mother of Pearl (*Pleuroptya ruralis*), Small Magpie (*Anania hortulata*), Angle Shades (*Phlogophora meticulosa*), Burnished Brass (*Diachrysia chrysitis*) (see plate Y), Snout (*Hypena proboscidalis*) and the delightful little Nettle-tap (*Anthophila fabriciana*) that can sometimes be found swarming around nettles in large numbers in sunshine.

In late summer you can often hear the soft zit-zit calls of Dark Bush-crickets (*Pholidoptera griseoaptera*) coming from a stand of nettles. A great deal of patience is required to find one of these large bush-crickets. If you're lucky, a calling male may well lure a female out into the open, or a rival male may put in an appearance. They are mostly active at night but start calling in late afternoon and at dusk.

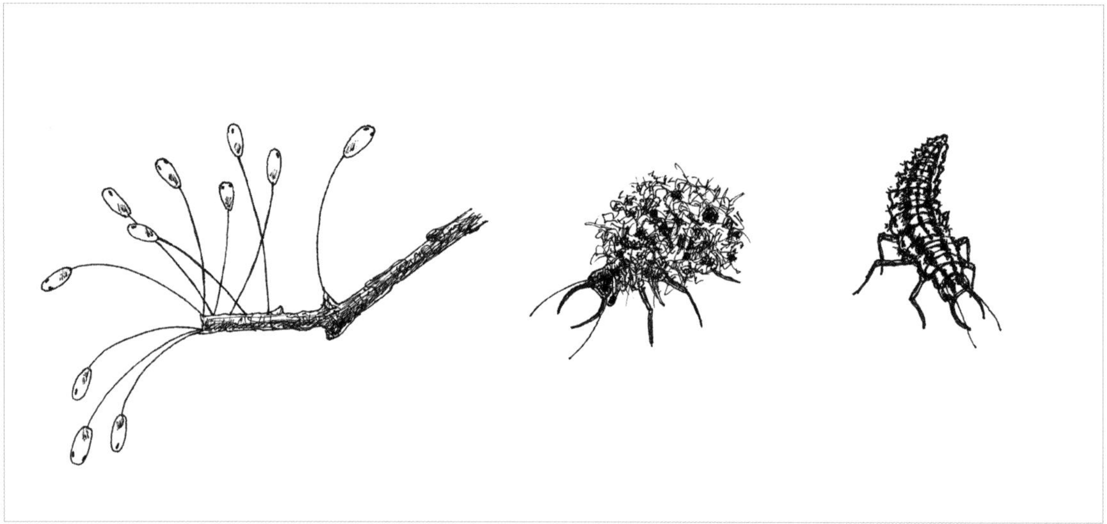

Alien life-forms: the strange stalked eggs of a lacewing and larvae with and without camouflage coating of aphid corpses.

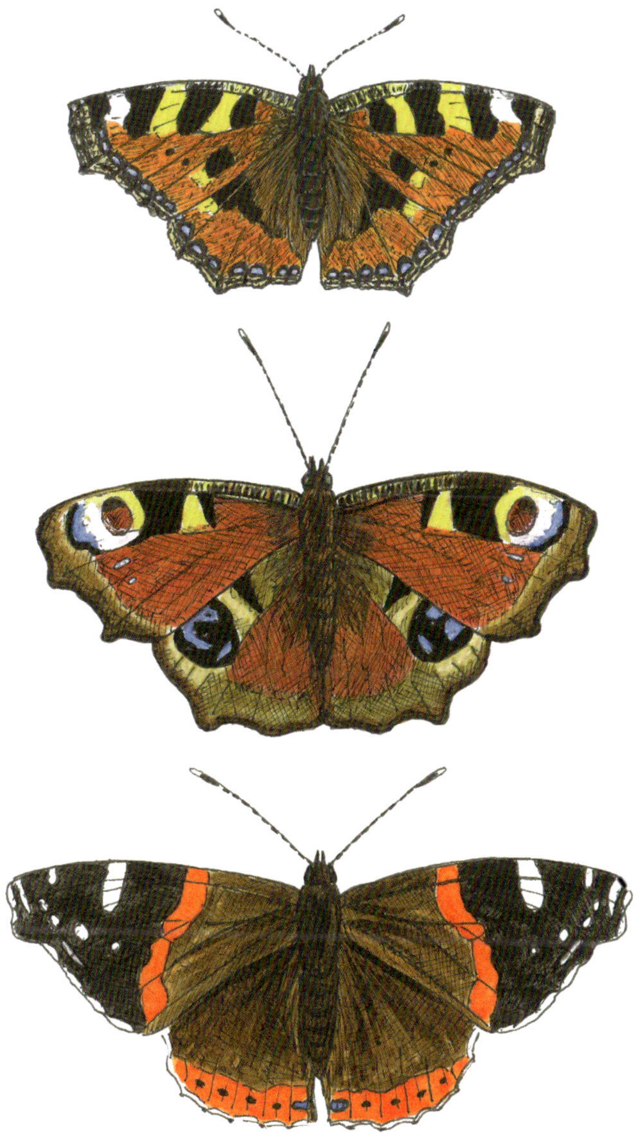

Three butterflies whose caterpillars can be found feeding on nettles: Small Tortoiseshell (top), Peacock (centre) and Red Admiral (bottom).

O *is for...* ORTHOPTERA

1 Meadow Grasshopper
2 Stripe-winged Grasshopper
3 Long-winged Conehead nymph ('Chocolate Lime')
4 Speckled Bush-cricket
5 Long-winged Conehead
6 Roesel's Bush-cricket
7 Wood Cricket
8 Field Cricket
9 Common Groundhopper

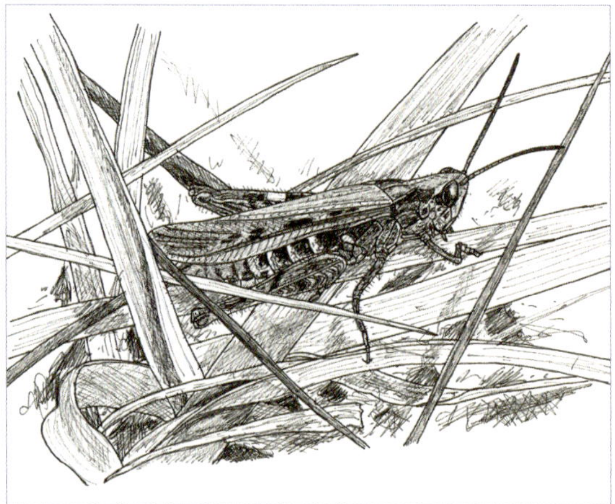

The soporific bzzt-bzzt of Field Grasshoppers (Chorthippus brunneus) calling to each other is one of the classic sounds of summer.

This is the order of grasshoppers and crickets, a page of sunny summer days spent searching meadows to track down stridulating songsters.

The Orthoptera are characterised by enlarged back legs that are modified to enable them to jump, and the ability in most to 'sing' by stridulating – that is, rubbing one part of their body against another. The bush-crickets and crickets have long antennae, and stridulate by rubbing their forewings together; while the grasshoppers have short antennae, and rub their hind legs against their forewings to sing.

In the bush-crickets, it is easy to tell a female from a male as she has an obvious ovipositor at the end of her abdomen. This fearsome-looking appendage is used to slit open plant tissues so that she can then insert her eggs.

Because they communicate largely through sound, the orthopterans have evolved complex hearing organs. In grasshoppers this is an opening in either side of the first abdominal segment, whereas the crickets have an opening in each side of the thorax linked to a 'tibial ear' on the front leg. The groundhoppers do not sing so they do not have any specialised organs for hearing.

If you have good hearing, you can track down many of these insects by listening for their distinctive songs, although some require exceptional hearing. Even if you can hear your quarry, finding and seeing them isn't always easy. Some species stay concealed (usually in brambles or nettles where you can't get at them), and the ones that sing in the open usually ping off the minute you move near them. The challenge of whiling away a sunny afternoon in a meadow or other nice spot searching for these lovely creatures is one I'll happily rise to. The great thing about searching for any invertebrates is that it can take you to some beautiful places, and even if you don't find your quarry something just as interesting is bound to turn up.

The UK is home to around 30 species of Orthoptera, most of which have a southerly distribution. Many are restricted by habitat, and found only in a very few locales, while some are extremely rare.

Field Crickets (*Gryllus campestris*) have always been somewhat localised in their distribution, requiring warm, south-facing, sheltered sites with areas of bare ground. Widespread on the Continent, they are on the northern limit of their range here, declining over the years and now extremely rare. Reduced to one site, efforts have been made to improve and create habitat, and there have been some successful re-introductions. I have never seen them in Britain but have been lucky enough to see them in Europe. In the Netherlands, we cycled around *De Hoge Veluwe National Park* and heard several calling males. We managed to track down a couple, along with

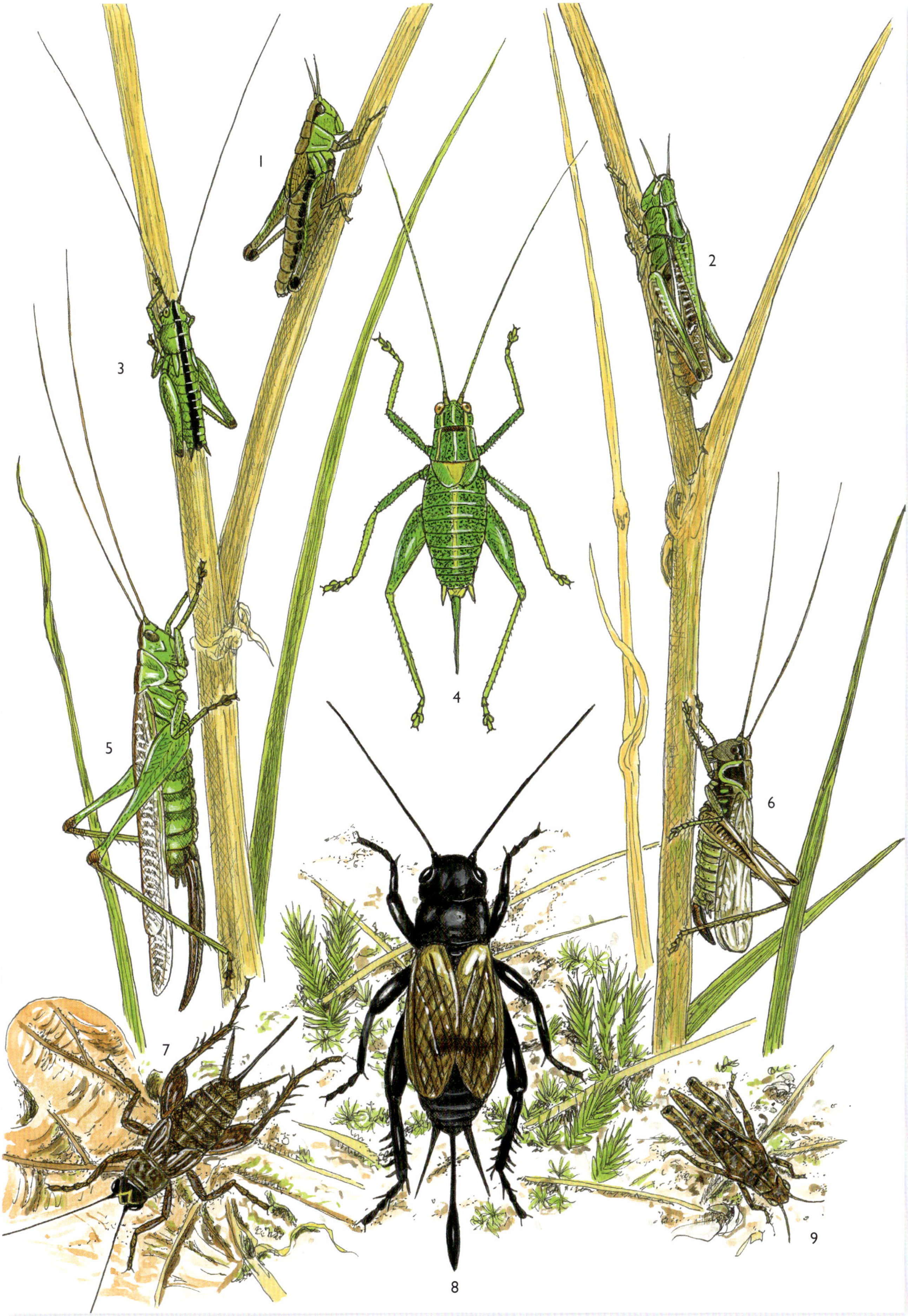
1
2
3
4
5
6
7
8
9

some females, finding them sitting at their burrow entrances. They are lovely insects to behold, all glossy black enveloped in warm yellowy wings.

The Wood Cricket (*Nemobius sylvestris*) is another very local species, found in Devon and Hampshire, with its stronghold in the New Forest. This is where we found a couple after hearing their call and diligently scanning the woodland floor for movement. If we hadn't heard them, I don't think we would have discovered them at all, as they are rather small and spend their time on the ground, disappearing into leaf litter or under logs when disturbed.

Whereas some species are struggling to keep a toe-hold in Britain, Roesel's Bush-cricket (*Metrioptera roeselii*) has undergone an incredible range expansion in recent years. It used to be a southern speciality, but with hotter, drier summers it has been spreading north. I now hear them on roadside verges and field edges all around Norfolk. Usually their wings extend to about half the length of the abdomen, but there is a long-winged form that I have depicted (see plate K for a normal winged specimen). The long-winged (macropterus) forms seem to appear in populations that have built up high numbers and from where they can disperse greater distances to start new colonies farther afield.

The Speckled Bush-cricket (*Leptophyes punctatissima*) is a stout, rather leggy-looking handsome beast, speckled all over with fine black dots. It lacks hindwings, and is completely flightless. The forewings of the female are tiny stubs, while those of the male are very much reduced and modified for stridulation, the right one being rubbed over a tooth-like peg on the left stub to produce the 'song'. The males have a warm reddish-brown band running down the centre of the top of the abdomen, making them hard to spot when they sit about on bramble leaves. The tiny nymphs look like spotty greenfly, and I have sometimes found several together on a leaf.

We were lucky enough to have Long-winged Coneheads (*Conocephalus fuscus*) take up residence on our allotment in 2010. I had gone up early one hot summer evening and discovered a couple of nymphs sunning themselves on wooden tree stakes in our mini-meadow. Utterly entrancing, deep green with a black stripe running centrally down their back, I christened them chocolate limes after the old-fashioned hard-boiled sweets. The adults have a rather quiet song but keep up their reeling for long enough to locate them. When you do find them they shimmy round the other side of the stem they are sitting on, out of view. If you move your hand slowly round the side of them, they will shimmy back so you can get a good look. We now have a thriving colony on the allotment, and in 2017 they appeared in our garden, about a quarter of a mile away. Here I have been able to observe their courtship display, mating and egg-laying.

The grasshoppers are all superficially similar, and need to be viewed from different angles to positively identify them. Characteristics to look for are the shape of the pronotum behind the head, and the shape of the forewings and the pattern of the wing-veins (wing venation). The adult female

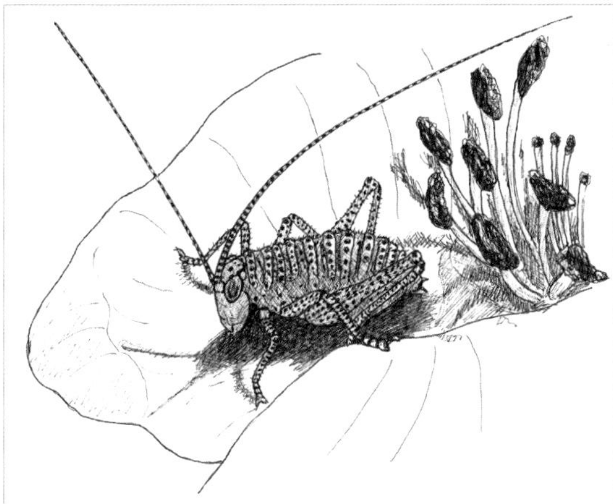

Tiny Speckled Bush-cricket nymphs can be hard to spot on a leaf. Luckily for me, this one was ensconced in an Evening Primrose flower so was rather more obvious.

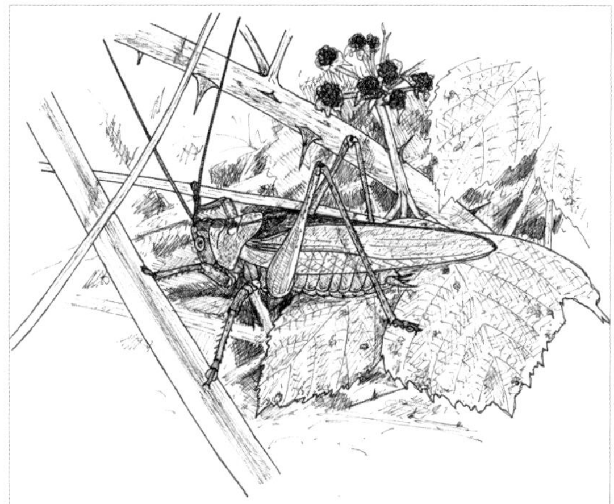

Great Green Bush-cricket (Tettigonia viridissima) skulking amongst brambles. This is our largest species of Orthoptera at around 50mm long.

Meadow Grasshopper (*Chorthippus parallelus*) usually has very short wings so is relatively straightforward to identify. The Stripe-winged Grasshopper (*Stenobothrus lineatus*) has a very characteristic song; in fact, it was the unknown song that led me to find my first one when I was looking for Large Blue butterflies (*Maculinea arion*) in Somerset. Fortunately, the Stripe-winged Grasshopper is one of the Orthoptera that is spreading north, and I have now had the pleasure of encountering it in Norfolk.

The groundhoppers are extremely well camouflaged and often overlooked. Not only are they rather small, they are silent, so you can't listen out for them. They are characterised by the elongated pronotum that stretches back over the abdomen. Three species are found in Britain. The Common Groundhopper (*Tetrix undulata*) usually has short wings, and the Slender Groundhopper (*Tetrix subulata*) has longer wings, extending well beyond the abdomen. The two species often occur on the same site, although I've always found the Slender in wetter areas than the Common. The third species is the much more local Cepero's Groundhopper (*Tetrix ceperoi*) that I have yet to see. All are very variable in colour and blend in superbly with their backgrounds.

P is for... POLLINATORS

1 Peacock Butterfly
2 Beetle
3 Andrena bicolor
4 Eristalis intricaria
5 Wasp (Dolichovespula saxonica)
6 Rhagonycha fulva
7 Sawfly Tenthredo omissa
8 Paracorymbia fulva
9 Leucozona laternaria
10 Varied Carpet Beetle
11 Graphomya maculata
12 Common Malachite Beetle
13 Pammene aurana
14 Bombus hortorum
15 Colletes daviesanus
16 Bombus pascuorum
17 Grammoptera ruficornis
18 Honeybee
19 Andrena haemorrhoa

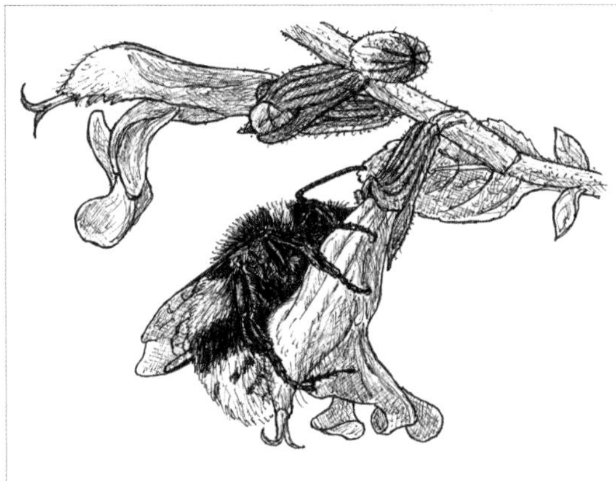

Getting one over – Bombus terrestris bumblebee circumventing the pollinating apparatus of a Blackcurrant Sage flower and robbing its nectar.

In order for a flowering plant to reproduce and set seed, it has to be pollinated. This involves the transfer of pollen from the male part of the flower, the anthers, to the female part, the stigma.

Pollen can be transferred by the wind or by animals. Examples of plants with wind-pollinated flowers include grasses and sedges, and trees such as the Hazel and oaks. In Britain the animals involved in pollen transfer are mostly insects, but in other countries some plants are bird-pollinated and others are pollinated by mammals, including bats.

Pollen can be transferred accidentally as an insect crawls about over the flower to eat pollen or nectar, to look for a mate or seeking another insect to eat. Some plants have evolved to have complex relations with insects, especially bees, where the plant produces copious amounts of nectar to encourage the bee to visit and thereby pollinate the flower. Although some plants are self-fertile and can pollinate themselves (sometimes as a last resort), most flowers are adapted so that they have to be pollinated by another flower of the same species. This is called cross-pollination and ensures genetic diversity.

There is a lot more to pollinators than honeybees and bumblebees, although these are undoubtedly important. For a start there are more than 200 species of solitary bee in Britain, compared with 1 Honeybee and 25 species of bumblebees. Add to that various wasps, sawflies, hoverflies and countless other flies. Also in the mix are numerous beetles and bugs. Doubtless there are other insects and invertebrates that we don't yet recognise as pollinators. If they clamber about over flowers as they go about their lives, they will almost certainly transfer pollen from anthers to stigmas.

Flies can be very important pollinators in early spring when many fruit trees come into flower. At this time of year the weather can suddenly turn very cold, and many of the bees become inactive whereas the flies will still be out and about. Beetles are perhaps surprising pollinators, but the first flowers to evolve were pollinated by them as there were no bees or wasps. Examples of these so-called primitive flowers are still around and tend to have large, open flowers. Magnolia is a classic example.

More complex flowers have evolved to have close relationships with bees, offering them lots of nectar as an attractant so that they then carry pollen to another plant. Different species of bumblebee have tongues of different lengths, enabling them to extract nectar from different flowers. The Garden Bumblebee, *Bombus hortorum*, has an especially long

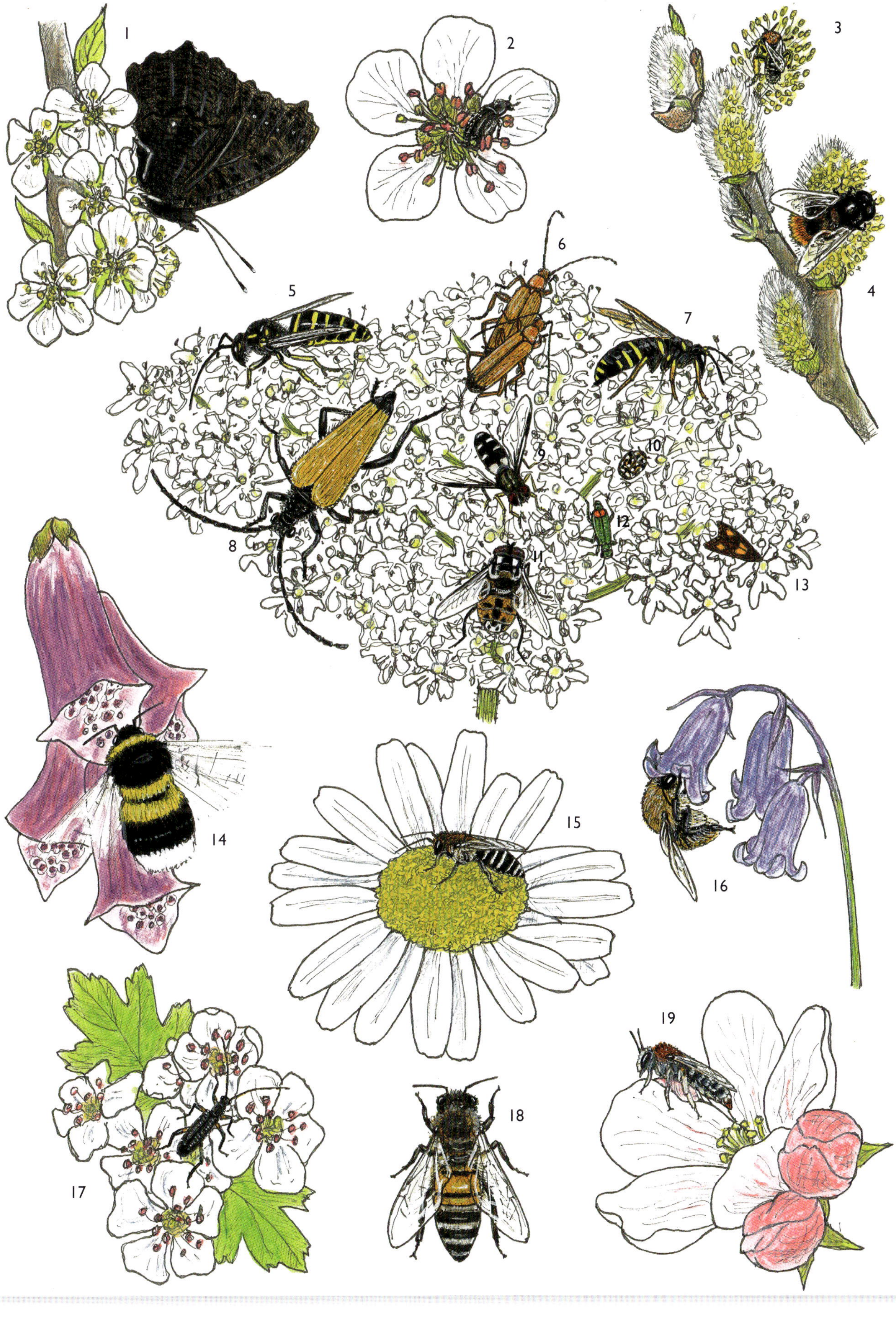
1
2
3
4
5
6
7
8
9
10
11
12
13
14
15
16
17
18
19

tongue to exploit such flowers as Foxgloves and Honeysuckle. While *Bombus pascuorum* is slightly shorter-tongued, it can still get nectar from deep inside Bluebell flowers, pollinating them in the process and helping to perpetuate our beautiful Bluebell woods. Some bees have learnt to cheat and carry out nectar-robbing, biting a hole in the base of a flower tube and extracting the nectar without pollinating the plant. This happens on Salvia flowers in our garden, especially Blackcurrant Sage, which is robbed by *Bombus terrestris* workers that have very short tongues (a *Bombus terrestris* queen is illustrated on plate B). Once a hole has been cut in a flower, other bumblebees may find it and exploit it too.

Umbellifer flowers (family Apiaceae) attract a wide array of pollinators. To appreciate their variety, take a close look at a head of Hogweed (like the one illustrated) in a grassy verge, the lush umbels of Wild Angelica on a grazing marsh or a Fennel head on an allotment. You will find all sorts of insects, large and small, from tiny bugs and beetles through moths, colourful flies and hoverflies to wasps and sawflies and large, lumbering longhorn beetles. You will probably see a few bees, too.

A single umbellifer head can have a whole assortment of critters crawling over it. Often a whole flowerhead will be swarming with the orange soldier beetles *Rhagonycha fulva*, known as Hogweed Bonking Beetles – for they are invariably paired up and copulating. Other species of beetle commonly found include Varied Carpet Beetle (*Anthrenus verbasci*) and the colourful Common Malachite (*Malachius bipustulatus*). Several species of longhorn beetle visit umbellifers, including the rare *Paracorymbia fulva*, which amazingly turned up in our garden.

Social Wasps like *Dolichovespula saxonica* are attracted to umbellifers along with sawflies such as *Tenthredo omissa*. One of my favourite flies to look out for is the super spotty *Graphomya maculata*. Only the male has the orange abdomen; the female's is a lovely silver grey. *Leucozona laternaria* is an attractively marked hoverfly found on Hogweed and Angelica along woodland edges and rides where its larvae feed on aphids.

The small micro moth *Pammene aurana* is found on Hogweed where its larvae feed in a web amongst the seeds. The adults crawl about the flower heads, searching for mates, transferring pollen as they go.

You may not think pollinators of umbellifers are particularly important, but it isn't just wild flowers that they pollinate. Umbellifers include vegetables such as carrots and parsnips and plenty of herbs – parsley, coriander and fennel, for example.

Many of our important fruit crops are in the same family, the Rosaceae, including apples and pears, plums, strawberries and raspberries. Peacock butterflies (*Aglais io*) regularly come to take nectar from the flowers of our Mirabelle Plum in early spring and accidentally transfer pollen. The Pear blossom attracts plenty of bees but I often find small, dark, unidentifiable beetles ensconced in the petals, covered in pollen. Solitary bees, such as *Andrena haemorrhoa*, are just as likely to be found on the allotment apple blossom, as are Honeybees (*Apis mellifera*) or bumblebees. And in the hedgerows, Hawthorn flowers (another member of the Rosaceae) attract all manner of insects from flies and bees to various longhorn beetles including *Grammoptera ruficornis*.

Pollinating insects need a source of nectar and pollen throughout the year to keep them alive. Sallows, with their well-known and loved pussy willow catkins, are a very important early source of pollen and nectar. They attract all sorts of insects in spring, especially hoverflies such as *Eristalis intricaria*, which hibernates over winter as an adult; or solitary bees that emerge early in the year, such as the diminutive *Andrena bicolor*.

At the other end of the year, one of the most important food sources for insects is Ivy (*Hedera helix*). A much maligned plant, Ivy is often the last native plant flowering in the year and can positively hum with insect activity. Dozens of Honeybees will be attracted to the heady scented flowers; you can buy single-variety ivy-blossom honey, although personally I find its flavour a bit strong. In amongst the Honeybees you will find hoverflies, butterflies and other bees, including one of the latest additions to our bee fauna, the Ivy Bee *Colletes hederae* (see plate B), which emerges late in the year, specifically timed to exploit the Ivy flowers. Ivy is so important, not only for providing nectar and pollen but also cover for hibernation, that I very nearly made it the subject of plate I – until, that is, I started learning about woodlice...

If you want to attract pollinators in your garden, as well as planting a range of plants that flower over a long period, it is also good to have flowers that are different shapes. While not everyone has room or actually wants to grow Hogweed or Angelica, other umbellifers such as Wild Carrot and the non-native *Ammi majus* take up a lot less room but are still good for all sorts of insects. Bumblebees visit more complex flowers, but the smaller solitary bees like platform flowers such as Oxeye Daisies, Corn Chamomile and Yarrow. In our garden these attract the delightful little plasterer bee *Colletes daviesanus*.

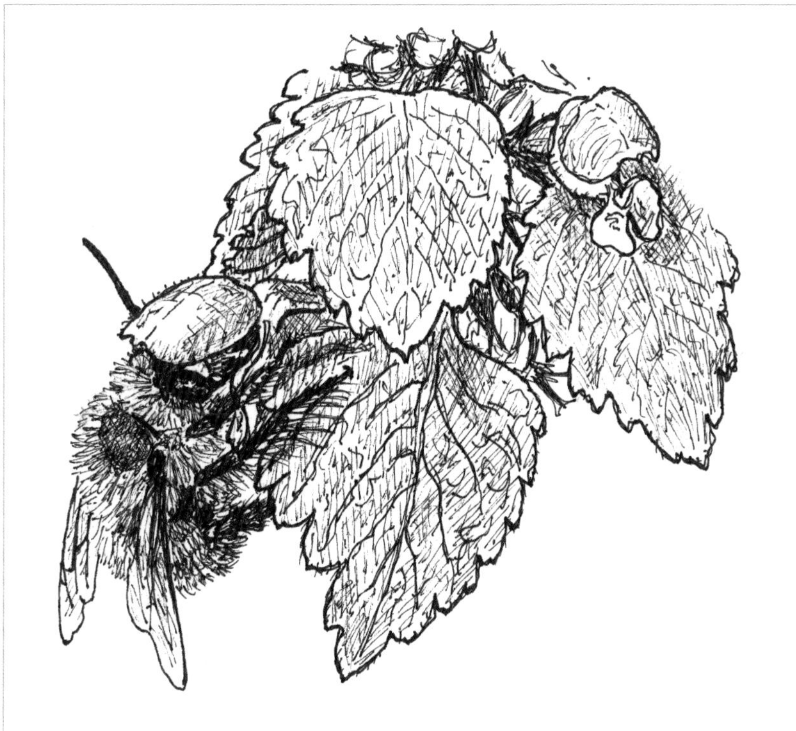

The long tongue of this male Anthophora plumipes enables it to get nectar from the deep flower tube of the Red Dead-nettle. The bee inadvertently picks up pollen on its head as it does so and transfers it to another flower and pollinates it. The English name for this bee is the Hairy-footed Flower Bee, after the long hairs on the middle tarsus (foot) of the male.

Q is for... QUERCUS

1 Tillus elongates
2 Cream Spot Ladybird
3 Purple Hairstreak
4 Festoon
5 Green Oak Tortrix
6 Green Silver-lines
7 Ledra aurita
8 Paidiscura pallens
9 Cixius nervosus
10 Pine Ladybird
11 Tetragnatha obtusa
12 Megacoelum infusum
13 Purple Hairstreak
14 Dryophilochoris flavoquadrimaculatus
15 Acorn Weevil

a Currant Galls
b Common Spangle Galls
c Smooth Spangle Galls
d Silk Button Spangle Galls
e Andricus grossulariae Gall
f Knopper Gall
g Leafmine

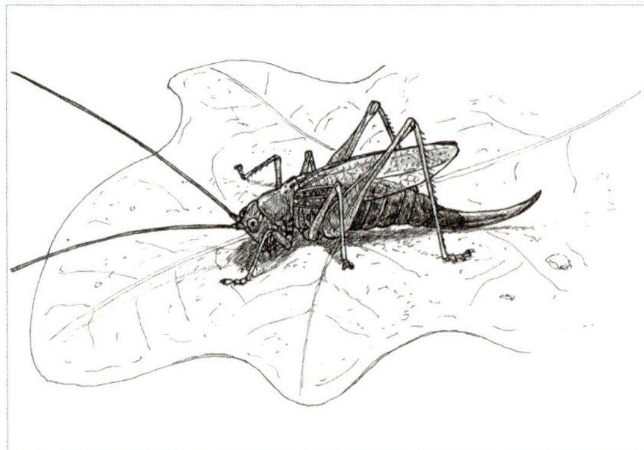

The Oak Bush-cricket (Meconema thalassinum) is commonly found in oak woods in southern England, becoming more localised farther north. They also inhabit gardens and parks where they live on various shrubs and trees. They are nocturnal hunters, feeding on various small invertebrates, and are not above preying on other crickets. They often turn up indoors, attracted to lights at night, and are regularly found sitting on ceilings (during the day they normally sit motionless on the underside of a leaf). They are unusual in that the males do not have wings modified for stridulating; instead, they drum on a leaf rapidly with a hind foot in order to advertise their presence and attract a mate.

Quercus is the generic name for oak trees. In Britain and Europe more species of insect can be found on oak trees than on any other plant. A mature oak can be a teeming metropolis of life. Moth caterpillars feed on the leaves, from large noctuids such as the Green Silver-lines, through to tiny micro moth species whose larvae mine the leaves, feeding between the upper and lower epidermis. There are beetles with wood-boring larvae; various true bugs that suck sap; and ladybirds that feast on aphids, scale insects and even mildew. Not all the species are exclusively on oak, but plenty are. Then there are spiders that entrap the varied insects. With so many invertebrate species on oak trees, a lot of birds are attracted to them, too, where a veritable banquet of creepy-crawlies awaits.

There are two species of oak native to Britain, the English (or Pedunculate) Oak, *Quercus robur*, depicted at the top of the plate, which has acorns borne on stalks; and the Sessile Oak, *Quercus petraea*, pictured lower down, with acorns attached directly to the twigs. Where both types of oak occur you can also get hybrids between the two. There are also various other species planted in parks and gardens and sometimes the wider countryside – Turkey Oak and the evergreen Holm Oak are common enough, and my local cemetery also has exotics from North America.

The Purple Hairstreak (*Favonius quercus*) is our only butterfly whose caterpillar feeds exclusively on oaks. The tiny white eggs are laid at the base of a bud and spend the winter this way, hatching the following spring when the buds start to open. The caterpillar spins a silken cocoon around the buds to hide away in during the day, emerging at night to feed on the fresh new leaves. The butterflies rarely come down from their tree-top haunts as they feed on aphid honeydew, but they can be seen spiralling together around the canopy on still, sunny days in July and August when the undersides of their wings flash silver in the sunshine. They will also bask with their wings open when the deep purple on the upper surface of the wings can be seen. Late afternoon and early evening seem to be the best times to see them.

Of the many moth species that occur on oak, the Green Silver-lines (*Pseudoips prasinana*) is one of the prettiest with its beautiful frosted green wings with white cross lines and deep pink antennae. Its boat-shaped cocoon can sometimes be spotted on the undersides of leaves. I found several in December one year on the undersides of the leaves of a Lucombe Oak, a hybrid between Cork and Holm Oaks and as such partially evergreen, retaining many of its leaves through the winter.

The Festoon (*Apoda limacodes*) is a scarce

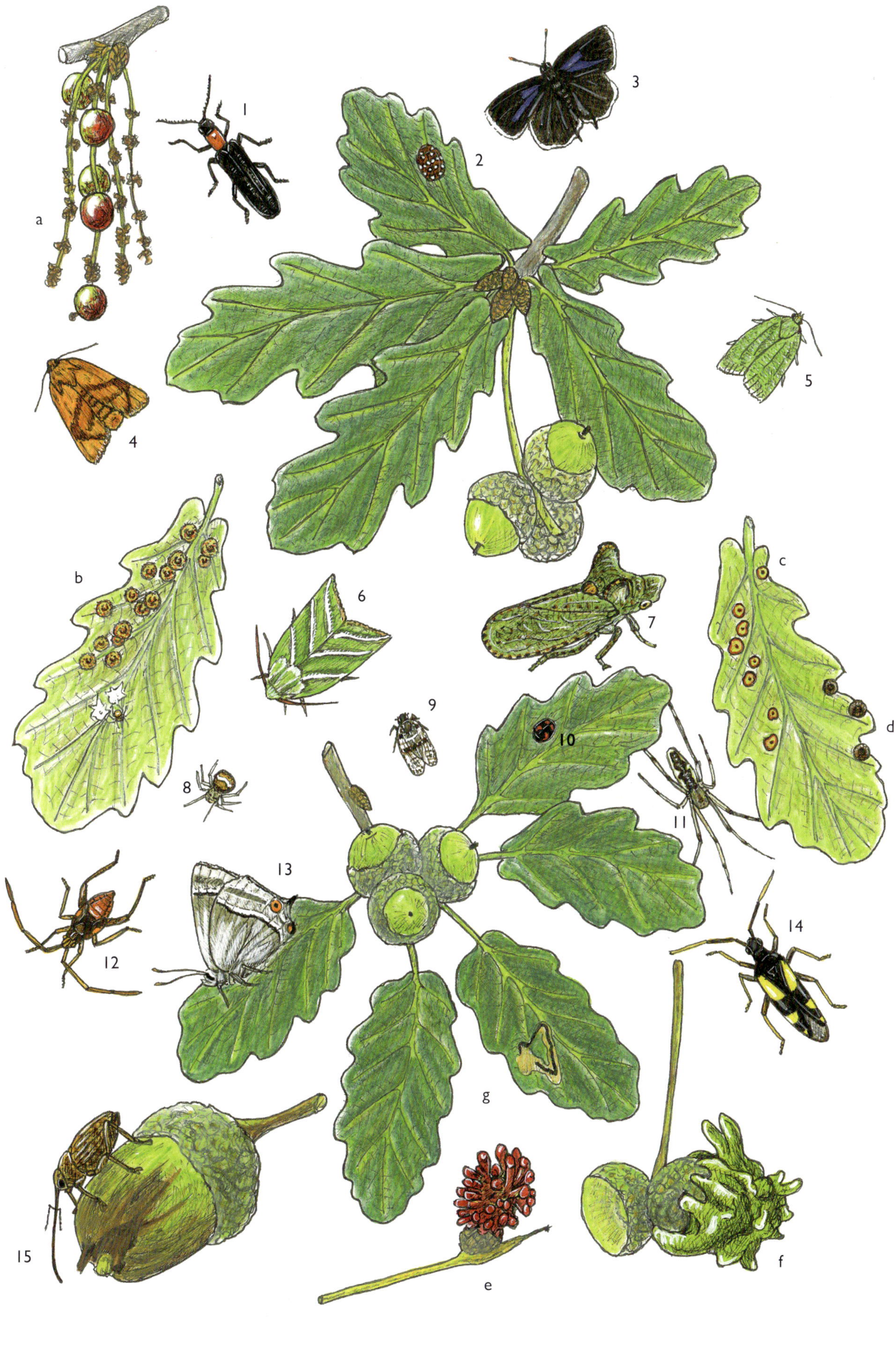
a
1
2
3
4
5
b
6
7
c
9
10
d
8
11
13
12
14
g
15
e
f

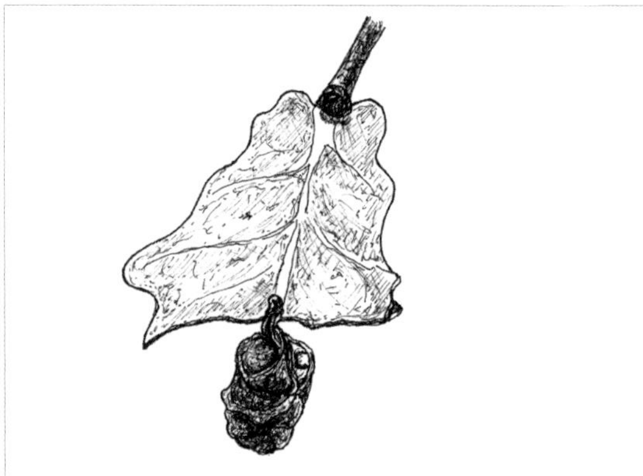

The Oak Leaf-roller Weevil, Attelabus nitens (pictured below), is a beetle that specialises in laying its eggs in oak leaves. A leaf is cut half way along its length from either side to the mid rib and then rolled up in a double layer to provide a safe home in which the larva can develop. The characteristic leaf roll (above) is probably seen more often than the adult beetle. The beetle is rather attractive, being a deep glossy red with contrasting black head and legs. This one flew in while I was watching solitary wasps on a sandy bank beneath some oak trees. Its wings are still protruding from the elytra (wing cases) after landing.

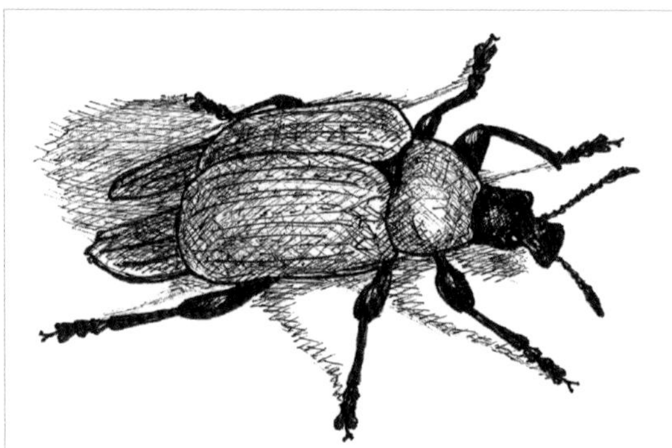

species that is occasionally seen during the day. Its caterpillar is very odd-looking, more like that of a blue butterfly or even a hoverfly larva. Of the many micro moths associated with oak, the Green Oak Tortrix (*Tortrix viridana*) is one of the larger species. There are numerous tiny leafminers, a few of which have distinctive enough mines, but many have to be reared to adult moth to confirm identification.

Bugs come in all sorts of shapes and sizes, and plenty can be found on oak trees. *Dryophilocoris flavoquadrimaculatus* is a striking black and yellow capsid bug with a name far longer than the actual insect. The specific name relates to the four yellow spots: flavo = yellow, quad = four and maculatus = spotted. *Megacoelum infusum* is another capsid bug. It is quite distinctive with its long legs and antennae, and is found exclusively on oaks where it feeds on small insects and sap. The one shown is a late instar nymph so it doesn't have the fully developed wings of the adult insect.

The lacehoppers are small bugs with delicate-looking lace-like wings. *Cixius nervosus* is the most commonly encountered. It can be found on the foliage of various trees and shrubs including oaks.

Ledra aurita, the Eared Leafhopper, is our largest leafhopper. It is beautiful and bizarre in equal measure. Its lovely greeny-grey coloration blends in perfectly with lichen-encrusted branches. Because of its superb camouflage it is seldom seen, but occasionally turns up in the moth trap in our garden. We affectionately call it 'The Hippo' because of the large, ear-like projections on the sides of its pronotum.

The beetle *Tillus elongatus* is associated with trees that are infested with the larvae of other beetles, and is usually seen around rotten stumps. The female lays her eggs in the holes bored by the other beetles, and her larvae feed on their larvae. According to what I've read, they are usually associated with Beech, but the only one I've ever found was on an oak. Things do have a habit of turning up where they aren't expected, bearing in mind that insects don't read guidebooks and therefore don't know where they are supposed to be!

Another beetle on oaks is the Acorn Weevil (*Curculio glandium*). It is quite distinctive, having a very long, down-curved 'snout', the rostrum, with its antennae attached part way along. It uses this elongated rostrum to bore a hole in an acorn into which it can then lay an egg. The grub-like larvae feed inside the acorn out of the way of predators. I came across the one illustrated probing acorns when I was out searching for galls.

Various ladybirds can be found on oaks. The Pine Ladybird (*Exochomus quadripustulatus*) is one such, despite its name. While it is generally found on conifers, it also occurs on a wide variety of broadleaved trees where it feeds on scale insects. It is a smallish, shiny black species with four red spots – of which the front two are comma shaped. It has a distinct lip or rim around the base of the wing cases (elytra). When English names were being assigned, most records of this species had come from conifers; it was therefore assumed to have a close association with them, and thus ended up being called the Pine Ladybird.

The Cream-spot Ladybird (*Calvia quattuordecimguttata*) also frequents a variety of broad-leaved trees including oak. Larger than the Pine Ladybird, it is a deep maroon-brown colour with 14 large, round cream spots. It feeds on aphids and psyllids (true bugs known as 'jumping plant lice').

A variety of spiders can be found on oak trees. If

you peer at the undersides of leaves in summer you may find the strange sputnik-like, spiky white egg sac of *Paidiscura pallens*. Although small, they are easy to spot but you have to look very closely indeed to see the tiny female spider that often lurks close by. *Tetragnatha obtusa* is one of the so-called stretch spiders. It has a characteristic elongated abdomen that helps camouflage it when it stretches out at rest. There are six species in Britain, most occurring in wetland habitats where they often spin their webs over water. However, *Tetragnatha obtusa* seems to prefer drier situations, and is found on trees in woodland including oaks.

GALLS

Signs of insect life are often easier to spot than the actual insect itself. This is particularly true of the gall wasps, which are tiny, generally black or brown and rather difficult to find. On the other hand, the galls that they induce the host plant to make are often both colourful and eye-catching, none more so than some of the oak galls. Galls are actually found on a variety of plants, and are basically defined as an abnormal growth caused by the presence of another organism living in or on the plant that causes its cells to expand or multiply and form a structure that houses and nourishes the gall inducer. They can be caused by bacteria, fungi and mites, but the majority are caused by insects, especially flies and wasps.

Oak trees are brilliant places to search for galls, harbouring far more than any other plant. The vast majority of these are caused by gall wasps in the family Cynipidae. The strange growth formations are produced by the plant after the eggs are laid, when the larvae hatch and start feeding. The oak gall wasps generally have two different, alternating generations: an asexual (or agamic) one that produces fertile females without the need for mating; and a sexual generation that has both males and females. The different generations create very different galls either on different parts of the same tree or sometimes even on different species of oak.

The various spangle galls are easily found on the underside of leaves in late summer or autumn. They are caused by the asexual generation of different *Neuroterus* gall wasps. The galls generally fall off the leaves in the autumn, and the single larva housed inside continues its development over the winter hidden down in the leaf litter. In spring the fertile females emerge and lay their eggs in different parts of the oak trees to produce new galls of the sexual generation. The Silk Button Spangle is caused by *Neuroterus numismalis*, and the Smooth Spangle is caused by *Neuroterus albipes*.

While the asexual generation of *Neuroterus quercusbaccarum* produces the Common Spangle Galls on the undersides of leaves, in the sexual generation the mated females lay their eggs on the male flower buds to produce Currant Galls on the catkins.

The *Andricus* species of gall wasp produce some of the largest and most noticeable galls to be found on oak trees. Many are formed on buds or developing acorns. *Andricus grossulariae* asexual galls develop on buds or acorn cups, starting off green but usually turning a deep reddish-purple. The sexual generation produces currant galls on Turkey Oak very similar to those of *Neuroterus quercusbaccarum* but with a prominent point.

The Knopper Galls are caused by the asexual generation of *Andricus quercuscalicis*, and develop on the acorns, often completely concealing them. When these were first found in England it was feared that the acorn crop could be reduced to such an extent that our oak woods would be in trouble, but that hasn't proved to be the case. In some years trees are seemingly infested with them, but in other years there are plenty of unaffected acorns.

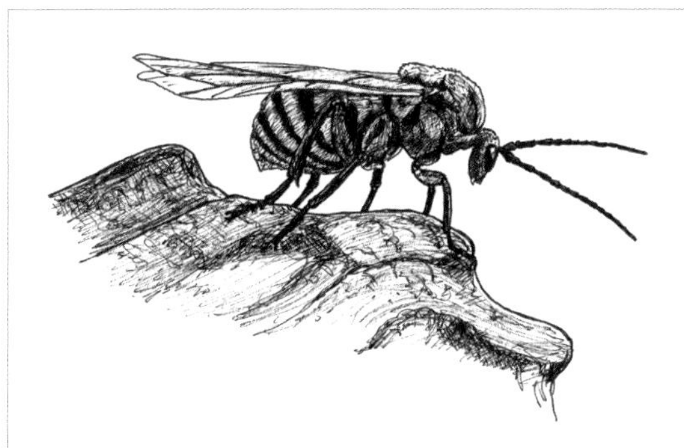

Cynipid wasp Andricus quercuscalicis newly emerged from the Knopper Gall I illustrated on this plate. They are only around three or four millimetres long and seldom seen.

Of the many types of gall found on oaks, I sadly had room for just six. Galls could really have done with their own plate. I was tempted, but while I have found a lot of very different and fascinating galls, on a wide variety of plants, it has been rare indeed that I have encountered the actual gall-causers themselves and I would have wanted to picture them alongside their galls. Probably the best way of finding them would be to collect up some galls and keep them in a container over the winter to see what emerges. If you do this, you may well be surprised at what you find as there are just as many, if not more, insects that are parasites or lodgers within the galls as there are gall-makers. Something to do one winter when I'm bored...

R *is for... rich, ruddy* REDS

1 Large Red-belted Clearwing
2 Maiden's Blush
3 Blood-vein
4 Cardinal Beetle
5 Red Admiral
6 Red Longhorn Beetle
7 Red-barbed Ants
8 Red-legged Shieldbug
9 Ruddy Darter
10 Red-tailed Bumblebee (male)
11 Red and Black Froghopper

A Red Letter Day for rare ants and a Large Red-belted Clearwing. The Red Admiral butterfly (*Vanessa atalanta*) is an autumn delight when spotted nectaring on ivy flowers, often one of the last species seen in the year. Until recently, all our early Red Admirals were migrants, arriving from Europe in spring, mating and egg-laying to provide a home-grown summer brood but then not being able to survive our winter. Now, with milder winters, many hibernate to emerge as early as February or March when the weather is warm, so often the first butterfly I see in the year is a Red Admiral, as is the last.

Sympetrum sanguineum is the scientific name of the aptly named Ruddy Darter, whose abdomen is a truly rich ruddy red. The word *sanguineum* comes from *sanguis*, meaning blood. Males have a distinctive bulge towards the end of the abdomen. The eyes are red, too, as are the wing spots (pterostigmas), and there is a subtle yellow flush to the wing bases. In common with other darters, they are often found in numbers on paths and boardwalks around pools soaking up the sun.

We have the early naturalists to thank for the lovely lyrical names of some of our moths. Maiden's Blush (*Cyclophora punctaria*) and Blood-vein (*Timandra comae*) poetically describe the subtle shading and patterning across the wings of these two geometer moths. Others are much more prosaic, and the muse was obviously out the day the Large Red-belted Clearwing (*Synanthedon culiciformis*) acquired its epithet. (At least it does what it says on the tin.) The clearwings don't even look like moths. They have thickened antennae, akin to the burnet moths (see plate Z) to which they are related. They are all day-fliers, and their larvae develop within trees or the woody stems of plants. In the case of the Large Red-belted Clearwing, the eggs are laid in freshly cut stems of birch trees, often on heathland or moorland. This is a rather scarce moth but worth seeking out for it is rather lovely, a deep blue black with contrasting red belt and bases to the wings.

There are a number of red beetles in Britain, of which the Cardinal is one. In fact, there are two species, the Red-headed Cardinal (*Pyrochroa serraticornis*) and the Black-headed Cardinal (*Pyrochroa coccinea*), both of which have distinctive serrated black antennae. The Red-headed is the commoner of the two and is often to be found sitting on foliage along woodland edges.

The Red Longhorn (*Stictoleptura rubra*) is a bit of an East Anglian speciality. It is more or less confined to woodlands where its larvae feed in the wood of conifers for two to three years. It used to be considered pretty rare but seems to have a stronghold in Norfolk and Suffolk where there are a lot of conifer plantations. One even turned up in our garden in Norwich. Like a lot of longhorn beetles, they can be found on umbellifer heads in the summer feeding on pollen.

There are five species of bumblebee in Britain that normally have really obvious large red tails, but it is the commonest, *Bombus lapidarius*, that has been singled out to be called the Red-tailed Bumblebee. The queens are really large impressive bumblebees, all black except for the deep orange-red tail. The smaller workers are the same colour; it is only the males that sport a yellow face and collar like the one illustrated.

The Red-legged Shieldbug, *Pentatoma rufipes*, is sometimes known as the Forest Bug as it is usually found in woodland although it also turns up in gardens and parks. The pale yellow or orange tip to the scutellum is more distinctive than the red legs for which it is named as these can vary in colour, especially in older specimens. The curved and pointed tips to the pronotum are also distinctive. The adults sometimes predate caterpillars and other insects. It is the only British shieldbug that overwinters as a small instar rather than as an adult.

The unmistakable Red-and-black Froghopper (*Cercopis vulnerata*) is one of our largest froghoppers and is the sole representative of its family in Britain (the Cercopidae). It can be found on nettles in damp areas, such as the edges of marshes or in wet woodland.

Last but by no means least, we have the Red-barbed Ant (*Formica rufibarbis*). This is Britain's rarest ant; indeed, one of our rarest insects altogether, found only on St Martin's in the Isles of Scilly and on a Surrey heath (although it may possibly be extinct there now). It is sometimes known as the Scilly Ant. We went to the Isles of Scilly hoping to see a Scilly Bee (a subspecies of *Bombus muscorum* – ssp. *scyllonius*) but, sadly, these may well be extinct so we had to make do with Scilly Ants instead. I have to say that they were very obliging as they ran about the hot granite rocks while we ate our lunch.

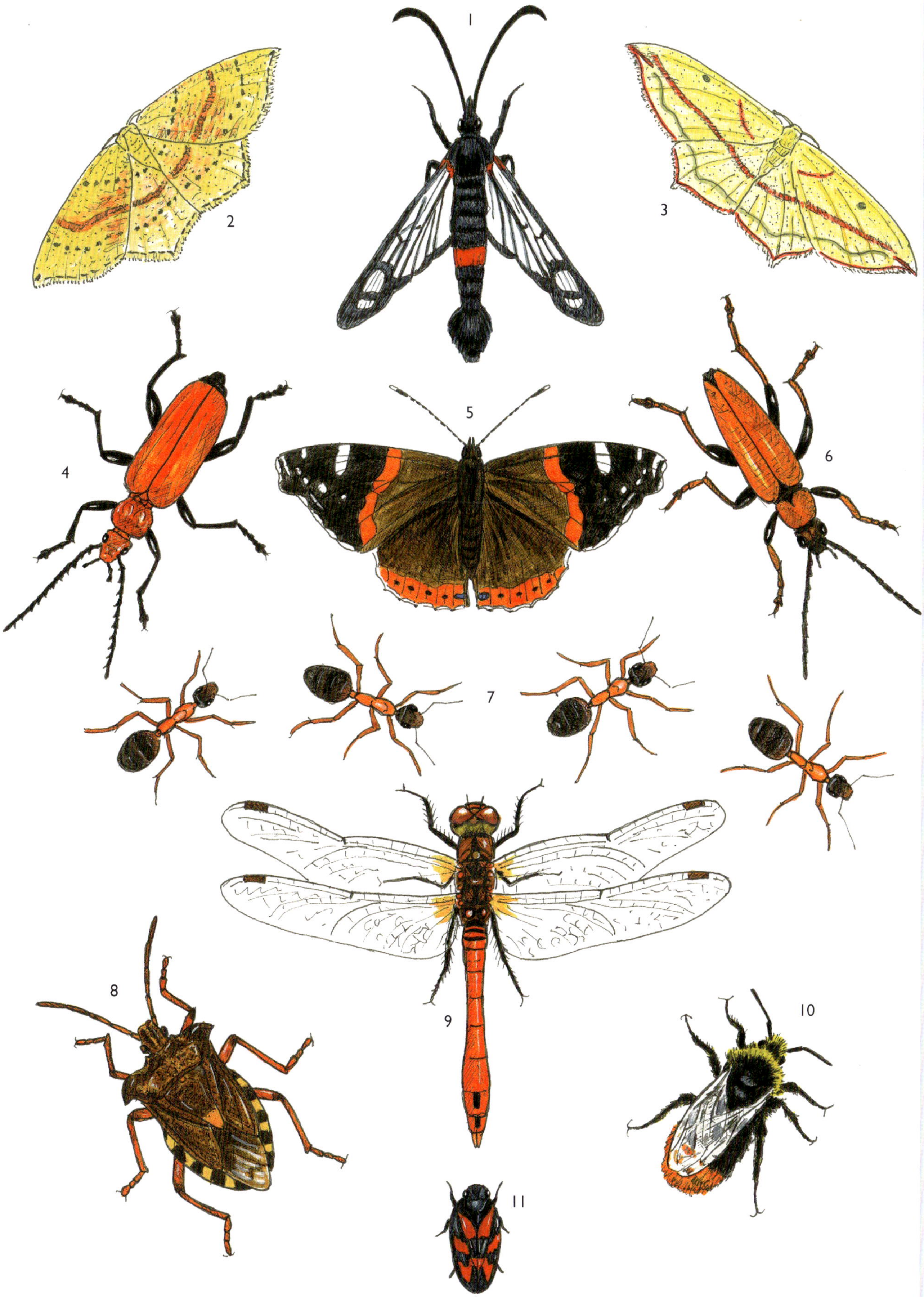
1
2
3
4
5
6
7
8
9
10
11

S is for... SHIELDBUGS

1 Bishop's Mitre
2 Parent Shieldbug and nymphs
3 Woundwort Shieldbug
4 Hairy Shieldbug
5 Juniper Shieldbug
6 Green Shieldbug
7 Hawthorn Shieldbug
8 Pied Shieldbug
9 Spiked Shieldbug
10 Tortoise Shieldbug

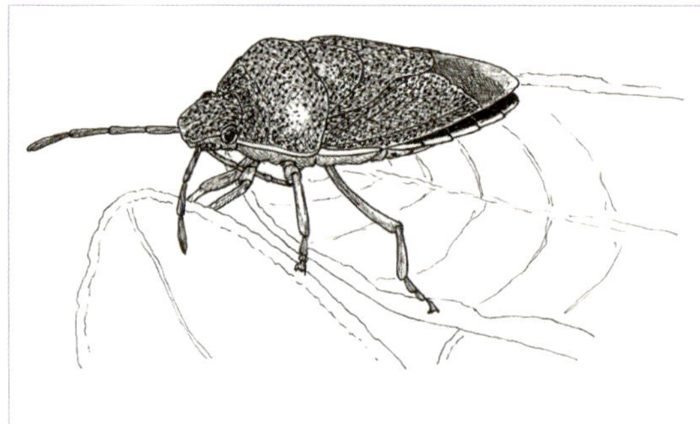

A Gorse Shieldbug (Piezodorus lituratus) showing its long, thin rostrum tucked out of the way underneath the front of its body.

The shieldbugs are a distinctive group of 'true' bugs in the order Hemiptera, named because of the shield-like shape of their enlarged scutellum (a plate present in many insects covering the top of the end of the thorax). In shieldbugs it stretches backwards and completely covers the first half of the abdomen. Shieldbugs resemble beetles somewhat, but rather than having mandibles for eating they have a long, pointed rostrum. This is a hollow tube that they use for piercing and sucking up juices, a bit like a syringe. It is kept folded underneath the body out of the way when they aren't feeding. Most of them are plant eaters but others are predatory – the rostrum is just as suited to sucking up the juices of a tasty caterpillar as it is the sap of a plant.

Shieldbugs are a real favourite of mine, being lovely to look at, nice to draw and relatively easy to identify. Most of them overwinter as adults, and many species can easily be found in spring when they emerge from hibernation and sit about basking in sunshine. Careful searching is required for a number of species, as they are found only around the bases of their foodplants, and some are very rare with a restricted distribution.

The shieldbugs are divided into several families, the largest of which is the Pentatomidae – known as the typical shieldbugs. The Green Shieldbug (*Palomena prasina*) is one of the most common, and one of the largest, species. Although it is usually bright green, in winter it can turn brown prior to hibernation. It is found in parks and gardens, and regularly turns up in our own garden.

The Hairy Shieldbug (*Dolycoris baccarum*) is also found in our garden where it can be surprisingly unobtrusive, with its pretty shades of purple and green blending in perfectly with vegetation. Up close they are noticeably hairy, a characteristic shared by the earlier stages or instars. In spring I look for them on clumps of Red Dead-nettles where I often find

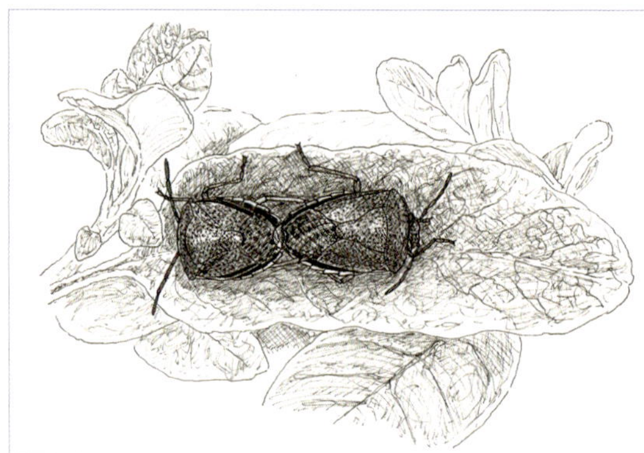

Gorse Shieldbugs (Piezodorus lituratus) mating back to back. Normally associated with Gorse, as their name suggests, this pair were found in our garden where they over-wintered in a dense evergreen Brachyglottis shrub.

them mating in their characteristic back-to-back position, looking like Dr Dolittle's pushmi-pullyu.

Another species to look for in spring is the Woundwort Shieldbug (*Eysarcoris venustissimus*), which can often be found in large numbers along hedgerows swarming over the ground around the foodplant, Black Horehound, a rather smelly herb. It can also be

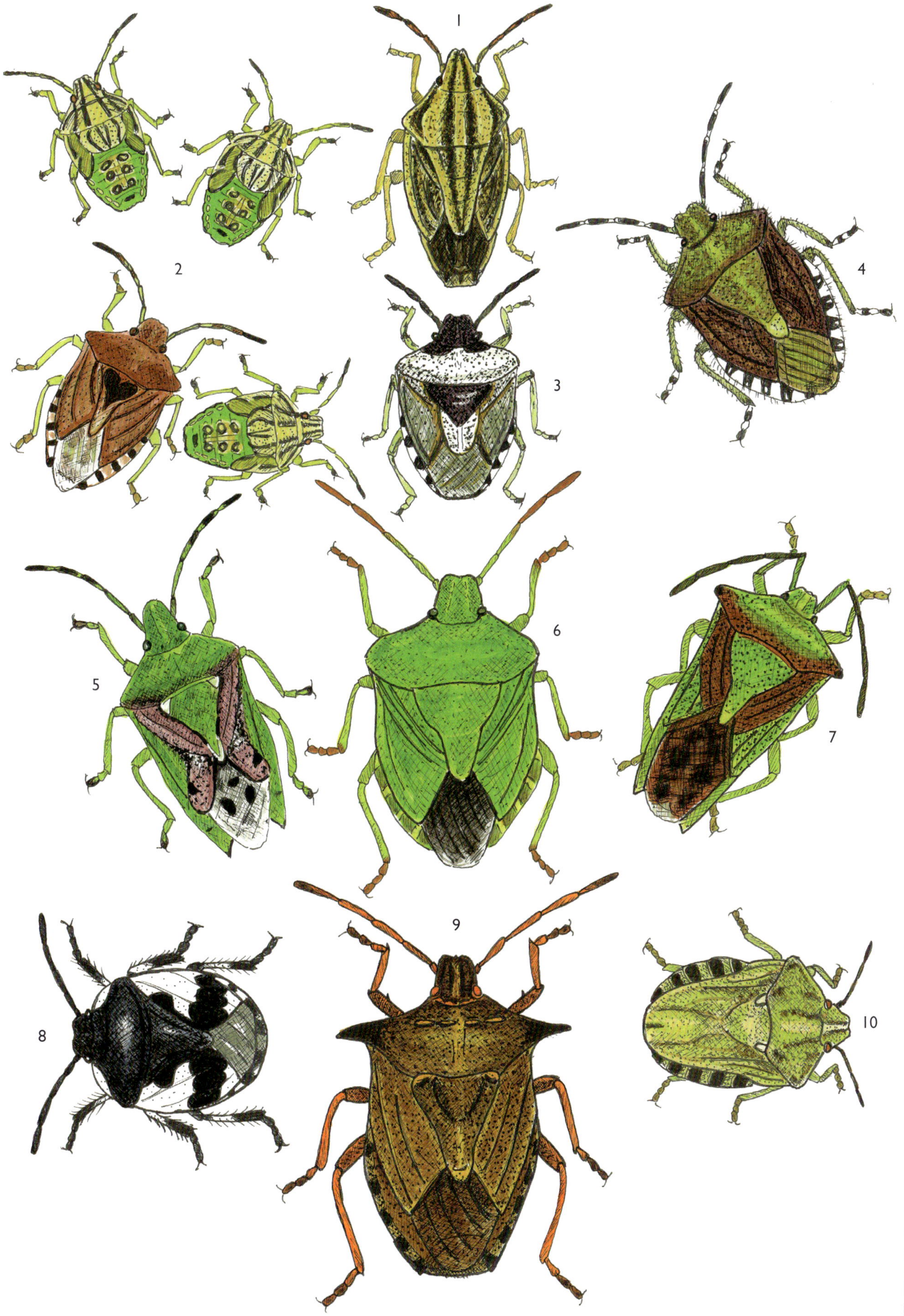
1
2
3
4
5
6
7
8
9
10

found on White Dead-nettle and Hedge Woundwort.

Also in the Pentatomidae is the Bishop's Mitre (*Aelia acuminata*), an attractively shaped and cryptically coloured species that is perfectly camouflaged for its grassland habitat. We have found the odd one or two on our allotment in the past, and they occasionally turn up in the garden, but they don't mind damp grassland either.

The Spiked Shieldbug (*Picromerus bidens*) is one of the predatory species, using its rostrum to pierce caterpillars and sawfly larvae and suck them dry. It has distinctive points on the pronotum, giving the English name. I've always found them on heathland, amongst heather, hunting for moth caterpillars. They happily tackle prey three or four times their size, stabbing in their rostrum and sucking the life out of them.

Another family is the Acanthosomatidae or keeled shieldbugs. These are distinguished from the Pentatomidae by having two, rather than three, segmented tarsi (feet). The largest is the Hawthorn Shieldbug (*Acanthosoma haemorrhoidale*). It is rather elongate, commonly associated with hawthorn as the name suggests, but also found on other trees and shrubs.

The Parent Shieldbug (*Elasmucha grisea*) varies in colour from green to pinkish brown, but invariably the scutellum has a dark heart-shaped mark in the centre. The female lays her eggs in a cluster on the underside of a leaf, often birch or alder, and sits over them until they hatch. She stays over them for the first couple of moults (when they shed their skins), and the young stay together even longer. I look for them on either alders or birch in late summer, often finding clusters of up to two dozen on a single leaf. The early instars are lovely, with a striped pronotum, and look quite different to the adults.

The Juniper Shieldbug (*Cyphostethus tristriatus*) is very pretty, green with distinctive pinkish bands. It is surprisingly difficult to spot when it sits motionless on a conifer, blending in superbly with the foliage. We find it every year when we trim a neighbour's Leylandii hedge on the allotments – we have to search through the debris and retrieve them from the garden waste bin. They are found exclusively on conifers. In our local cemetery I've come across them on Lawson's Cypress and also on Larch in spring.

The Scutelleridae is a small family containing the Tortoise Shieldbugs (*Eurygaster testudinaria*). These are grassland specialists, and require diligent searching as they are very well camouflaged. I've found them on the seedheads of Lesser Knapweed as well as on grass stems.

Known as the burrowing shieldbugs, the family Cydnidae are characterised by having strong spines on their tibiae (legs). All the species in this family are black, sometimes with a bluish sheen, and many have areas of white on them. They have to be searched for on the ground around or under their foodplants. The Pied Shieldbug (*Tritomegas bicolor*) is the commonest and the most prominently marked. We are lucky to have them on our allotment, and generally find one or two in spring as they cross bare ground between patches of White Dead-nettle, one of their foodplants. The other is Black Horehound.

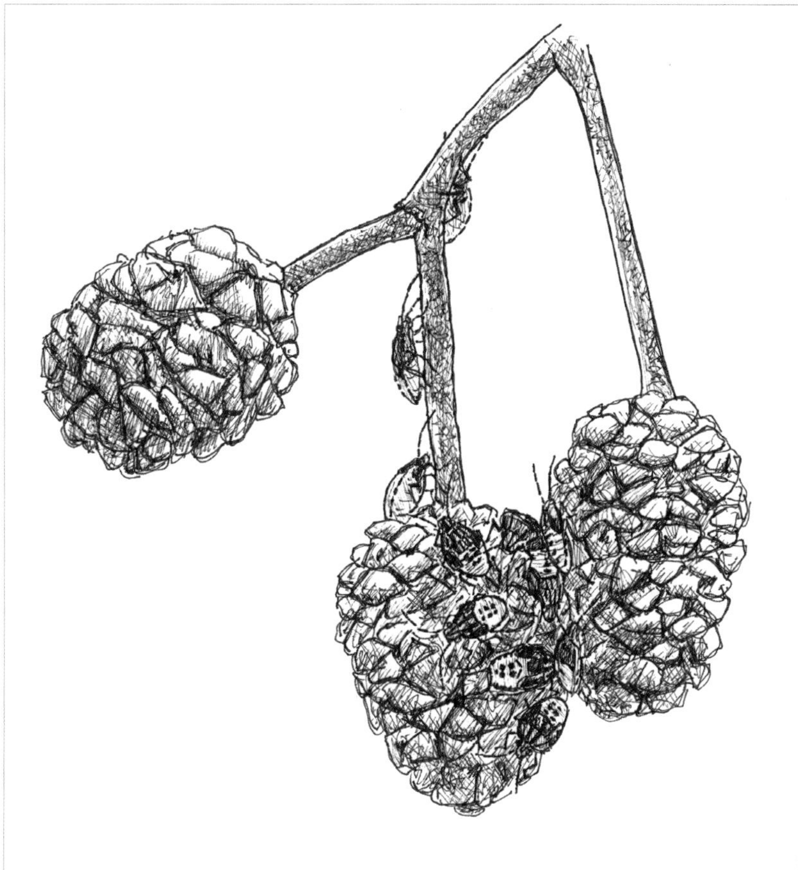

A cluster of Parent Shieldbug nymphs were perfectly camouflaged on a group of Alder catkins, until they started running away up the stem away from me!

T is for... TIGERS

1 Green Tiger Beetle
2 Cinnabar Moth
3 Scarlet Tiger Moth
4 Cinnabar caterpillars ('Tiger-tails')
5 Garden Tiger caterpillars ('Woolly Bears')
6 Garden Tiger Moth
7 Scarlet Tiger Moth
8 Ruby Tiger Moth
9 Cinnabar Moth

The 'Tigers' on this plate are some of my favourite insects. As a child, I raised the caterpillars of the Garden Tiger moth, rushing home from school to watch the moths emerge from their silken cocoons, their crumpled wings gradually swelling out as the moth pumped fluid into them. The magic culmination of metamorphosis was a thrilling delight to witness, and fired my interest in natural history.

Tiger moths were originally called leopard moths – after all, they are spotty rather than striped – but later naturalists preferred the name tiger. Ironically, they are actually named after bears, being in the Arctiidae after the Greek arcturus/arktus – meaning bear. This is a reference to their hairy caterpillars, commonly called woolly bears. The hairs on the caterpillars make them unpalatable to birds, although the Cuckoo is adapted to cope with them and is one of the few birds that will readily eat big hairy caterpillars. (I call them 'nattipillars' as they are very nattily attired.) The adult tiger moths are also distasteful, and have the red/black/yellow warning colours to ward off would-be predators.

There are several species of tiger moth but I've seen only a few. The Ruby Tiger (*Phragmatobia fuliginosa*) is probably the least spectacular but is attractive, nonetheless, the brownish forewings hiding a striking red and black abdomen and dark pink hindwings. The day-flying Scarlet Tiger (*Callimorpha dominula*) can be found in southern England in water meadows and along riverbanks where there is plenty of Comfrey, one of the main foodplants of the caterpillar. We found several sitting openly on Green Alkanet leaves at Hestercombe Gardens in Somerset, their dark forewings shining an iridescent green in the bright sunshine.

The Cinnabar (*Tyria jacobaeae*) is another member of the tiger family. They get their name from the mineral cinnabar that artists used for a reddish-pink pigment. They used to be called the Pink Underwing but I would describe the hindwings as red rather than pink. The caterpillars feed almost exclusively on Ragwort, and used to be a lot more common when I was a child. We would search derelict building sites for the ubiquitous plants, and each would have its cluster of black and yellow caterpillars that we called 'tiger-tails'. Again, the black and yellow coloration warns would-be predators of their distastefulness. The caterpillars' toxins are absorbed from their foodplant.

Garden Tigers (*Arctia caja*) are my absolute favourite moths. They are truly beautiful, and the white forewings with their rich dark brown markings look like velvet or damask silk. The furry deep brown head has a red collar and white antennae, and the amazing scarlet hindwings bordered with black spots are really sumptuous. Garden Tiger caterpillars will eat a wide range of plants. When I was a child, these woolly bears lived on Lupins in the tiny back yard of our terraced house. They used to be a really common garden species, also being found on waste ground and in a variety of other habitats. Sadly, they have suffered a massive decline in many of their former haunts – due probably to loss of habitat, increased pesticide use and over-tidying of gardens. Climate change is also a significant threat. The caterpillars overwinter when only half grown and need a good cold spell to hibernate properly. Mild, wet winters are detrimental to their survival.

The final tiger is the Green Tiger Beetle (*Cicindela campestris*), a fast-running beetle of heathland and sandy sites. Like nearly all beetles, the Green Tiger can fly but in practice this is more of a quick dash, jump and short glide with a crash landing. Often, all you see is a bright green flash and then they disappear. If you get a close view they are beautiful, a shiny metallic green with iridescent flashes of purple, yellow spots on the wing cases and huge pale-yellow scything mandibles.

The Green Tiger Beetle is a formidable predator with an equally impressive larva. The adult deposits her egg in a tunnel at the bottom of a shallow, funnel-shaped depression. Here, the larva lurks with just its massive mandibles poking out. Any insect that wanders too close tumbles into this perfect pitfall trap and the waiting jaws. However, the larva doesn't get things all its own way. There is a tiny ant-like wasp, *Methocha articulata*, that deliberately enters the trap, luring the larva farther out. Just as she is grabbed by it, she curls her abdomen round and stings it. She then drags the paralysed larva into its own burrow and lays an egg on it. Finally, she seals up the tunnel to provide a safe nest site with a fresh food supply, still living but immobilised, for her own larva.

There are four other species of tiger beetle in Britain – Northern Dune, Dune, Heath and Cliff – but the Green Tiger is by far the most common and widespread. The others are all rare or very rare, with only one of them present in Norfolk. Hopefully one day I will get to see them.

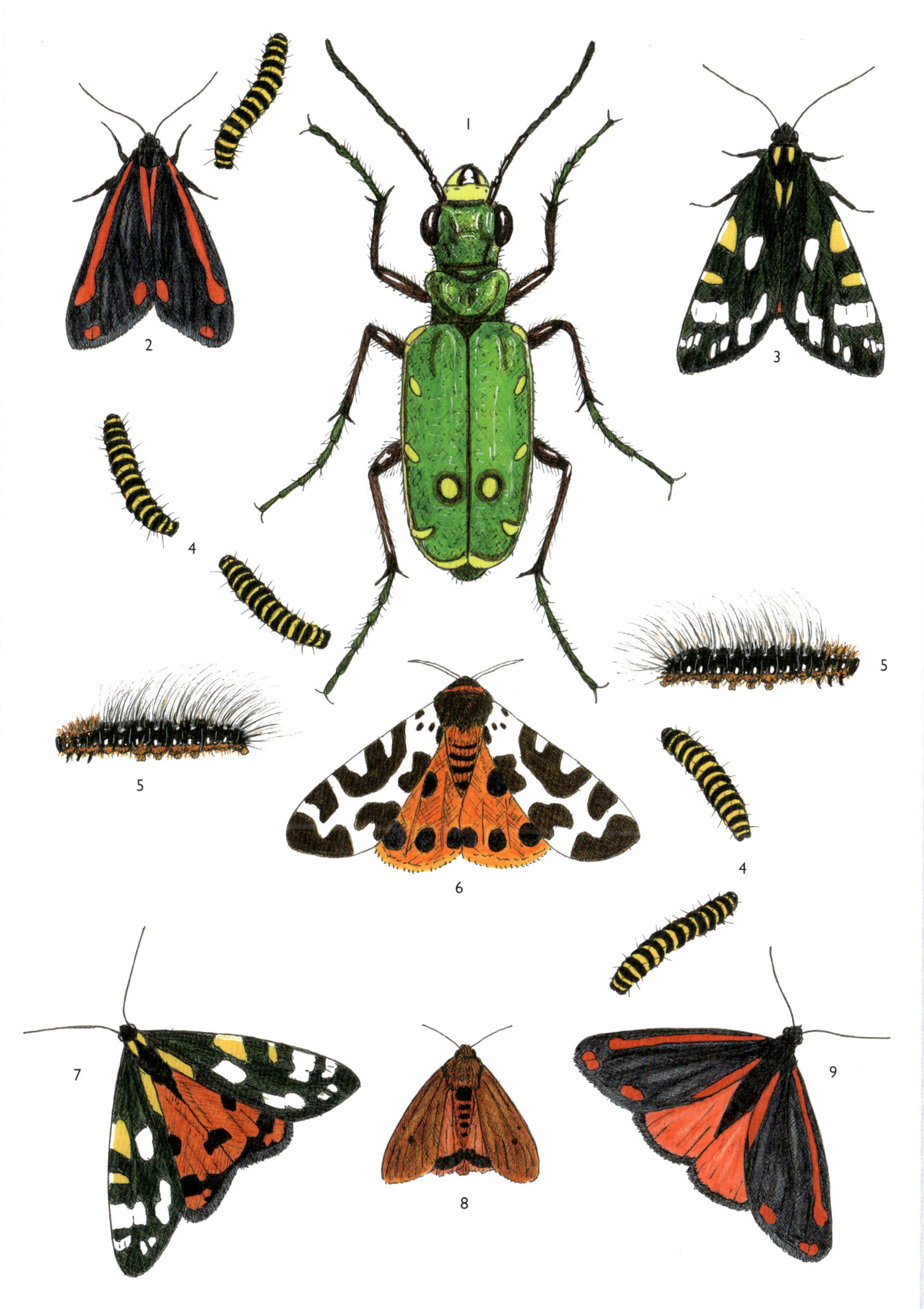
1
2
3
4
4
5
5
6
7
8
9

U is for... UNDERWINGS

1 Orange Underwing
2 Lesser Yellow Underwing
3 Lesser Broad-bordered Yellow Underwing
4 Red Underwing
5 Large yellow Underwing
6 Copper Underwing
7 Straw Underwing
8 Beautiful Yellow Underwing

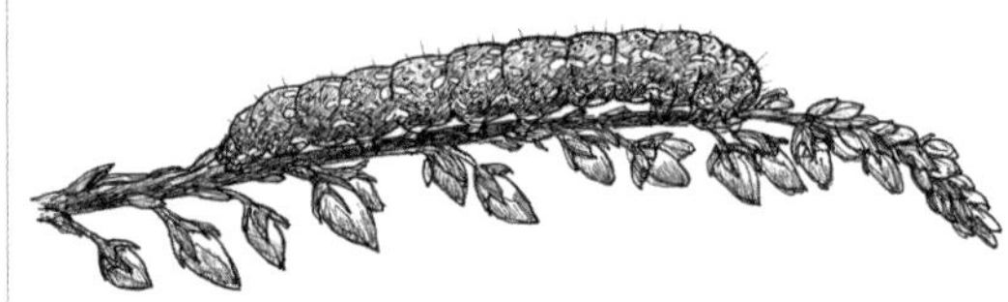

The caterpillar of the Beautiful Yellow Underwing lives up to the moniker of the adult moth, being rather lovely – unlike the brown or greenish jobs of many of the others. Although bright green, it can be difficult to spot reclined along a sprig of Heather.

Drab, grey-brown and uninteresting. Moths are often written off as dull and unattractive; but, while it is true that many are brown or grey (the equivalent of 'little brown jobs' in the birding world), on close inspection they all have a subtle beauty. And a number of them have an ace up their sleeves – or, rather, under their wings: brightly coloured hindwings, often in reds and yellows, which are hidden away when the moth is at rest. These moths are the aptly named 'Underwings'.

Most of them are members of the noctuid family, rather robust medium to large species. Their upper wings are perfectly coloured for camouflage when they are at rest on tree trunks, hiding them from birds and other potential predators. When disturbed or feeling threatened, they can give a quick flash of their brightly coloured underwings with their bright warning colours. This is usually enough to scare predators away, or to distract them long enough for the moth to make an escape.

The odd one out on the plate is the Orange Underwing (*Archiearis parthenias*), which is a geometer (see plate G). It is an early spring species, on the wing in March and April when it flies during the day. The larvae feed on birches, so look for them in open birch woodland or around scattered birches on heathland. A warm, sunny day when birch trees are in tight green bud just before the leaves burst forth is the ideal time to search for them. They are often seen high up around the tops of birch trees but will come down to settle and have been found drinking from puddles.

The Red Underwing (*Catocala nupta*) definitely has the wow factor. Even without the rich red underwings it is an impressive moth and one of our larger species. The forewings are lovely soft shades of grey with pale dogtooth markings and jagged cross-lines. Then there are those gorgeous hindwings, likened by some to gaudy petticoats. The eminent Swedish naturalist Carl Linnaeus certainly thought so. He seems to have had a thing about the underwing moths, and gave them specific Latin names alluding to marriage (*nupta* for the Red meaning bride, and *pronuba* for bridesmaid for the Large Yellow). Maybe the great man enjoyed a naughty flash of red and black petticoats!

Red Underwing caterpillars feed on poplars and willows, and old guide books recommended searching the trunks of trees along river valleys where the adults could easily be seen at rest. Hah! I've lost count of trees such as these that I've scanned, and nary a moth of any sort. But I have seen one, my very own, that I found all by myself. I sat at the kitchen table one day and happened to glance outside. There, tucked under the overhang of the window embrasure, sat a huge grey moth. Large as life. I knew what it was straight away, having dreamed of seeing one for years. I couldn't quite believe it. We managed to reach up and catch it in a pot so we could look at it closely and I could draw it. We have no decent photograph, for as soon as the lid was off the moth was gone – vroom! – rocketing off stupendously fast right over the rooftops at dizzying speed. It was never seen again, but was never forgotten either.

Back down to earth, we have the Beautiful Yellow Underwing (*Anarta myrtilli*). Found on heathland and moorland where its larva feeds on heathers, an attractive caterpillar, bright green with broken white lines that serve to break up the outline and hide it amongst the stems of its food plant. The moth flies during the day in sunshine, taking nectar from heather flowers. When the forewings are closed, the overall effect of rich reddish brown marbled with white is perfect camouflage amongst the heather.

The other yellow underwings on the plate are all frequently recorded in our garden. The Large Yellow Underwing (*Noctua pronuba*) is very common and widespread. It is a real blunderer of a moth, creating havoc in the moth trap as it refuses to settle, instead disturbing everything else that has nestled down

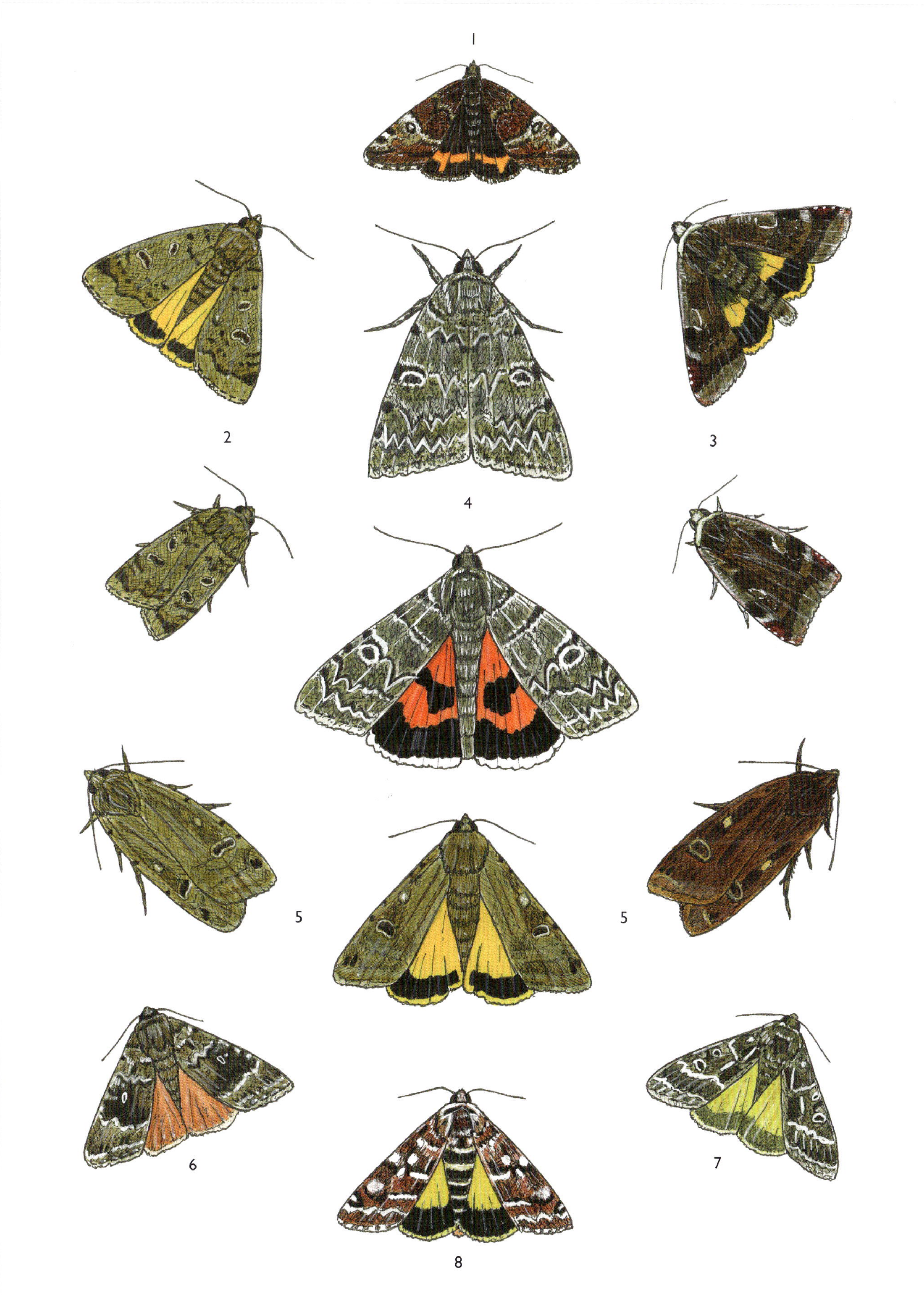
1
2
3
4
5
5
6
7
8

quietly under the egg boxes. I've had them fly up my trouser leg, down my T-shirt and even rescued one from a cup of tea I'd taken outside while inspecting the trap. The long, narrow shape lets them burrow off through vegetation to hide away when released in the morning. If you disturb one during the day the yellow flash of the underwings is quite startling even when you know what to expect.

Other yellows are better behaved and not nearly so rambunctious. The Lesser Broad-bordered (*Noctua janthe*) is probably the most attractive of these species. Its upperwings are beautifully marked with rich browns and greys, flecks of almost silver run along the costa (wing edge), and a patch of rich reddish purple completes the glorious cloak. It has a pale lemon-yellow collar behind the head, and then there are the deep yellow underwings with their contrasting wide black border.

The Lesser Yellow Underwing (*Noctua comes*) lives up to its name, and is altogether a more understated moth, lacking anything really distinctive on the forewings. In my experience, it also seems somewhat reluctant to show off its hindwings.

Lastly, we have the Copper Underwing (*Amphipyra pyramidea*) and Straw Underwing (*Thalpophila matura*). Both are at the more subtle end of the spectrum, with unfussy forewings and softer shades on the hindwings. The Copper Underwing is a common visitor to gardens, and can easily be found by searching Buddleia flowers after dark with a torch. This is also a good way to find Large Yellow Underwings.

When it comes to underwings, the greatest prize of all is the Clifden Nonpareil (*Catocala fraxini*). Unfortunately, it has lately been given the far too dull and prosaic name Blue Underwing. It is similar to the Red Underwing, to which it is closely related, but is larger and greyer with a pale whitish spot almost in the centre of each forewing. The black underwings have a glorious violet blue band across the centre. It is a truly magnificent creature.

I have yet to find one of these beauties for myself. Even the great Moses Harris never saw a live one. In his day there were only two known specimens in the country, and he had to copy one of those for his great work on butterflies and moths. The first one was caught at Cliveden (originally spelt Cleifden) in Buckinghamshire, hence the name. The nonpareil bit is from the French, meaning unmatched or beyond compare.

Nearly everyone who is interested in moths dreams of finding one of these great rarities. Years can go by with no records, and then a flurry will turn up from the Continent, usually on the east or south coast and quite often in Norfolk. In fact, there were colonies established in Norfolk in the 1930s and in Kent in the 1950s but they were short-lived. The caterpillars feed on Aspen and poplars so there is no shortage of food plant. When only a handful of them arrive on our shores the chances of a pair meeting up and breeding must be fairly slim, but perhaps they will re-establish and I may yet have the thrill of finding one.

Most moth enthusiasts employ a light trap of some sort to capture and record moths. This consists of a light bulb mounted over a waterproof

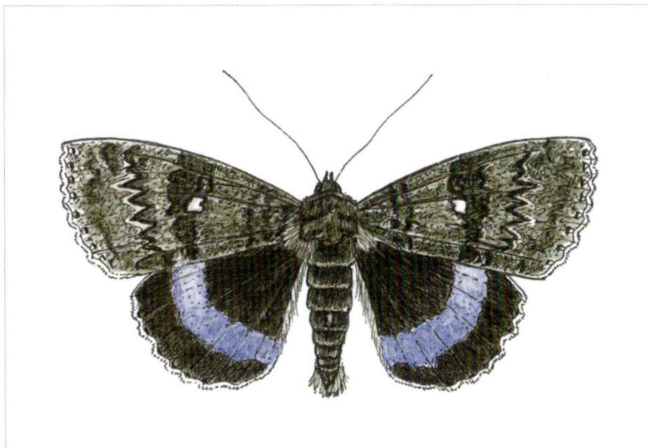

Clifden Nonpareil, a pinned specimen from Norwich Castle Museum. Like Moses Harris, I had to borrow a specimen from a collection in order to include this superb moth in my book.

box that is lined with egg boxes, giving the moths somewhere to settle down and hide. These traps are run overnight with the catch examined in the morning and then released at dusk. Mercury vapour lamps are often used as they give off ultraviolet light, but these are very bright; many people use more energy-efficient lamps that are less bright, a consideration if you have close neighbours.

Before electric lights, people had to look for moths on tree trunks or search out eggs and caterpillars to rear. Another method that was eagerly adopted was 'sugaring' after it was noted that moths were attracted to empty sugar barrels. A concoction of Barbados sugar, black treacle and beer was cooked up with some rum added. The resulting sticky gloop was painted on tree trunks and fence posts at dusk when it attracted moths which could then easily be caught.

Even with the advent of the mercury vapour lamp, sugaring was still used as certain moths – notably, the copper and red underwing species and the Old Lady – didn't come to light but were reliably attracted to sugar. This was also the best way of finding the elusive Clifden Nonpareil.

V is for... VOLUCELLA

1 Volucella zonaria
2 Volucella inanis
3 Volucella zonaria
4 Volucella inanis
5 Volucella pellucens
6 Volucella bombylans
7 Volucella bombylans

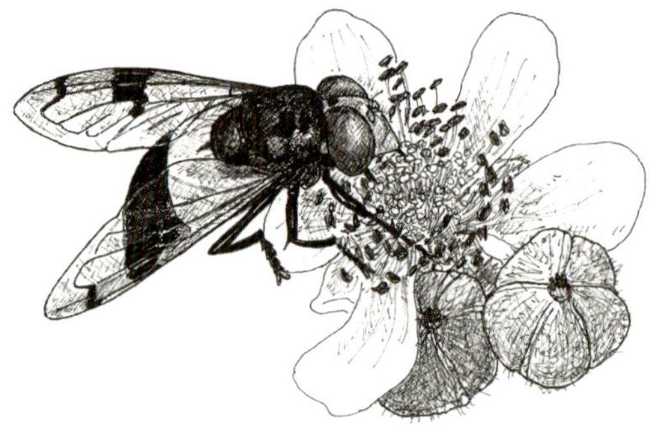

Volucella pellucens is instantly recognisable with its black and white livery. Here, a female is taking nectar from a bramble flower.

There may be only five species of hoverfly in the genus *Volucella* in Britain but they are all rather large and impressive and include our largest hoverfly, *Volucella zonaria*. The larvae of these hoverflies develop in the nests of bumblebees and social wasps where they scavenge on debris or feed on the host larvae. Four species are illustrated as I haven't yet managed to catch up with the fifth, *Volucella inflata*.

The Great Pied Hoverfly is the name sometimes given to *Volucella pellucens*, and it is easy to see why. The large size and bold black and white abdomen makes it a very distinctive species. It is widespread and common across the country, frequenting woodland rides and edges where it is often found on bramble flowers. The larvae are scavengers in the nests of social wasps.

Volucella bombylans is the bumblebee mimic of the group, and is polymorphic, having three different colour forms. I have depicted the commonest two. The black and red form mimics the Red-tailed Bumblebee (*Bombus lapidarius*), and the black and yellow form mimics the white tailed bumblebees (*Bombus lucorum* agg.). They visit a wide range of flowers, including bramble and Hogweed. Territorial males will sit on a sunlit leaf on the lookout for females and also other males that they will chase off. The larvae have been found in the nests of bumblebees as well as in those of social wasps, feeding mainly on debris. The colour mimicry that makes these harmless hoverflies look like bees armed with a defensive sting is thought to help avoid predation by birds.

Volucella inanis and *Volucella zonaria* are superficially very similar. They are regular visitors to gardens in the south of England, where they can be seen feeding on the flowers of Buddleia and *Escallonia*. *Volucella inanis* is the more widespread of the two although both species have increased dramatically in recent years, spreading farther north and being seen more frequently. Gone are the days (the 1970s) when a sighting of *Volucella zonaria* was so rare that it was featured in the Bulletin of the Amateur Entomologists' Society. It was almost the equivalent of announcing the arrival of the first Cuckoo of spring in *The Times*.

Volucella inanis is the smaller of the two species, and although the abdomen is yellow the overall appearance can seem quite dull. This is especially true when the wings are closed, so all you see is the darker thorax and rather dull brown scutellum. *Volucella zonaria* is larger and a much deeper, warmer yellow with a rich reddish-brown thorax and scutellum that gives it a shiny, polished appearance. The obvious distinction is the dark second sternite (abdominal plate) on the underside of *zonaria*, clearly visible in the side view illustration, which is yellow in *inanis*.

Volucella inanis is a wasp mimic, and its larvae are known to feed on the grubs of social wasp species, notably *Vespula germanica*. *Volucella zonaria* is known as the Hornet Hoverfly, and it really does resemble a Hornet (*Vespa crabro*) at first glance. Often, one has droned past me and I've thought it was a Hornet from the size and colour; but they have a lazier, less purposeful flight than the great Hornets, which are really rather zippy. The larvae do indeed live in Hornet nests, but have also been found in the nests of other social wasps where they scavenge debris as well as sometimes attacking wasp grubs.

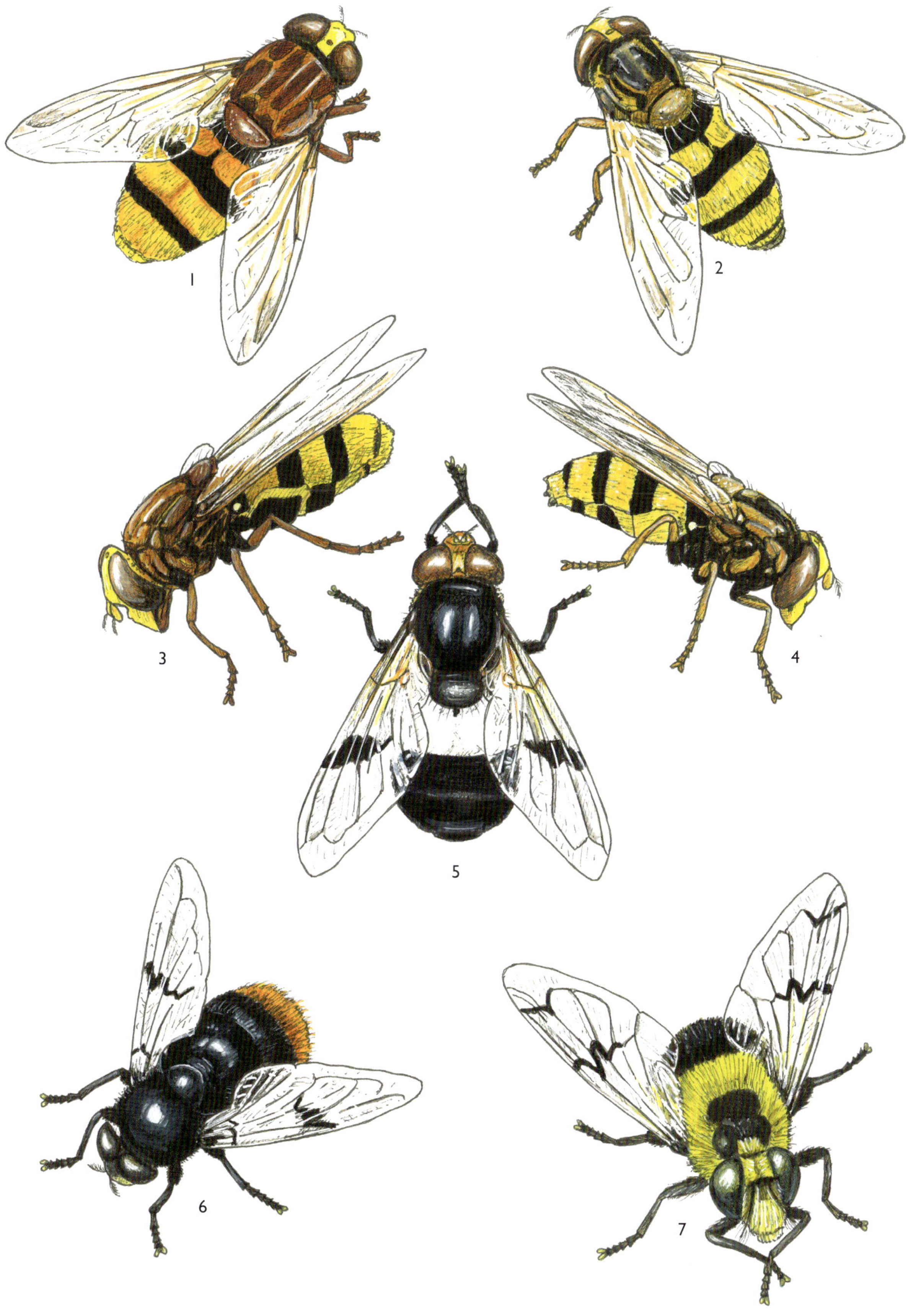
1
2
3
4
5
6
7

W is for... *WASPS*

1 Oxybelus uniglumis
2 Philanthus triangulum
3 Cerceris rybyensis
4 Pompilus cinereus
5 Vespa crabro
6 Ammophila sabulosa
7 Gasteruption assectator
8 Sapyga quinquepunctata
9 Ormyrus nitidulus
10 Vespula vulgaris
11 Torymus sp.

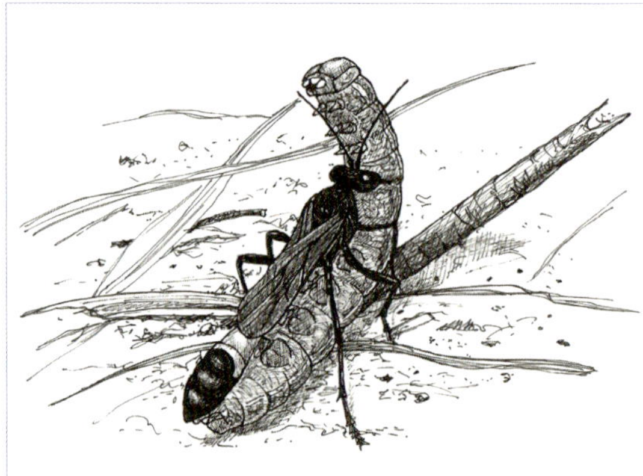

The solitary wasp Ammophila sabulosa with a large juicy moth caterpillar. She straddles the paralysed prey with her long legs and drags it back to her nest burrow in a sandy bank.

It seems that nearly everybody loves to hate wasps. Yes, they can be a nuisance, but they are the gardener's friend, our very own pest control, snatching up aphids, caterpillars, flies and all manner of creepy-crawlies that are hell-bent on munching through our favourite plants.

There is a lot more to wasps than the perceived black-and-yellow peril. They belong to the order Hymenoptera that also includes bees, ants and sawflies, and is the largest insect order in Britain. As well as the social wasps, there are solitary spider-hunters, sand wasps, digger wasps and parasitic wasps.

The social wasps live in colonies, all working for a single queen, building nests out of paper, which they make by chewing wood to a pulp. The largest of the social wasps is the Hornet (*Vespa crabro*), something of a gentle giant and wonderful to watch close up when frequenting Ivy flowers in the autumn. Hornets post guards around their nest entrances and, understandably, will defend their homes if disturbed. The Common Wasp (*Vespula vulgaris*) is no longer as common as a few years ago. We always see several queens early in the spring when they emerge from hibernation, but workers and actual nests seem few and far between later in the year.

With solitary wasps, individual females make their own nest burrows, but you can get several together forming a nesting aggregation like that of solitary bees. Each individual works on her own, provisioning her nest cells with live food that has been stung and paralysed so it can't attack the wasp's larva, a living larder that won't go off or escape.

Sand wasps are long, leggy beasts. There are only four species in Britain, all similar, black and red in colour, with *Ammophila sabulosa* being the commonest. They burrow in sand, and provision each nest cell with a live but paralysed caterpillar (usually that of a moth, but butterfly or even sawfly larvae are also taken). The caterpillars are often considerably larger than the wasp, and can weigh a great deal more. Sometimes the wasp will find its burden too heavy and will abandon the caterpillar if it has too far to drag it. I have watched one struggling along dragging a huge caterpillar for at least 10 minutes before it reached its burrow, only to discover that its prey was too big to fit in the hole. It then had to expend even more energy enlarging the tunnel in order to squeeze it in.

The spider-hunters are similar to the sand wasps in having long legs but are generally shorter in the body. They specialise in hunting spiders, darting about the ground or making short flights as they hunt for their prey. Spiders are quickly stung and paralysed then dragged off to a nest burrow where they are squeezed in to provide a fresh, tasty food supply for the larva. Many of these wasps are black and red but *Pompilus cinereus* is a distinctively dark species with a grey pubescence – giving it a leaden or silvery appearance (*cinereus* means ashen). Its English name is the Leaden Spider Wasp.

Digger wasps make up the large family Crabronidae, with more than 100 species, many of

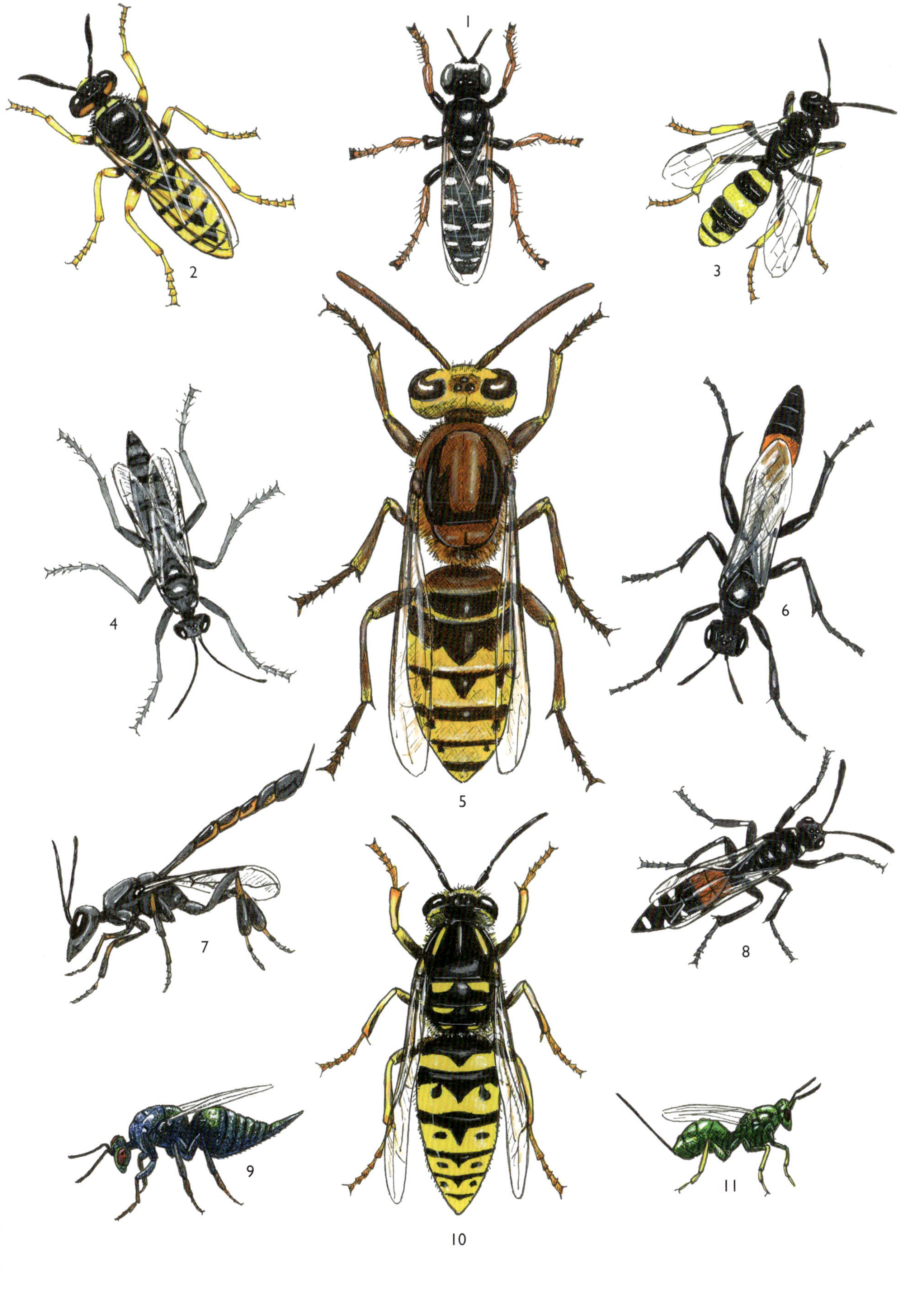
1
2
3
4
5
6
7
8
9
10
11

them black and yellow. The Bee Wolf (*Philanthus triangulum*) is the largest and most spectacular, and hunts Honeybees. I watched one stalking Honeybees on Kelling Heath in Norfolk, shadowing them across the heather before jumping on one from behind and curling up its abdomen to sting the bee in the neck where it is vulnerable, avoiding the bee's own sting. On the cliffs at nearby Weybourne I have seen them flying back to their nest holes with their cumbersome load tucked underneath them. They land and drop the bee next to the nest entrance then disappear underground, quickly re-emerging to drag the prey backwards down the hole.

The Bee Wolf is the only digger wasp that takes Honeybees. Other species take different prey including grasshopper nymphs, weevils, flies, solitary bees or froghopper nymphs. The *Cerceris* species are easily distinguished from other digger wasps by the pinched constrictions between their abdominal segments, but different species can be hard to separate from each other. *Cerceris rybyensis* is readily recognised in the field as it is the only one with yellow at the front of the first abdominal segment, where the others have black. It is sometimes called the Ornate Tailed Digger Wasp, and preys on various species of solitary bees.

Oxybelus uniglumis (Common Spiny Digger Wasp) is one of the species that isn't black and yellow. It catches flies, impaling them on its sting before dragging them off to its burrow. Like other digger wasps, they can be found visiting flowers and have even turned up in our garden.

The various parasitic wasps are amazing. These include the ichneumons (see plate K), colourful chrysid cuckoo wasps (plate J) and the tiny gall wasps and chalcid wasps.

The gall wasps have intriguing life histories but are seldom seen, unlike the flamboyant galls that are created by the action of their egg-laying (see plate Q for examples of oak galls). You are more likely to come across the equally small chalcid wasps such as *Ormyrus nitidulus*. These are best looked for around oak trees as they lay their eggs into the tissues of galls where the larvae then feed on the larva of the wasp that induced the gall in the first place. Some *Torymus* species also target oak galls but aren't necessarily parasitoids. These are the so-called inquilines whose larvae feed on the gall tissue rather than the host.

Sapyga quinquepunctata is a parasite on various solitary bees. It is often seen visiting Thyme flowers, but we have also recorded it in our garden on Tea Tree and Corn Chamomile. They are often around our bee hotels but will investigate holes in any timber including the dodgy woodwork of our crumbling summerhouse. Only the female has red on the abdomen, the male's being simply black but still with the white spots.

Another bee parasite is *Gasteruption assectator*, which seeks out nests of *Hylaeus* species in which to lay its eggs. They are usually seen visiting flowers, with Oxeye Daisies being favoured in our garden. They have a very distinctive posture – head down with a pair of upright antler-like antennae and the abdomen stuck up in the air at about 45 degrees while the wings are held horizontal. The sexes are alike except for the female's short ovipositor.

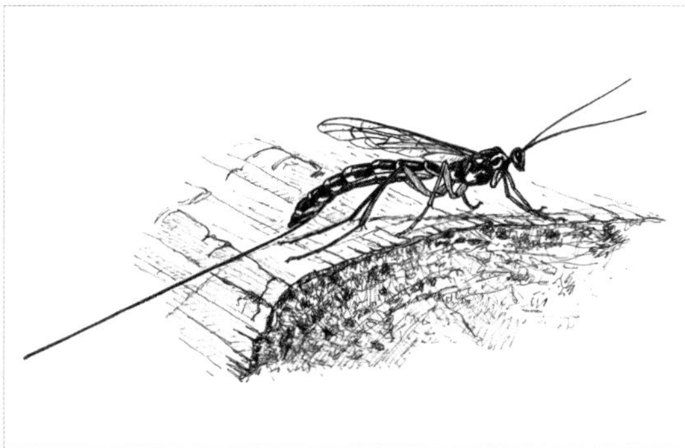

The magnificent Rhyssa persuasoria is our largest ichneumon. The female uses her extremely long ovipositor to lay her eggs deep into timber where her larvae parasitise the larvae of the Greater Horntail (Urocerus gigas). She locates the larvae by detecting the smell of a fungus that they use to break down the cellulose in the timber.

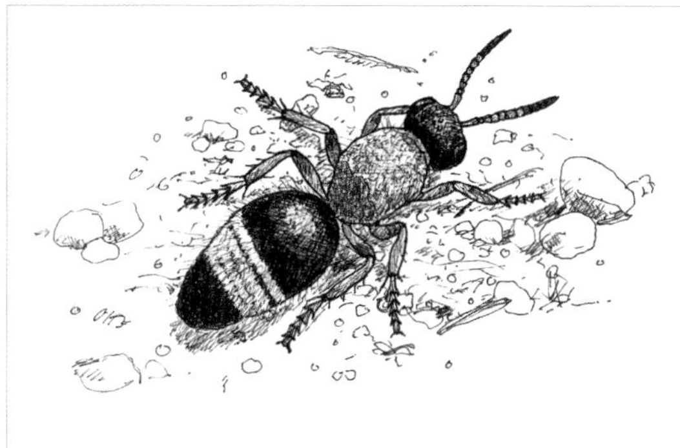

Velvet ants are in fact wasps; the name comes from the likeness of the wingless females to ants. There are only three species in Britain, and they are all parasites on species of solitary wasps and bees. The Small Velvet Ant (Smicromyrme rufipes) is confined to a few sandy areas in the south-east of the country, including heaths and coastal areas. I chanced upon this one in Orwell Country Park near Ipswich when I was searching for nesting solitary bees. It was running fast across bare, sandy ground and did indeed look much like an ant. Under magnification the body is densely hairy, giving it the velvety appearance to which the English name alludes.

X is for... anything beginning with X

1 Xysticus lanio
2 Xestia c-nigrum
3 Xestia xanthographa
4 Xanthorhoe fluctuata
5 Xanthorhoe biriviata
6 Xanthogramma pedissequum
7 Xanthia citrago
8 Xanthia aurago
9 Xysticus cristatus
10 Xylota sylvarum
11 Xylota segnis
12 Xylocampa areola

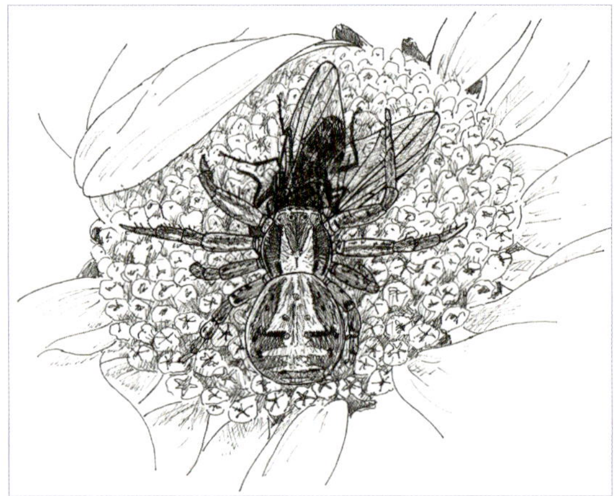

A female Xysticus cristatus with her prey – a fly – on an Oxeye Daisy.

I was rather stuck with 'X' as no big group starts with that letter. There is *Xiphydria*, the woodwasps, but I haven't seen any, and there aren't that many of them – so I had to cheat a bit here.

There are several critters whose scientific name begins with an X so I've plumped for a selection of those. I found a number of moths that start with X, notably some carpets and sallows, less than a handful of hoverflies and a whole family of crab spiders. Luckily, I had seen several of them as well. The plate is a bit of a hotchpotch, with seven moths, three hoverflies and two spiders, but I managed to get what I think is a pleasing design out of them.

The *Xysticus* spiders are all fairly similar in appearance and are rather tricky to identify to species, most requiring microscopic examination of an adult's reproductive organs – the male's pedipalps or the female's epigyne, which is located underneath at the front of the abdomen. Fortunately, this can be done with live specimens so I am slowly identifying the species in my garden.

They are species of crab spider and are rather squat in appearance with relatively short, stout legs – crab-like, in fact, hence the name. They skulk about on low vegetation or sit boldly in the middle of a flower waiting for some unsuspecting insect to visit, when they quickly grab them with their spiny front legs and sink their fangs in. They are perfect little sit-and-wait predators. The commonest is *Xysticus cristatus*, which I often find lurking on Oxeye Daisy flowers in our mini-meadow. Males of *Xysticus lanio* are quite distinctive, and I was lucky enough to find one at my local nature reserve posing on top of a Creeping Thistle flower.

Of the carpet moths, which are members of the Geometridae (see plate G), I picked *Xanthorhoe fluctuata* (Garden Carpet), often found in our moth trap; and *Xanthorhoe biriviata* (Balsam Carpet), an uncommon and rather localised species, first recorded in Britain in the 1950s. In Norfolk it can be found in damp woodland where it feeds on Orange Balsam, an introduced plant.

The sallows (members of the Noctuidae) are a group of generally bright yellowy-orange or brownish-coloured moths that are around in the autumn. *Xanthia citrago* (Orange Sallow) is really lovely, a deep orangey yellow with darker cross lines and flecks giving it a spangled appearance. *Xanthia aurago* (Barred Sallow) is a more lemon yellow with bold, dark reddish-brown markings, almost pinkish in some specimens.

Xestia c-nigrum (Setaceous Hebrew Character) and *Xestia xanthographa* (Square-spot Rustic) are common in our moth trap, too, but *Xylocampa areola* (Early Grey) is less often encountered as it flies early in the year, in March and April, when we trap less often and tend to get few moths anyway. Trapping in a city with the attendant light pollution generally means much lower catch numbers than in the countryside, but is still worth doing as you never know what may turn up.

The *Xylota* hoverflies are dark, elongate hovers that are marked with reddish or yellow areas on the abdomen. The commonest is *Xylota segnis*, which has a large, light-reddish area on its abdomen. It is usually seen running rapidly over a leaf surface where it feeds on aphid honeydew. Slightly larger is *Xylota sylvarum*, more of a woodland species (*sylvarum* is from *sylva*, meaning woodland). It has tufts of yellow at the end of the abdomen giving it a golden 'tail'. It, too, can be found feeding on honeydew on leaves, but is also attracted to umbellifer flowers for pollen.

The third hoverfly is the wonderfully named *Xanthogramma pedissequum*. Black and yellow with dark wing stigmas, it is a good wasp mimic. Its larvae are believed to feed underground on root aphids.

Belatedly, I found out that there is an entire tribe of hoverflies called the Xylotini, but I think a mixed plate worked better than another one of just hoverflies.

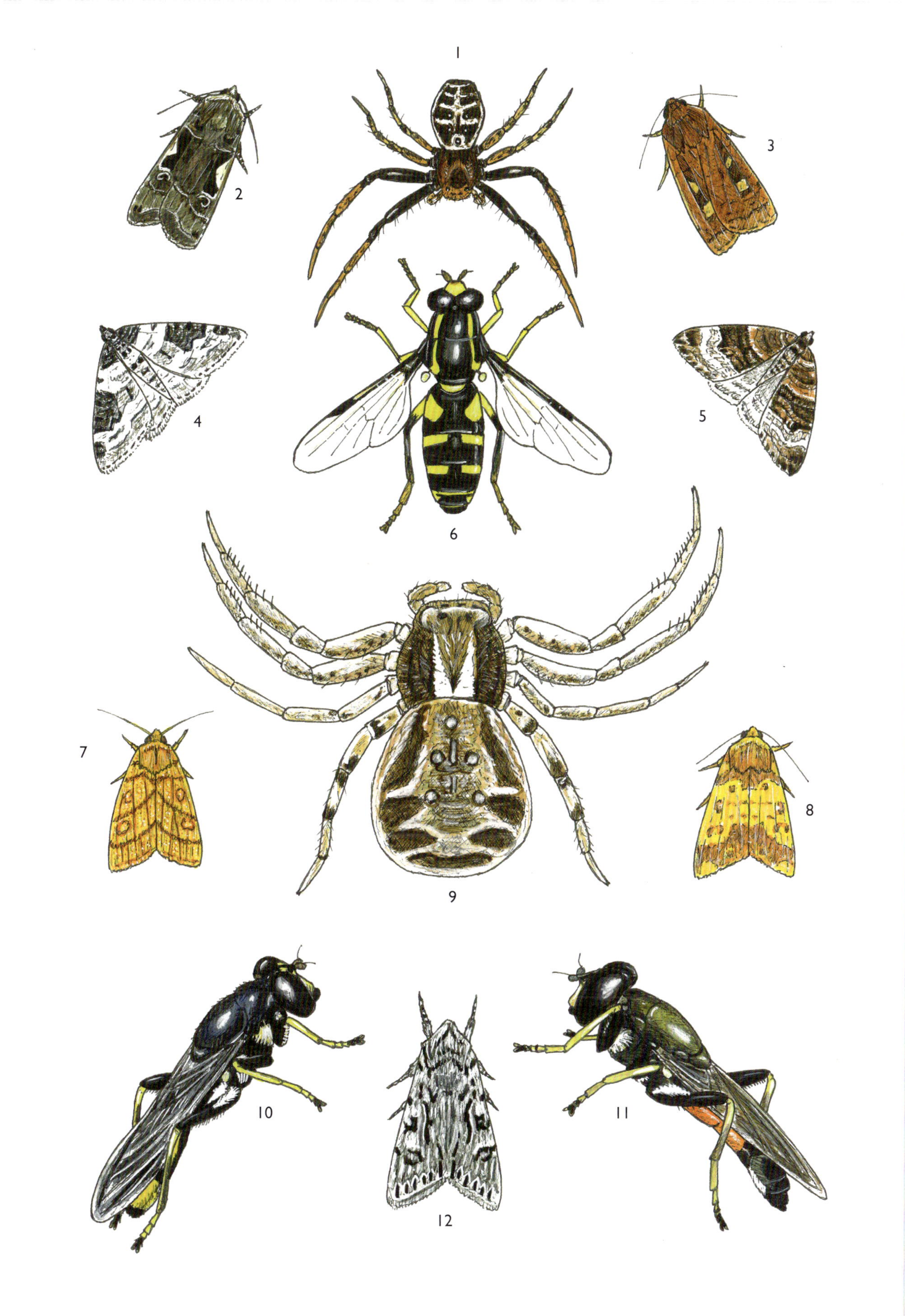
1
2
3
4
5
6
7
8
9
10
11
12

Y is for... YELLOW

1 Barred Yellow
2 Yellow-tail
3 Burnished Brass
4 Golden-ringed Dragonfly
5 Yellow Meadow Ant
6 Brimstone
7 Clouded Yellow
8 Yellow Shell
9 Yellow Dungfly
10 Yellow-legged Mining Bee
11 Canary-shouldered Thorn

A yellow-themed plate. The Brimstone butterfly (*Gonepteryx rhamni*) is named for its sulphur-yellow colour. Some think it may have been the original 'butter (coloured) fly', although the true origins of the word 'butterfly' are shrouded in the mists of time. It is a welcome sight in spring, when the bright-yellow males emerge from hibernation and fly furiously by on the hunt for the more elusive females. The brighter-hued Clouded Yellow (*Colias croceus*) is a migrant butterfly that turns up in varying numbers every year and is avidly sought after by butterfly watchers. The tips of the deep-yellow forewings are tipped with black on the upper surface. We don't always manage to see one every year as they are not that frequent in Norfolk, but they are much more common in the south of England.

The beautiful Golden-ringed Dragonfly (*Cordulegaster boltonii*) is a majestic black and yellow dragonfly with bright-green eyes which haunts clear-running acidic streams. I have rarely encountered one so they are all the more memorable for it. They are on the wing from late May into September. The males are very territorial and will chase off other males but will often return to the same perch and reward the patient naturalist. I watched one female in an idyllic valley in Cumbria, hovering over a pool midstream below a boulder and dipping the tip of her abdomen into the water, presumably egg-laying. Afterwards, for a few beautiful moments, she perched on a Foxglove a couple of yards across from where I sat before disappearing off upstream.

Little Yellow Meadow Ants (*Lasius flavus*) inhabit many a garden but live underground in the soil where they feed on honeydew from root aphids. They are seldom seen, except sometimes when you dig over the soil or when they emerge to swarm on a warm summer evening or afternoon. In old grasslands and ancient meadows they can make huge nest mounds. After being left to do their thing in our mini-meadow for five years we have three mounds around a foot across and more than six inches high. They have the added bonus of potentially housing Ant Woodlice (see plate I) or even attracting a Green Woodpecker (called a Yaffle in some parts of the country after the laughing call), although I'm not sure they'd appreciate the attentions of the latter!

The plate includes a small collection of moths, including Barred Yellow (*Cidaria fulvata*) and Yellow Shell (*Camptogramma bilineata*). The latter are often disturbed during the day from privet hedges or grassy corners. Their caterpillars feed on a variety of plants including cleavers, bedstraws and docks. The curious Yellow-tail (*Euproctis similis*) is a lovely white furry-looking creature that unnervingly twists its abdomen upright to flash its yellow tail to ward off would-be predators. The Burnished Brass (*Diachrysia chrysitis*) is a striking moth with metallic brassy-yellow wings and foxy orange head with a prominent tuft. They are common and widespread, their larvae feeding on Stinging Nettles.

The thorns are geometer moths with ragged-edged wings, some of which hold their wings upright rather like butterflies. They are all pretty with wings coloured in various shades of yellows, oranges and browns. The Canary-shouldered Thorn (*Ennomos alniaria*) is particularly striking with its bright canary-yellow head and thorax. I well remember my first one, attracted to the lighted window of a toilet block on a campsite in the Lake District one September night. Campsite wash blocks are great places to find interesting moths; for some reason, the best finds are always in the Ladies!

The Yellow-legged Mining Bee (*Andrena flavipes*) is slightly smaller than a Honeybee with long yellow pollen hairs on its hind legs and a markedly striped abdomen. It has spread north from its stronghold in southern England into Norfolk and beyond, bringing its cleptoparasite *Nomada fucata* with it (see plate B for more bees).

Last but not least is the lovely furry Yellow Dungfly (*Scathophaga stercoraria*). They are habitual haunters of cow pats and fox scats, pairing up on excrement and scattering their strange, arrowhead-shaped eggs over the rich substrate. Their 'maggot' larvae develop in the dung while the adult flies eat other small flies that are attracted to the dung. On a fresh, semi-liquid cow pat, the females can almost be subsumed into the rich organic matter when a male scrambles on top to mate.

The dedicated entomologist (well, this one anyway) will always be drawn to cow pats to observe their wonderful community of varied invertebrates.

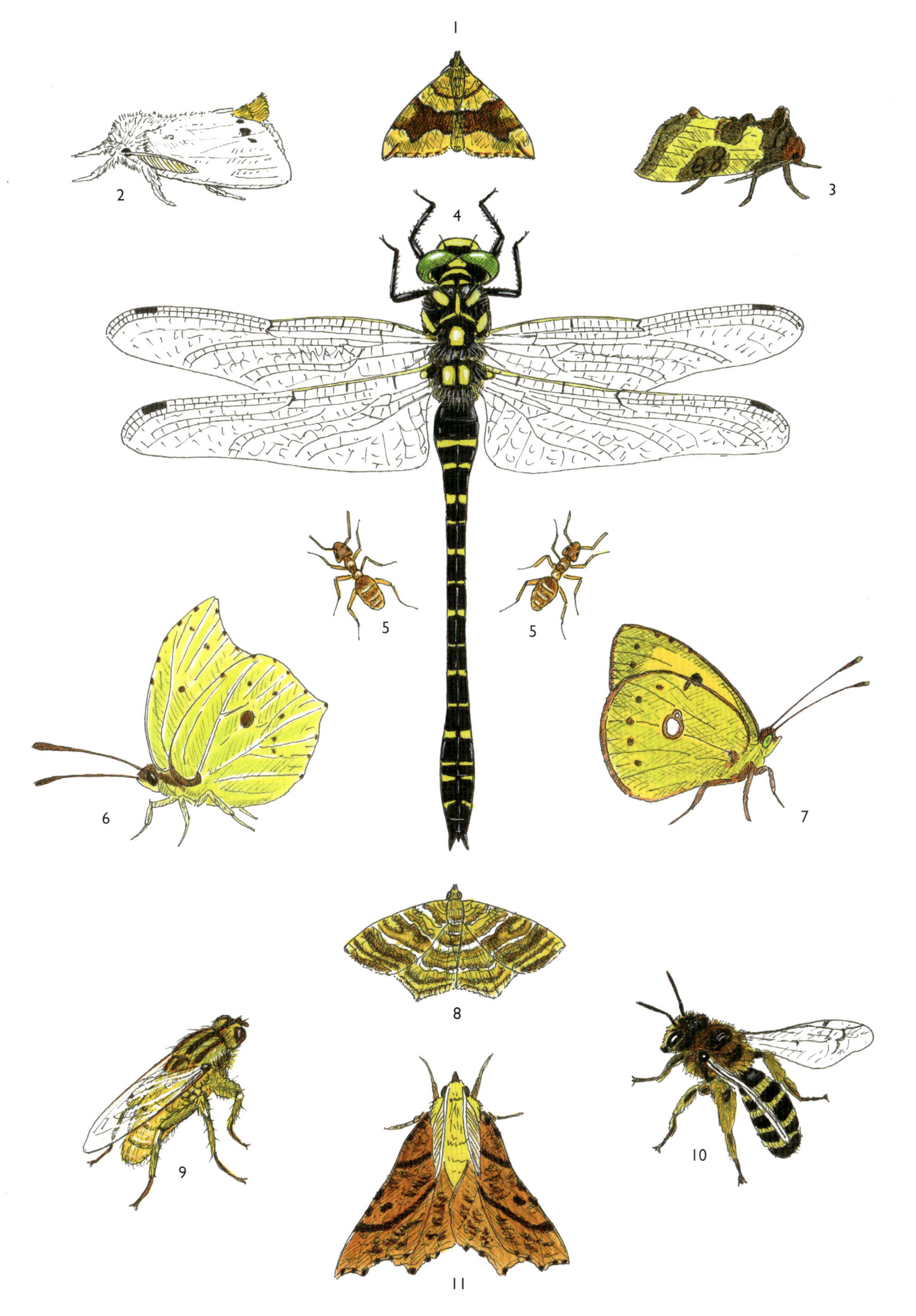
1
2
3
4
5
5
6
7
8
9
10
11

Z is for... ZYGAENIDAE

1 Five-spot Burnet
2 Forester (male)
3 Forester (female)
4 Six-spot Burnets
5 Six-spot Burnet cocoons
6 Narrow-bordered Five-spot Burnet caterpillar
7 Narrow-bordered Five-spot Burnet
8 Six-spot Burnet
9 Six-spot Burnet caterpillars

The Zygaenidae is the family of burnet and forester moths. These are brightly coloured day-flying moths that live in colonies. Most species are associated with flower-rich grassland. It used to be thought that they were fairly primitive moths, having stout, forward-pointing, almost clubbed antennae – more like those of butterflies than moths. Nowadays, they are just deemed to be different!

There are three species of forester, all very similar: a light burnished green, named after the colour, Lincoln Green, that was worn by mediaeval foresters rather than having anything to do with actual forests. The burnets are very striking. Their iridescent blue-black forewings usually have bold red spots, and the hindwings also have red on them. Occasionally, very rare aberrations are found where the red is replaced by yellow. These are warning colours that tell would-be predators that the moths are distasteful.

Of the seven species of burnet, only three are particularly common with just two being widespread. The others are very rare and restricted to isolated areas of Scotland, with one also found in Ireland.

The Six-spot Burnet (*Zygaena filipendulae*) is the commonest species, being widely distributed across the country. We have a small colony on our allotment where we have established a tiny wildflower meadow. Here I can study them at leisure, watching the stubby green and black caterpillars feeding openly on the leaves of Common Bird's-foot Trefoil. When fully grown, they climb up a grass or plantain stem and spin a delicate papery cocoon in which to pupate. The moths take nectar from a variety of flowers, especially thistles, knapweeds and scabious, and on hot summer days you can find flower heads crowded with them. On our allotment they have a particular liking for lavenders.

The Five-spot Burnet (*Zygaena trifolii*) and Narrow-bordered Five-spot Burnet (*Zygaena lonicerae*) are almost identical, being separated by very subtle differences in the shape of their wings. The Five-spot does have a common variant where the spots on the forewing are fused and run into each other – although this can very occasionally be seen in the Narrow-bordered, too. The only sure way of knowing what species you have is to hunt for their larvae and take note of the length of their bristles! (They are shorter in the Five-spot.) The larvae also have different foodplants. The Five-spot feeds on Greater Bird's-foot Trefoil, while the Narrow-bordered Five-spot prefers clovers and vetches. Both species do sometimes occur on the same site, but generally you find one or the other.

And, finally, the Forester (*Adscita statices*). I had never seen Foresters but I was determined to track one down to complete the plate. Fortunately for

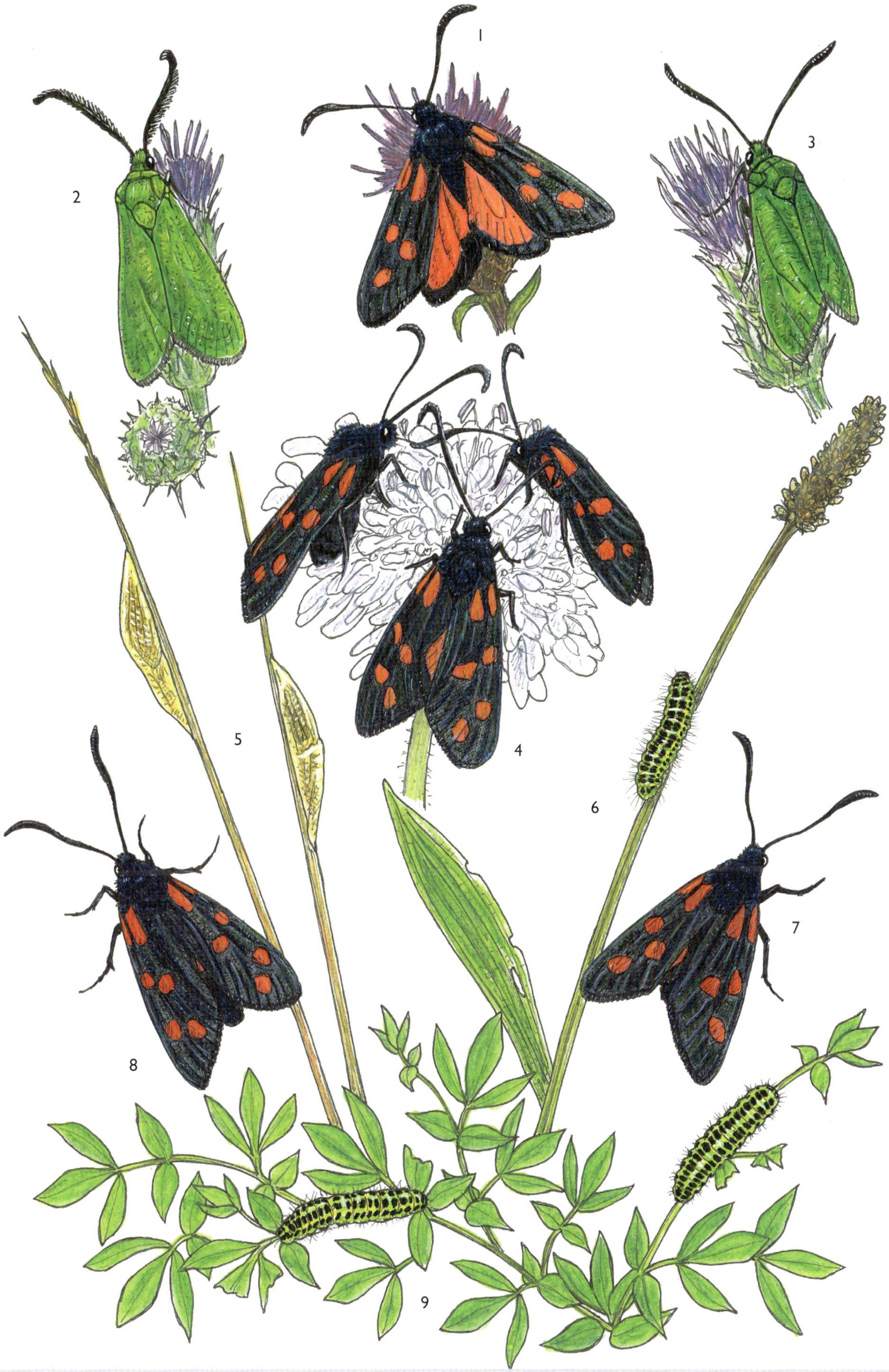
1
2
3
4
5
6
7
8
9

me, they do occur in Norfolk, and one day we heard on the grapevine that they had been seen on New Buckenham Common, just south-west of Norwich, within easy cycling distance. So we pedalled out on a hot July day with the seemingly daunting task of exploring the whole of the large common. We found a likely spot with plenty of thistles, and within five minutes of searching we had found a male with his lovely combed antennae feeding on a flower. Further searching brought the tally up to five, both males and females, which sat perfectly still so that I could sketch them as well as taking photos. Job done, easy-peasy, for once. As is often the way, a few days later we found more Foresters at two other sites. Like buses, you wait ages for one to turn up, then several appear at once...

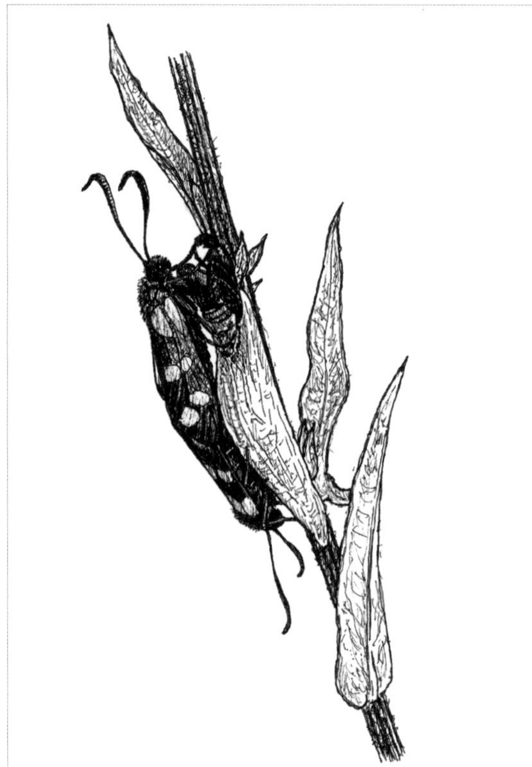

Time is of the essence. Female moths, and butterflies for that matter, give off a powerful pheromone to attract a mate as soon as they emerge. This female Six-spot Burnet had barely crawled out of her pupal case and was still perched on her empty cocoon with her wings drying when a male turned up and mated with her.

A garden for wildlife

As noted in the introduction, not only have many of the species covered in this book been found in my native county of Norfolk but a lot of them have actually turned up in my own modest suburban back garden. The garden is not especially grand or big, although a lot larger than the terraced house plot we used to have. We moved in during the spring of 2013, when it was just lawn, gravel, concrete slabs, four Leylandii and a rather nice honeysuckle. Straight away we began creating borders with plants that were not only attractive to us but that were also beneficial to insects.

We have always kept a garden diary, recording wildlife as well as which plants have been put in, when they flower and what they attract. It was surprising how quickly things began to colonise the new garden. To start with, a lot of creatures were just passing through and not staying very long, but as plants became established the list of invertebrates increased, showing that the habitat was improving. We were fortunate in that the two gardens either side were well established – one with mature trees and shrubs, the other with an abandoned wilderness at the bottom comprising a decent 'hedge' of tangled lilac, bramble and Leylandii. This was a great shrub layer and canopy, making our plot into a kind of sunny glade in between. What was missing was the floral ground cover, layers that provide a supply of pollen and nectar to nourish invertebrates throughout the year, and this is what we set out to provide.

Planting native wild flowers provides food for insect larvae (such as Garlic Mustard for Orange-tip caterpillars) as well as nectar and pollen for the adults (butterflies, bees, etc). But it is important to provide nectar and pollen for as much of the year as possible – and to achieve this you need to plant non-native flowers, too. Winter-flowering shrubs such as *Viburnum* and *Mahonia* are great for bees, followed in spring by Flowering Currant (*Ribes sanguineum*), which brightens up any garden. One of the best early spring flowers in our garden is the large Mediterranean spurge *Euphorbia characias*. It attracts numerous flies as well as bumblebees and mining bees such as *Andrena nigroaenea*. It is right by our front door and is a beautiful, cheery sight every time we come home, and a welcoming talking point for visitors.

We transplant young Red Dead-nettles (*Lamium purpureum*) from the allotment every year and grow them in a tub in a sunny spot. They are favourites of Hairy-footed Flower Bee (*Anthophora plumipes*) and early bumblebees. The non-native perennial Wallflower *Erysimum* 'Bowles' Mauve' flowers all year

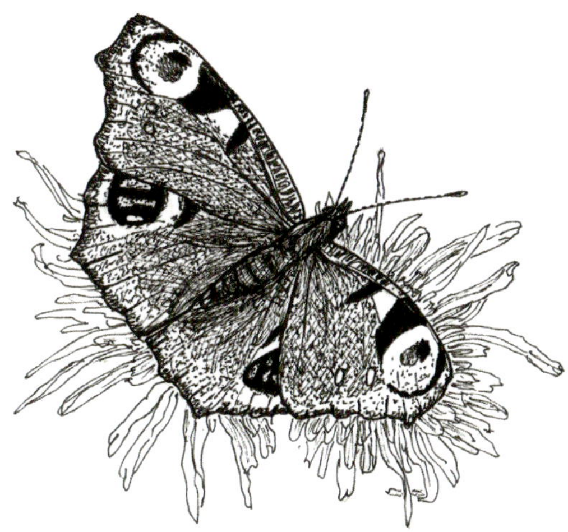

Dandelion flowers are a real boon for bees and butterflies such as this Peacock (Aglais io), providing an early source of pollen and nectar.

in our garden, and attracts both bees and butterflies, including Painted Ladies (*Vanessa cardui*).

As well as thinking about what time of year a plant is in flower, it is important to consider the shape of the flower. Many bumblebees can exploit deep tube-shaped flowers such as the native

Foxglove and non-native sages (*Salvia* sp.), whereas a lot of the solitary bees prefer shorter-tubed flowers such as Primroses. Open flowers, including Lesser Celandines, Plum, Apple and Pear blossom, and open-flowered roses such as the beautiful yellow *Rosa xanthina* 'Canary Bird', will cater for beetles and hoverflies as well as for bees. Lungwort is a good early spring flower that attracts Bee-flies (*Bombylius major*) and Hairy-footed Flower Bees. Forget-me-nots and Speedwells (*Veronica* sp.) are also useful, and include native and non-native species.

Flowers that form a large open platform will be visited by hoverflies, flies, beetles and bees. The best native ones are umbellifers such as Hogweed and Angelica, but these can become a bit thuggish in a small garden so we grow more delicate ornamentals such as *Ammi majus* and the Mediterranean herb Fennel as well as native Wild Carrot. Other examples of platform flowers are Yarrow, Oxeye Daisy and Corn Chamomile. These are favoured hunting grounds for crab spiders, which sit motionless and wait for an insect to land then pounce on them.

Dandelions are considered weeds by most gardeners, but we love to have a few flowering in our lawn and borders. Not only are they bright and beautiful to look at, but they are also a fantastic resource early in the year for insects that have hibernated over winter and need to refuel when they emerge in spring. Spare a few and you will find butterflies such as Small Tortoiseshell (*Aglais urticae*) and Peacock (*Aglais io*) enjoying them, along with various bumblebees. Later in the year, other yellow Composites (family Asteraceae), such as Catsear and Ragwort, are very much appreciated by solitary bees.

A lawn is a lovely thing to have if space allows. But by lawn I don't mean a shorn green sward constantly under the blades of a mower. The lawn we inherited was a straggly affair, mostly Perennial Rye Grass but also Fescues and Yorkshire Fog, then remnants of wild flowers including Dovesfoot Cranesbill, Common Catsear, Smooth Hawksbeard and White Clover.

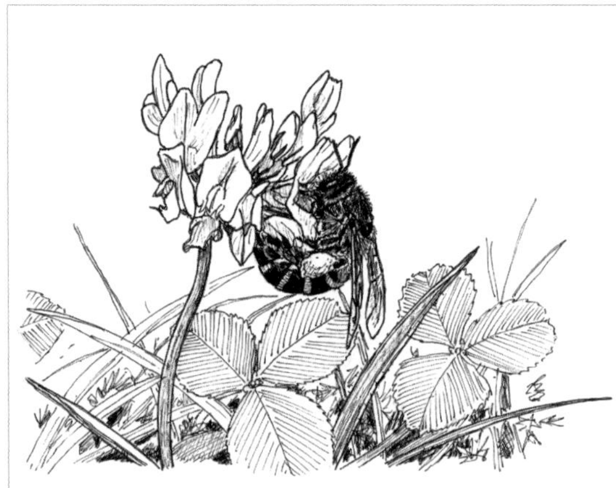

Clover Melitta (Melitta leporina) foraging on White Clover in the unkempt lawn.

We allowed it to get stragglier, leaving it longer in places during the summer, enabling the flowers to seed and spread. The action of ants (*Lasius* sp.) creates odd little patches of soil on the lawn in summer, which has enabled more wild plant seeds to germinate and colonise the garden. Now, in a square metre of lawn, I can count more than a dozen species of wildflower amongst the grasses. The plants that make up a lawn other than the grasses (and sedges and rushes) are known as forbs. The more forbs you have, the better your lawn is likely to be for invertebrates.

In summer the lawn is mown but only to enable us to get around the garden (and hang the washing out!). Leaving it uncut around the edges encourages the Common Catsear to proliferate which attracts the wonderfully named Pantaloon Bee *Dasypoda hirtipes* (see plate B), which collects pollen solely from yellow Composites (family Asteraceae). Patches of White Clover are left in the middle of the lawn for another specialist bee, the Clover Melitta (*Melitta leporina*), which, as its

Opposite page: Meadow Life, a selection of invertebrates that are typical of a summer's day (see www.arthropedia.co.uk for a list of the invertebrates depicted)

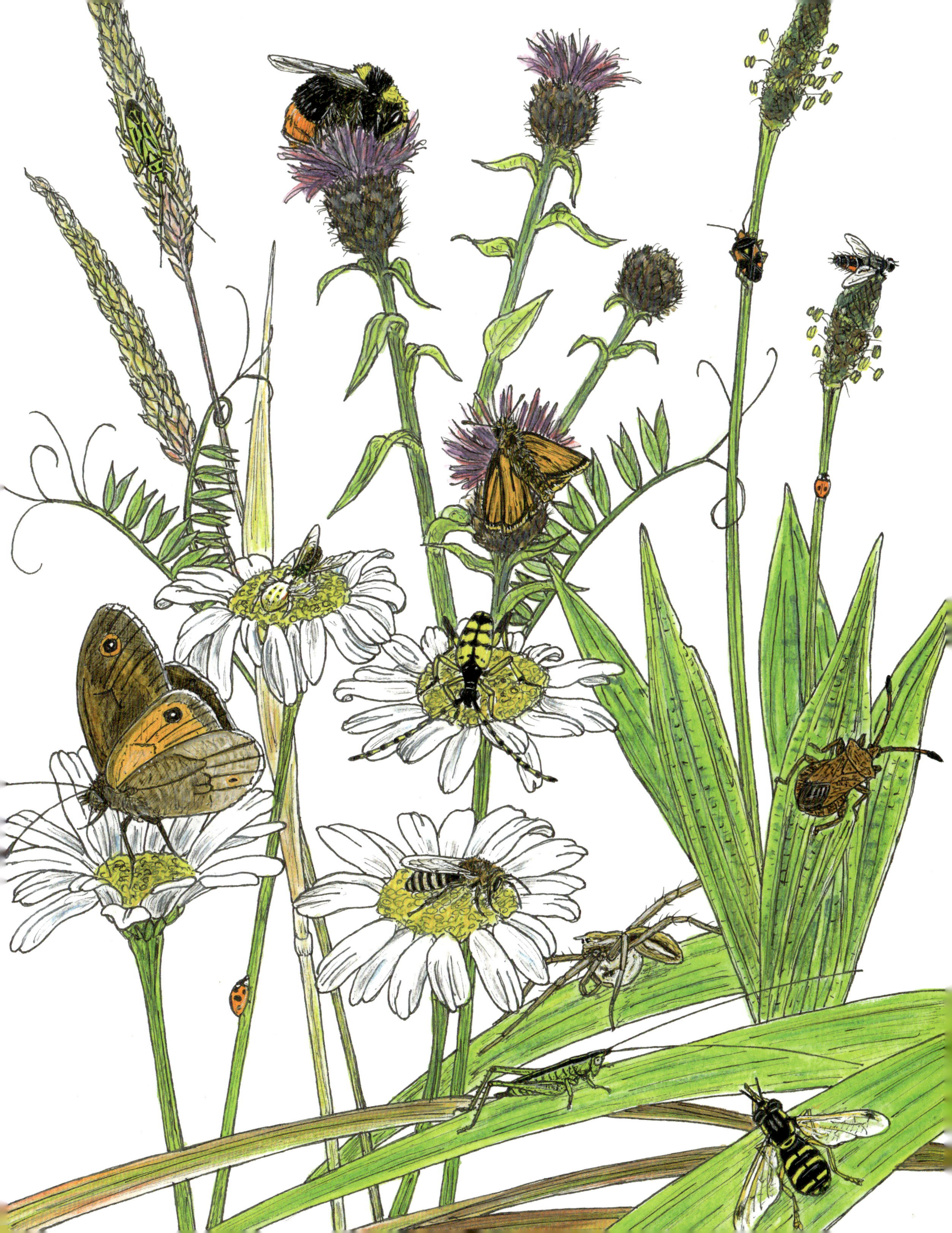

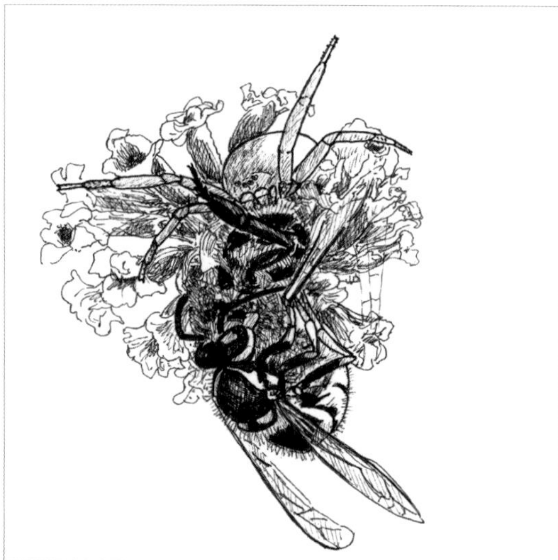

Everyday drama: the garden is a great place to observe the daily trials of life. Here, a crab spider (Misumena vatia) has caught a Honeybee (Apis mellifera) only to have a wasp (Vespula germanica) come and steal part of her meal by cutting the bee in half with her powerful mandibles and then flying off with it.

name suggests, collects pollen from clover flowers.

We established a mini-meadow by removing a bit of the lawn and sowing a wild flower meadow seed mixture which had delicate grass species as well as wild flowers. This provides a great place for all sorts of spiders and is home to Long-winged Coneheads (*Conocephalus fuscus*). The plentiful Oxeye Daises in it are very good for attracting butterflies, hoverflies and some of the small solitary bees.

Layers are important in a garden. Some invertebrates dwell low down amongst groundcover plants, some like to be up in the canopy of trees and tall shrubs, while others exploit everything in between. The transition zone between layers is important with many invertebrates exploiting this 'edge' habitat. We have short lawn; longer grass in the meadow; dense groundcover in the form of Crosswort, Sweet Woodruff and plenty of Primroses; then taller perennials such as hardy geraniums and Lesser Knapweed. This is followed by a woody shrub layer, including *Brachyglottis* (great for overwintering ladybirds and shieldbugs, with flowers for butterflies in summer), Purple Sage and Lavenders, and a 'canopy' layer created by honeysuckle, clematis and fruit trees (as well as that 'borrowed' from the neighbouring gardens).

It pays not to be over-tidy in the garden. A pile of leaves and or logs will provide an ideal habitat for woodlice, centipedes, spiders and beetles. Dead stems and seed heads left overwinter will give shelter to all sorts of hibernating invertebrates.

We have a few bee hotels dotted about the garden that have been used by several different species, mostly leafcutters and mason bees. They are best positioned facing south, but we have them on a west-facing shed about four or five feet off the ground above a flower border. We also have an old hole-entrance bird box on the fence, again west facing, that has been used by the Tree Bumblebee (*Bombus hypnorum*) in which to make a nest. Other bees like bare soil, preferably sandy, to nest in. Our garden lacks larger patches of bare soil, but a few solitary bees have managed to nest at the bases of plants in the borders. Several species will nest in the ground in closely mown lawns.

When it comes to bees, perhaps the most important plant in our garden is Catmint (*Nepeta*). We have four plants close together in the gravel area near the pond where they have also started seeding themselves. Some days the Catmint patch literally hums with activity. Catmint flowers over a long period and produces nectar throughout the day. Bumblebees are frequent visitors along with various solitary bees. Their most important visitor is the solitary bee *Anthophora quadrimaculata* (see plate B), which appeared in our garden the very first year we were there, a few weeks after we had planted the Catmint.

Between 2013 and 2017 our garden was one of only a handful of locations in Norfolk where *Anthophora quadrimaculata* was seen. It is a lovely charismatic bee, and its presence in our garden has led to our wider fascination with and interest in solitary bees. The very hot summer of 2018 produced a couple of sightings elsewhere in

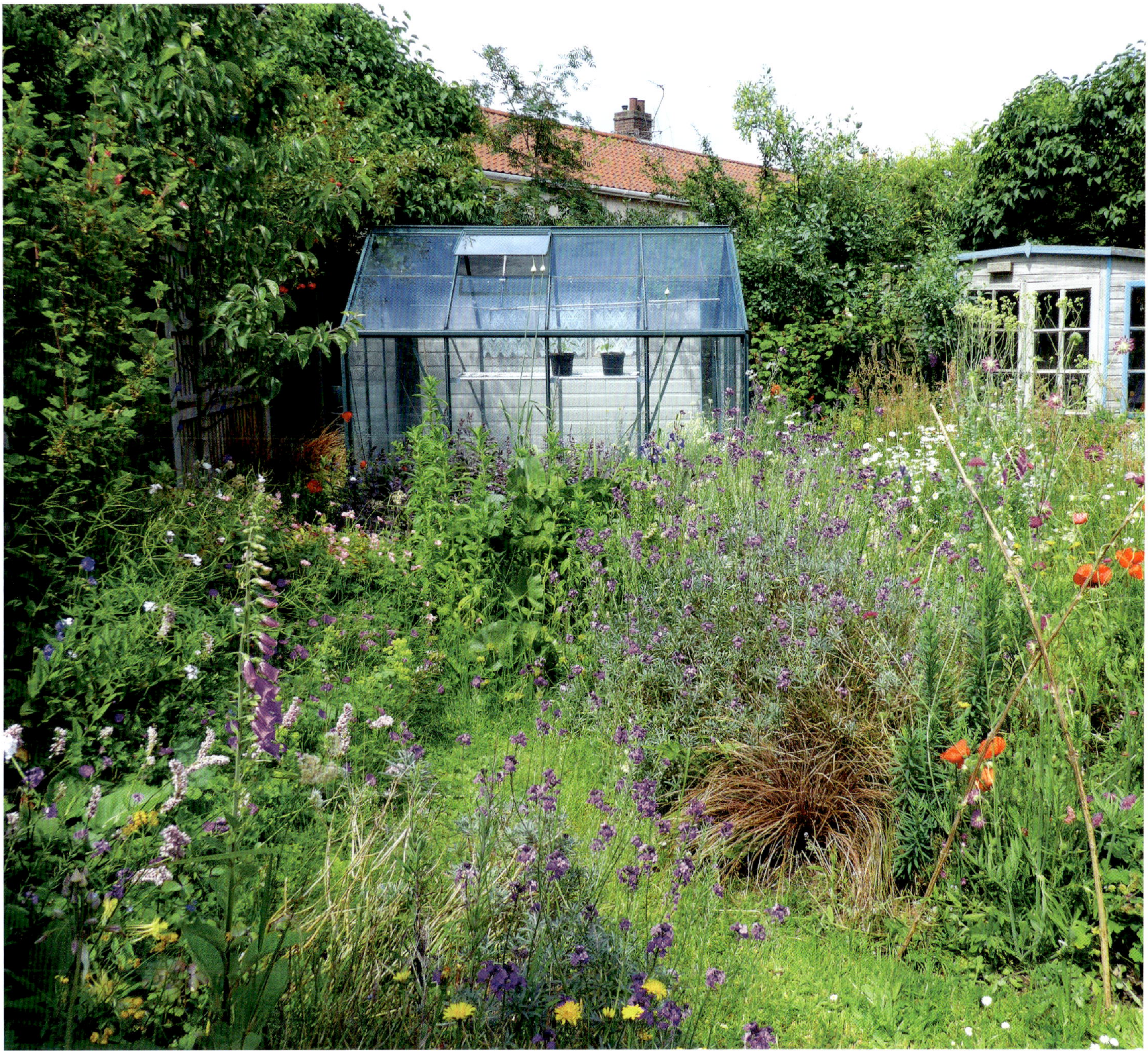

The author's garden in early summer. It pays not to be over-tidy... Dead stems and seed heads left overwinter will give shelter to all sorts of hibernating invertebrates.

Norwich, so I carried out a search of front gardens, churchyards and municipal plantings around the centre of the city to look for it and map its presence. It appeared to be doing well, and sightings increased again in 2019. As well as Catmint, I recorded it on

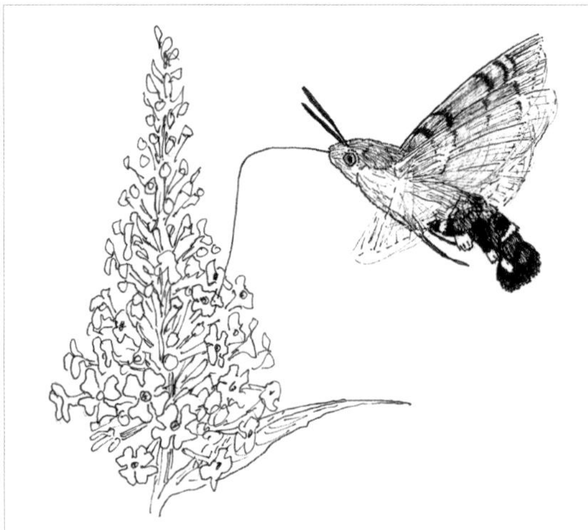

A touch of the exotic: Hummingbird Hawkmoths (Macroglossum stellatarum) are occasional visitors to the garden during summer. They flit from flower to flower, hovering on fast-beating wings as they sup nectar with their long proboscis. Buddleia is often favoured, as are the flowers of Red Valerian.

Lavenders, Ivy-leaved Toadflax and Red Valerian. The bees nest in old walls, of which there are plenty in the city, especially the old flint ones surrounding churches, but I have yet to find a nest site.

One important wildlife feature that we put in pretty quickly was a small pond. Not only did this provide a place for Common Frogs to spawn, it also attracted Smooth Newts and various insects including Water Boatmen (*Corixa* sp.), Backswimmers (*Notonecta* sp.), Pond Skaters (*Gerris* sp.) and a tiny Water Measurer (*Hydrometra stagnorum*). Various flies were attracted to the pond, including those with larvae that prey on pond snails, and hoverflies which have aquatic larvae. These are known as rat-tailed maggots and they live submerged with a telescopic breathing tube reaching up to the surface for air. Damselflies were soon ovipositing (egg-laying) in the pond, mostly Large Red (*Pyrrhosoma nymphula*) but also Azure Damselflies (*Coenagrion puella*), and even a Southern Hawker Dragonfly (*Aeshna cyanea*) visited.

Small China-mark moths (*Cataclysta lemnata*) also discovered the pond and laid eggs, their tiny caterpillars living a strange watery existence in a case made from duckweed. Another moth, the Water Veneer (*Acentria ephemerella*), also colonised the pond. Its larvae are totally aquatic and have been found at depths of up to two metres below the surface. Sometimes, on a warm summer night, we get lots of males in the moth trap but never females as these generally have only rudimentary wings and can barely fly although a fully winged form also occurs. Social wasps (*Vespula* sp.) and Hornets (*Vespa crabro*) occasionally visit the pond for a drink, as do honeybees.

The rich invertebrate fauna that our garden supports attracts other visitors. We have a reasonable number of birds for a city garden, including breeding Blue Tits, Robins and Blackbirds, along with a small colony of House Sparrows. The frogs in the pond do eat a fair number of aquatic invertebrates, but I wouldn't want a pond without them – especially in spring when the males croak through the night – and, anyway, their numerous tadpoles are food for the newts that have discovered our garden and made it their home, too. Hedgehogs have also taken to visiting, doubtless munching beetles that I have yet to identify along with various slugs and worms.

The garden is attractive to humans, too, with pretty flower borders, an apple tree, pear and fig and sprawling wild strawberries that provide a few handfuls of fruit for breakfast in summer. There is a bench by the pond to sit on and daydream, a Daisy-sprinkled lawn, space for a couple of chairs in sun or shade depending on the time of day, and a dilapidated summerhouse that doubles as a hide for watching the birds that visit the garden. A friend once joked that I wouldn't want to leave the garden: how true – it has become a mini nature reserve with an astonishing wealth of invertebrates. I often record more species in a day in the garden than on a trip out into the countryside.

Meet the author

Vanna Bartlett (www.arthropedia.co.uk and www.vanna-art.co.uk) is a wildlife artist and naturalist based in Norwich, Norfolk. She combines a love of drawing with a passion for wildlife, to explore the interconnections between plants and animals and their environment in her paintings and prints. Field observations are key to her work; time spent sketching and studying her subjects gives her an invaluable insight into their lives and behaviour.

As a life-long fan of invertebrates, Vanna wanted to help promote a wider interest in them and came up with the idea for her 'alphabet'. *Arthropedia* is the culmination of three years' work, dedicated to searching out different species, designing and painting the plates, distilling observations and knowledge into the text, and completing the numerous pen and ink drawings. It is informed by more than 50 years of fascination with and appreciation of our amazing invertebrate world.

Vanna's linocuts have been exhibited in the Society of Wildlife Artists' annual exhibition, 'The Natural Eye', at the Mall Galleries in London, and she has taken part in The Norwich Print Fair. She has also had prints used in designs for Christmas cards for the RSPB and Amnesty International. Her work has featured in several Mascot Media books, including *The Artful Hare*, *Wings Over Water* and *The Elegant Fowl*.

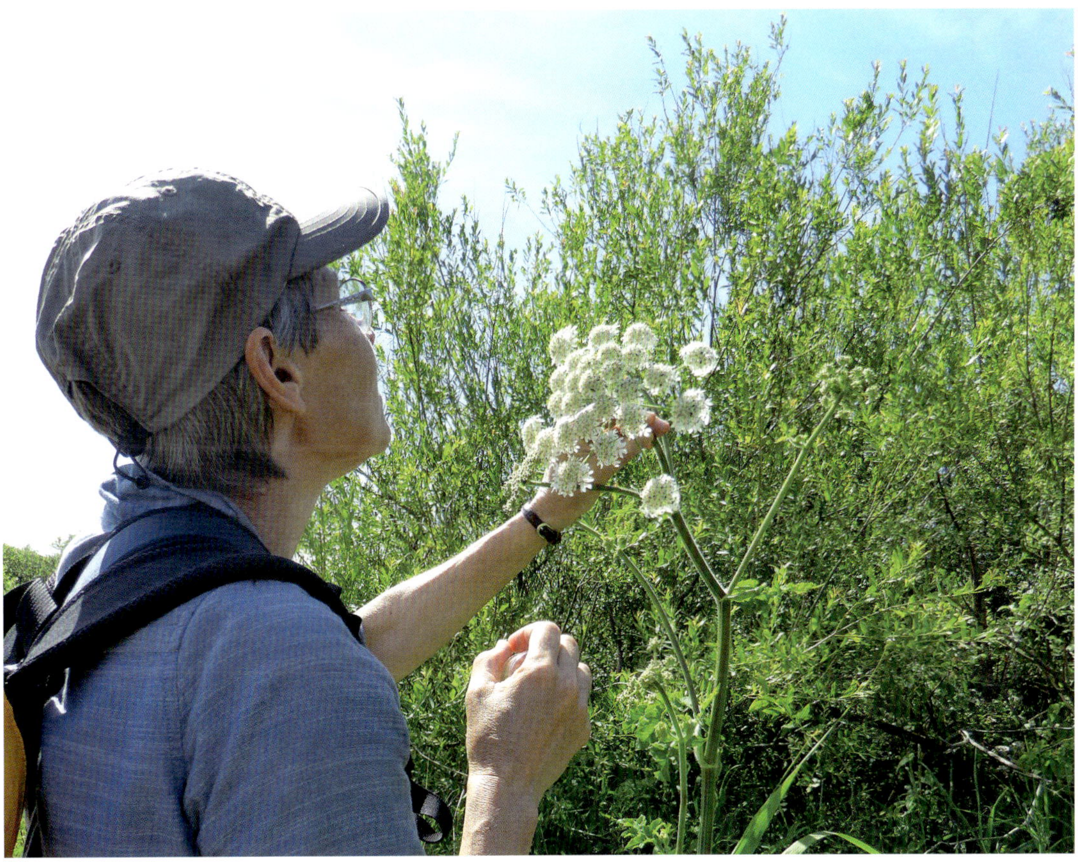

Further reading

There is a much more comprehensive list of further reading on the *Arthropedia* website (https://arthropedia.co.uk/)...

ARTWORK
The work of three artists has been a key inspiration in the making of this book:

● *Art Forms in Nature: Prints of Ernst Haeckel* by Olaf Breidbach, Irenaeus Eibl-Eibesfeldt & Richard Hartmann (2008). Prestel, Munich. A good introduction to Haeckel's work, with beautiful, symmetrical plates featuring a wide range of life forms.

● *The Aurelian* by Moses Harris, with an introduction by Robert Mays (1986). Country Life Books, Twickenham. A facsimile reprint of Moses Harris' 1766 book, featuring superb copperplate engravings of the life cycles of butterflies and moths, depicted with food plants, many reared and drawn by the author.

● Maria Sybilla Merian's amazing depictions of invertebrates and her work on studying metamorphosis. There is a good introduction to her life and work in *Amazing Rare Things: The Art of Natural History in the Age of Discovery* by David Attenborough, Susan Owens, Martin Clayton and Rea Alexandratos (2007). Royal Collection Enterprises, London.

GUIDE BOOKS
For identifying invertebrates some really good books are now available, chiefly those illustrated by Richard Lewington, one of the greatest entomological artists ever.

Digital photography has made huge advances in photographic guides, and the best general guide to British insects is:
A Comprehensive Guide to Insects of Britain & Ireland by Paul D. Brock (2014). Pisces Publications, Newbury. The book features over 2,100 species.

I especially recommend the WILDGuides series of guide books published by Princeton University Press and the Bloomsbury Wildlife Guides (formerly British Wildlife Guides), published by Bloomsbury.

Britain's Hoverflies: A Field Guide by Stuart Ball & Roger Morris (2015). Princeton University Press, Princeton & Woodstock. A photographic guide.

Britain's Spiders: A Field Guide by Lawrence Bee, Geoff Oxford & Helen Smith (2017). Princeton University Press, Princeton & Woodstock. A photographic guide.

Field Guide to the Bees of Great Britain and Ireland by Steven Falk & Richard Lewington (2015). British Wildlife Publishing, London.
Field Guide to the Moths of Great Britain and Ireland by Paul Waring, Martin Townsend and Richard Lewington (2018). Bloomsbury, London.

Pocket Guide to the Butterflies of Great Britain and Ireland by Richard Lewington (2019). Bloomsbury, London.

Field Guide to the Ladybirds of Great Britain and Ireland by Helen Roy, Peter Brown & Richard Lewington (2018). Bloomsbury, London.

Spiders of Britain and Northern Europe by Michael J. Roberts (1996). Collins, London. Exquisitely illustrated, with keys.

Collins Guide to the Insects of Britain and Western Europe by Michael Chinery (1986). William Collins, London. Old, but still good, with lots of information.

OTHER
Wildlife of a Garden: a Thirty-year Study by Jennifer Owen (2010). Royal Horticultural Society, Peterborough. Reveals the amazing diversity of life that can be found in a suburban garden.

The Butterflies of Britain & Ireland by Jeremy Thomas & Richard Lewington (2014). British Wildlife Publishing, Oxford. The ultimate book on British butterflies.

Bugs Britannica by Peter Marren & Richard Mabey (2010). Chatto & Windus, London. General information and folklore on all sorts of invertebrates.

INTERNET
The iRecord website (https://www.brc.ac.uk/irecord/) provides a useful way of submitting wildlife recordings.

Facebook has a number of arthropod identification groups. For more details see the *Arthropedia* website (https://arthropedia.co.uk/).

ORGANISATIONS
Buglife, the Invertebrate Conservation Trust (https://www.buglife.org.uk), is campaigning to prevent the decline of British arthropods; and Butterfly Conservation (https://butterfly-conservation.org) is campaigning for Britain's butterflies and moths. Other conservation organisations are worth supporting, too, including the RSPB and county wildlife trusts (https://www.wildlifetrusts.org), such as Norfolk Wildlife Trust (https://www.norfolkwildlifetrust.org.uk/). It is also worth joining your county natural history group (eg, Norfolk and Norwich Naturalists' Society, https://norfolknaturalists.org.uk/).

K is for... KALEIDOSCOPE (key to species on page 51)

INSECT TYPE	SCIENTIFIC NAME	ENGLISH NAME
Bug	*1 Corizus hyoscyami (x4)*	
Beetle	*2 Cryptocephalus sp (x2)*	
Moth	*3 Anania funebris (x2)*	
Butterfly	*4 Carterocephalus palaemon (x2)*	*Chequered Skipper*
Beetle	*5 Rhagium bifasciatum (x4)*	*Two-banded Longhorn Beetle*
Fly	*6 Stratiomys potamida (x4)*	*Banded General*
Bug	*7 Eurydema oleracea (x1)*	*Crucifer Shieldbug*
Bug	*8 Podops inuncta (x1)*	*Knobbed Shieldbug*
Bug	*9 Leptopterna dolabrata (x4)*	
Beetle	*10 Elaphrus cupreus (x1)*	*Copper Peacock*
Beetle	*11 Badister bullatus (x1)*	
Beetle	*12 Platyrhinus resinosus (x1)*	*Cramp-ball Fungus Weevil*
Beetle	*13 Phyllobrotica quadrimaculata (x1)*	*Skullcap Leaf Beetle*
Bug	*14 Pantilius tunicatus (x2)*	
Dragonfly	*15Libellula quadrimaculata form praenubila (x1)*	*Four-spot Chaser (form praenubila)*
Dragonfly	*16 Libellula quadrimaculata (x1)*	*Four-spot Chaser*
Grasshopper	*17 Omocestus viridulus (x1)*	*Common Green Grasshopper*
Grasshopper	*18 Myrmeleotettix maculatus (x1)*	*Mottled Grasshopper*
Bush-cricket	*19 Metrioptera brachyptera (x1)*	*Bog Bush-cricket*
Bush-cricket	*20 Metrioptera roeselii (x1)*	*Roesel's Bush-cricket*
Butterfly	*21 Melitaea cinxia (x1)*	*Glanville Fritillary*
Butterfly	*22 Erebia aethiops (x1)*	*Scotch Argus*
Butterfly	*23 Lasiommata megera (x1)*	*Wall Brown*
Butterfly	*24 Euphydryas aurinia (x1)*	*Marsh Fritillary*
Butterfly	*25 Plebejus argus (x1)*	*Silver-studded Blue*
Hoverfly	*26 Dasysyrphus albostriatus (x1)*	
Butterfly	*27 Callophrys rubi (x1)*	*Green Hairstreak*
Butterfly	*28 Celastrina argiolus (x1)*	*Holly Blue*
Hoverfly	*29 Sericomyia lappona (x1)*	
Butterfly	*30 Satyrium w-album (x1)*	*White-letter Hairstreak*
Beetle	*31 Sphaeridium scarabaeoides (x1)*	
Beetle	*32 Aphodius obliteratus (x1)*	
Beetle	*33 Anatis ocellata (x1)*	*Eyed Ladybird*
Beetle	*34 Anisosticta novemdecimpunctata (x1)*	*Water Ladybird*
Beetle	*35 Tytthaspis sedecimpunctata (x1)*	*16-spot Ladybird*
Beetle	*36 Subcoccinella vigintiquattuorpunctata (x1)*	*24-spot Ladybird*
Beetle	*37 Onthophagus similis (x1)*	
Beetle	*38 Aphodius fimetarius (x1)*	
Moth	*39 Olethreutes arcuella (x1)*	
Sawfly	*40 Tenthredo scrophulariae (x1)*	*Figwort Sawfly*
Moth	*41 Nemophora fasciella (x1)*	
Bug	*42 Syromastus rhombeus (x1)*	*Rhombic Leatherbug*
Bug	*43 Grypocoris stysi (x1)*	
Fly	*44 Villa modesta (x1)*	*Dune Villa*
Bug	*45 Harpocera thoracica (x1)*	
Bug	*46 Arenocoris falleni (x1)*	*Fallen's Leatherbug*
Moth	*47 Griposia aprilina (x1)*	*Merveille du Jour*
Wasp	*48 Diphyus quadripunctorius (x1)*	
Moth	*49 Phlogophora meticulosa (x1)*	*Angle Shades*
Moth	*50 Bryophila domestica (x1)*	*Marbled Beauty*
Wasp	*51 Ichneumon stramentor (x1)*	
Moth	*52 Thyatira batis (x1)*	*Peach Blossom*
Bug	*53 Coriomeris denticulatus (x1)*	*Denticulate Leatherbug*
Bug	*54 Calocoris roseomaculatus (x1)*	
Fly	*55 Phasia hemiptera (x1)*	
Bug	*56 Rhabdomiris striatellus (x1)*	
Bug	*57 Coreus marginatus (x1)*	*Dock Bug*
Moth	*58 Esperia sulphurella (x1)*	
Sawfly	*59 Eriocampa ovata (x1)*	*Alder Sawfly*
Moth	*60 Agapeta zoegana (x1)*	
Beetle	*61 Cteniopus sulphureus (x4)*	*Sulphur Beetle*
Bee	*62 Megachile leachella (x1)*	*Silvery Leafcutter Bee*
Bee	*63 Coelioxys conoidea (x1)*	

Index

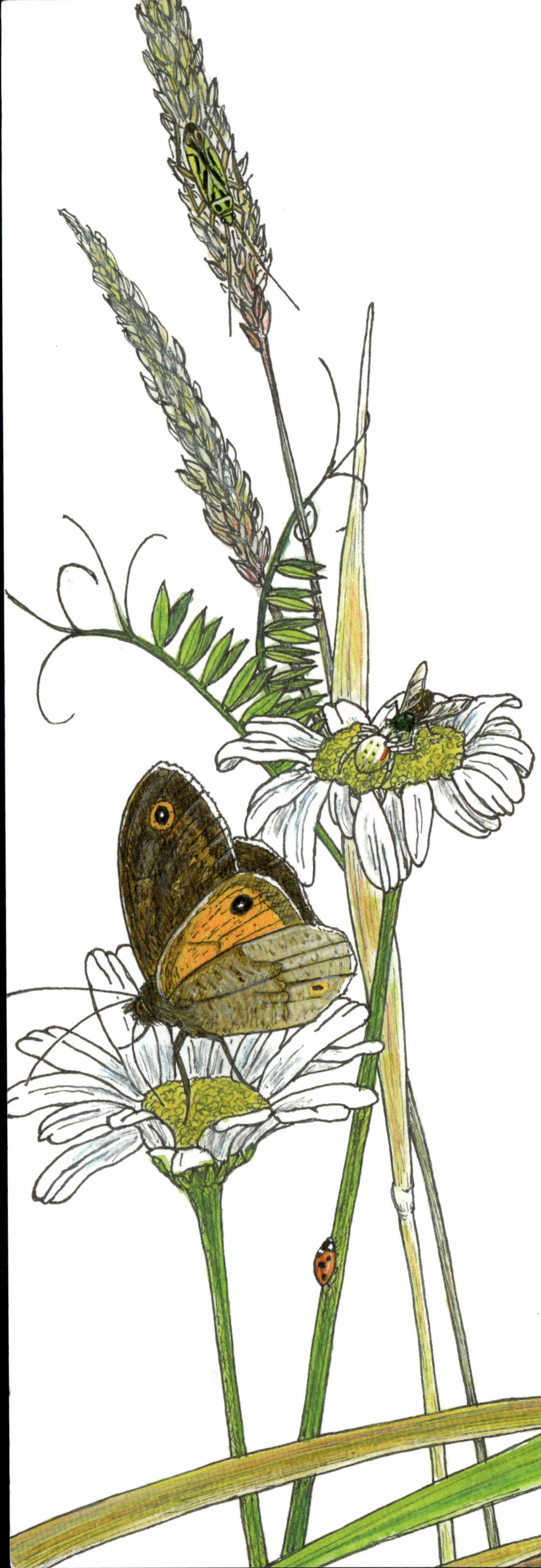

Acknowledgements

Thanks to my husband Jeremy who has accompanied me on numerous outings to look for wildlife. He has patiently waited (well, gone off and botanised or found something just as interesting as the thing I was looking at) while I have keyed out bees, scribbled notes or made quick field sketches. He proof-read, corrected and edited the chapters before handing them over to Mascot Media. He is also responsible for planning, planting and maintaining (ie, allowing nature to run its course) our lovely wildlife-friendly garden, which has been the source of many of the creatures and observations that feature in this book.

Various people have given lifts to out-of-the-way (of public transport) places or tagged along on trips and helped find things; and others have offered expertise on identification or told me where to look for particular species. Thanks, therefore, to Ian Senior, James Emerson, Nick Owens, Tony Irwin, Tim Strudwick, Stuart Paston, Janice Darch and Steve Ecclestone, Sarah Barney, and Simon and Anne Harrap at Natural Surroundings.

Hopefully, I haven't forgotten anyone!

And a big thank-you to Alan and Marion Marshall of Mascot Media for believing in the book and bringing it to publication.

Disclaimer

Any mistakes in this book are all mine, whether in the artwork or text. I have read a lot of books on different invertebrates over the years and assimilated a great deal of knowledge which has been 'regurgitated' here along with my own field observations. I have checked my facts as much as possible, correcting a few glaring mistakes along the way as I've misremembered things I thought I knew. The old phylum Arthropoda that I learnt about at school is no longer neatly divided into the four classes of Insecta, Arachnida, Crustacea and Myriapoda. However, I have kept to this straightforward division within the book for simplicity (and for the sake of the sanity of author and readers!). New discoveries change our understanding of things, and it isn't always easy to keep up with the latest theories. Even scientific names change sometimes. Species' distributions alter, sometimes dramatically, especially with changes in climate. So the text is as accurate and up to date as possible, to the best of my knowledge.

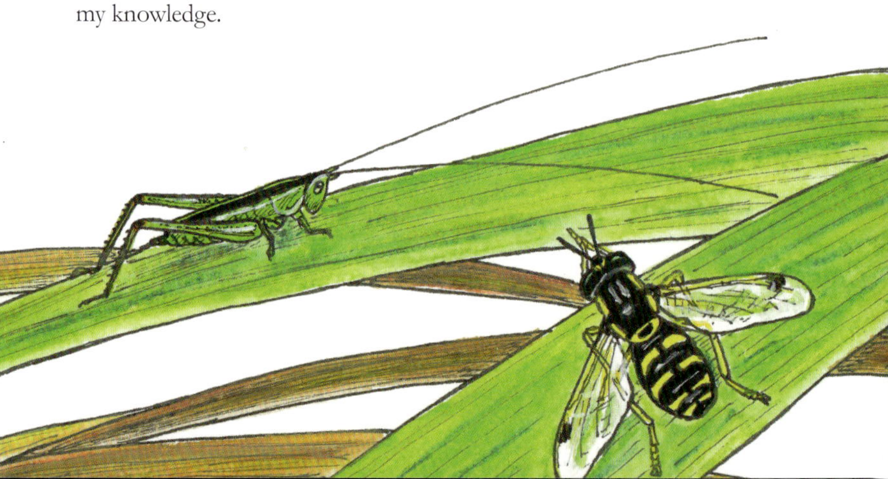